UNRAVELLING GLOBAL APARTHEID

This book is dedicated to Nozipho, her family and everyone
working for a fair, sustainable future

Unravelling Global Apartheid

An Overview of World Politics

Titus Alexander

Polity Press

The right of Titus Alexander to be identified as author of this work has been asserted in accordance with the Copyright, Designs and Patents Act 1988.

First published in 1996 by Polity Press in association with Blackwell Publishers Ltd.

2 4 6 8 9 10 7 5 3 1

Editorial office:
Polity Press
65 Bridge Street
Cambridge CB2 1UR, UK

Marketing and production:
Blackwell Publishers Ltd
108 Cowley Road
Oxford OX4 1JF, UK

Blackwell Publishers Inc.
238 Main Street
Cambridge, MA 02142, USA

ISBN 0–7456–1352–7
ISBN 0–7456–1353–5

A CIP catalogue record for this book is available from the British Library and the Library of Congress.

Typeset in 11 on 12 pt Stempel Garamond
by CentraCet Ltd, Cambridge
Printed in Great Britain by T J Press Ltd, Padstow, Cornwall

This book is printed on acid-free paper.

Contents

A Note on Terminology

'Majority World' refers to countries sometimes called the South, 'Third World', 'developing countries', 'emerging markets', NICs (Newly Industrializing Countries) and LDCs (Less Developed Countries), sometimes grouped together as the G77 and China. In 1993, their population was about 4.4 billion, almost 80 per cent of the world's people. In money terms, they had less than 20 per cent of world income, up from 15 per cent in 1970.

The 'West' refers to twenty-two industrialized countries of the OECD, including Australia, New Zealand, Western Europe, Japan and the United States, sometimes referred to as the North, the developed, or the industrialized countries, with the G3 and G7 group of most powerful countries as its core. In 1993, they had a population of about 800 million people, about 15 per cent of the world total, and over 70 per cent of world income. The United States is sometimes referred to as America.

This broad distinction between the West and the Majority World is based on differences in political power in international affairs. There are huge social, economic and political differences within and between all countries. Both the 'Majority World' and the 'West' include immense diversity as well as extremes of poverty and wealth.

The main reference point for South Africa is 1986, when most apartheid legislation was still in place. White, Coloured, Indian and Black (formerly Native) were political classifications by the apartheid state. In 1986 people in the first three categories had separate chambers in parliament and most Blacks were legally assigned to tribal homelands, most of which were nominally independent. Lower-case 'white' or 'black' is used for people of

European or African descent and the concept of race is rejected in this book.

Apartheid was never static. As between the West and the Majority World, political distinctions between White, Coloured, Indian and Black obscured wide disparities of wealth, power and influence. The 'homelands' are included in South African statistics given throughout.

Unless otherwise stated, financial statistics are exchange rate values converted into US dollars. Although these are not an accurate description of economic differences, they reflect the relative purchasing power in international markets and therefore the economic power under the present global regime.

The 'Western Economic System' refers broadly to the many varieties of mature mixed economies prevailing in the West.

Acknowledgements

The origin of this book owes a great deal to people in Mexico, Central America, China and Morocco, where I learnt about global apartheid at first hand. Also to Pat and John Bardill, Dawn and Patrick Mokhobo, Sylvan Golden and his family, who introduced me to South Africa, and endless conversations with Dave Spooner. I owe an intellectual debt to the books cited as references, and many more not quoted. Television, particularly Britain's Channel Four and BBC2, has been a source of background knowledge. I am particularly grateful to David Boyle, Professor Desai, Jay Derrick, Harold Goodwin, Judith Hanna, Nick Robbins and Danyal Sattar who took the time to read the manuscript and comment critically. Their disagreements were always constructive. I am also grateful to Polity Press for taking the risk of publication and for their superb professionalism throughout the process. Finally I would like to thank my friends and family for their patience.

Preface

Unravelling Global Apartheid provides a critical overview of the institutions, issues and underlying forces shaping the modern world. It is written in a clear, accessible style suitable for undergraduates and general readers who want a comprehensive introduction to global history, economics, environment, international relations, law, media, politics, security and society, with booklists for further study on each topic. It includes a wide-ranging analysis of the Western Economic System from Adam Smith to the present, highlighting the dangers of both unrestrained free trade and protectionism.

The many parallels between the modern world and apartheid in South Africa are used as an analogy to illustrate profound inequalities between the West and the rest of the world.

Although *Unravelling Global Apartheid* outlines the terrible problems facing humanity at the start of the twenty-first century, it is a manual of hope, presenting recommendations for reform and strategies for change at local, national and global levels.

Introduction: What is Global Apartheid and Why does it Matter?

We have about 50% of the world's wealth, but only 6.5% of its population ... In this situation, we cannot fail to be the object of envy and resentment. Our real task in this coming period is to devise a pattern of relationships which will permit us to maintain this position of disparity without detriment to our national security. To do this, we will need to dispense with all sentimentality and day-dreaming; and our attention will have to be concentrated everywhere on our immediate national objectives. We need not deceive ourselves that we can afford today the luxury of altruism and world-benefaction ... We should cease to talk about vague and – for the Far East – unrealistic objectives such as human rights, the raising of the living standards, and democratization. The day is not far off when we are going to have to deal in straight power concepts. The less we are then hampered by idealistic slogans, the better.[1]

George Kennan, 24 Feb. 1948
Chief Planner, US State Dept

SHIFTING STRANDS IN THE NEW GLOBAL SETTLEMENT

There are times when societies need to revise the fundamental rules by which they conduct their affairs. Such periods may be marked by revolution, war or less dramatic changes in the law, constitution or particular institutions. However it happens, changing the ground rules transforms society. By making it easier to do some things and almost impossible to do others, certain developments become virtually inevitable. Decisions made during these critical periods have momentous importance, greater than even their makers foresee.

At these times it is essential to take stock of history and underlying principles shaping society. Fundamental changes in ground rules and structures of society usually follow shifts in the balance of power between social groups. When sections of society no longer accept customary ways of doing things, the prevailing settlement between groups is challenged, modified and sometimes overthrown.

The creation of a global society, in which all human beings are linked through telecommunications, trade, international institutions and our common environment, means that a new global settlement is inevitable. It is no longer possible for any portion of the planet to act independently without affecting the rest in some way.

One of the most visible and powerful changes in international relations is increased integration of the world economy. Deregulation of finance, globalization of production and greater free trade are just three strands in a complex realignment covering at least six distinct sets of issues:

- *Trade*, managing global markets created by transnational corporations through institutions such as the European Union, NAFTA, GATT, World Trade Organization (WTO) and UNCTAD, as well as the Asia-Pacific Economic Cooperation Forum (APEC) and other trading areas.

- *Finance*, overhauling the International Monetary Fund (IMF), World Bank, central banking system and international investment regime as well as Majority World debt.

- *Global governance*, which currently means strengthening the G7, expanding the Security Council, streamlining the United Nations and creating powerful regional blocs such as the European Union.

- *Military security*, through the extension of NATO, the UN Security Council and the European Union as a military power, as well as unpredictable realignments within the former Soviet Union, Islamic world and Pacific states.

- *Environment*, coping with climate change, biodiversity, forests, hazardous wastes and other problems.

- *Information, knowledge and culture*, whereby entirely new global infrastructures of telecommunications, electronic databanks and media are being created together with new rules for intellectual property rights.

Global negotiations on these issues raise fundamental questions about how we share the planet and its resources. Concerns about poverty, health, hunger, human rights, civil war, population and women's equality are often at the margins of these negotiations, although they are central for over a billion people in the Majority World.

Whether we live in Dallas, Guildford or Bombay, decisions on these issues have a far-reaching influence on the food we eat, the price of goods, job prospects, peace and the long-term security of our environment. It is no longer possible for any one group or nation to escape the effects of international trade or environmental degradation. Yet change is happening faster than decision-makers can comprehend. The power of global communications means that actions anywhere in the world can influence events anywhere else almost instantaneously. A stockbroker responding to radio news on her company car in rural New England can make decisions to buy or sell over her mobile phone that create factory jobs in distant Chengdu and make workers in Birmingham redundant. At the same time, low-cost trading in Shanghai could put her out of business overnight. Indian software engineers earning under $3,000 a year are already taking knowledge-intensive jobs from the West.

As global traders hunt the planet for the highest rates of return, even the largest economies are shaken by fluctuations in exchange rates, share prices, interest rates, investment and unemployment. For countries like Mexico, Pakistan or Rwanda, the effects can be devastating, intensifying struggles for subsistence, land and power. And wherever there are conflicts, the second-hand cold war arsenal supplies a savage solution. Scenes of slaughter in distant wars cross the world instantaneously, stirring political passions in unpredictable ways.

These issues are all linked. But they are being argued through separate channels, by different negotiators who are often seeking incompatible solutions on behalf of the same political masters. The most ambitious attempt to bring these strands together was Agenda 21, a unique agreement signed in 1992 at the Rio Earth Summit, the world's largest-ever gathering of political leaders. But critical issues such as armaments, population, the role of transnational corporations and the financial system were avoided and the agreement expressed aspirations rather than actions. The real negotiations, where binding decisions are made, happen elsewhere, often out of sight of the world's press, parliaments and people.

In a disjointed, *ad hoc* fashion, the postwar settlement which established the UN, IMF/World Bank, GATT and other international institutions is being replaced by a new world order. Many different proposals for reform are being developed by the G7, the UN and independent agencies such as the Club of Rome,[2] the South Commission,[3] the Wuppertal Institute[4] and others. The eminent Commission for Global Governance made comprehensive recommendations in *Our Global Neighbourhood*,[5] drawing on extensive experience at senior levels of the global system as well as selective consultation. This very considered, practical report even includes a ten-year implementation process. Many of its arguments and recommendations are consistent with the proposals in this book. The main difference is that, in my view, it does not adequately confront the driving forces of global restructuring already taking place.

The most powerful participants in the new global politics are Western finance, transnational corporations, and the United States and its allies, for whom these issues are an extension of domestic interests. They set the agenda, fix the framework and have the final say. Leaders of the Majority World participate on Western terms, rarely winning more than rhetorical concessions, while people in the West do not know what is being said or signed in their name.

The danger is that piecemeal bargaining over the global political jigsaw may provide temporary protection for a few while the majority sacrifice their families, communities, cultures and environment in a scramble of global competitiveness. Most dangerously of all, Western leaders are pursuing a single solution – economic growth through free trade – which threatens the stability of every society in the world. By pursuing narrow economic solutions without addressing wider social, political and ecological consequences, Western leaders are jeopardizing the very values they espouse. As tens of millions of people throughout the Majority World leave the land to seek work in overcrowded cities and in the West itself, Western voters demand more controls on immigration and imports to protect their communities. Right-wing populists, nationalists and racists are gaining political support as voters fear for their security.

The scale of our predicament is entirely new in human history. None of our experiences or existing models of society can cope with the complexity of managing our crowded, divided planet. Few communities, companies or countries can say they have resolved the conundrums that confront them. Western Europe took over forty years to create a single market, with many economic and political problems still unresolved. Yet the World Trade Organization will take us towards a single global market even more diverse and unequal than Europe in just ten years. Who can honestly say there will be no losers as global competition intensifies? And who knows how the losers will fight back? Increased competition means that everyone fights for themselves and their particular interests, a fight in which the strongest or smartest may win in the short term, but where all could lose before the fighting is finished.

Humanity needs a better way of resolving collective problems than it has achieved so far. Our species has faced similar dilemmas on a smaller scale in the past: when rural vagrants threatened the urban prosperity of medieval Europe; when impoverished workers demanded the vote, higher wages and social protection during the last century; or when competition between the first industrial nations fuelled protectionism and war in the first half of this century. South Africa was a microcosm of North–South conflict. It provides the most dramatic example of the running battle between rich and poor seeking a new settlement. Its experience may offer fresh insights into the new world now being created.

Comparison between apartheid and the global system is not new. 'The World in One Country' was a slogan of the South African tourist industry. More seriously, the parallel was used by Gernot Kohler.[6] Arjun Makhijiani,[7] Vandana Shiva,[8] and others. It was used by scenario-planners of the Anglo-American Corporation to make the case for negotiated majority rule in South Africa in the mid-1980s,[9] and the Group of Lisbon presented global apartheid as one of seven possible scenarios for the future.[10] More recently, Anthony Richmond described the impact of globalization on international migration, racial conflict and ethnic nationalism as global apartheid.[11] These references have much in common with this book, but they do not address its central argument, namely, that apartheid was a form of exclusive protectionism in response to economic competition.

The close analogy between South African apartheid and international inequality does not mean they are the same. While structural similarities are sufficient to justify the term 'global apartheid', there are also significant differences. This book tries to convey the complexity of the issues through the historical context and examples while drawing out the central thread. Many issues left out or mentioned only in passing may be followed up through the bibliography provided for each chapter.

DIFFERENCES BETWEEN THE WEST AND SOUTH AFRICA

Apartheid was a very specific system of discrimination which classified each individual according to race and ruthlessly divided people into separate groups. Western systems of exclusion are more sophisticated. They also involve a hierarchical ranking of group privileges (see pp. 178–9), but the West is publicly opposed to racism. Most Western countries have laws against racial discrimination and active anti-racist movements. Yet much Western thought, law and action are exclusive, operating through institutional and indirect discrimination rather than overt racism. National interest rather than race justifies double standards in international relations, while appeals to national identity are often coded forms of racism in domestic politics.

The West is not a unitary state. Neither the USA nor the G7 group of the seven richest countries can easily impose decisions on other countries within the West. Agreement must be reached through negotiation between leaders jealous of their power and parochial interests. Western states also have different relationships with groups of countries in the Majority World, such as the Commonwealth, Lomé Convention or Organisation of American States. These historical ties cut across the Western Alliance, so that solidarity cannot be taken for granted, as it was between most white South Africans.

The Majority World is more varied and powerful than the non-white communities of South Africa. It includes widely differing political-economic systems, some even more oppressive than apartheid. Several Majority World states have considerable influence in international affairs. China has a permanent seat on the UN Security Council, others possess nuclear weapons, and a few have bigger economies than most Western countries. This prevents the West from exercising unconditional power in international affairs.

Lawful opposition is easier within the West than it was in South Africa. But it is often more difficult in Central America, Indonesia and much of the Majority World where the effects of global apartheid are experienced most acutely.

Inequality between white and black in South Africa was almost entirely due to apartheid. The relatively greater autonomy of Majority World states means that some pursued policies which brought greater prosperity while corruption, dictatorship and incompetence debilitated others. The West cannot be blamed for all the world's ills, although its legacies of imperialism, trade discrimination and postwar intervention are a major factor in continuing inequality.

Moreover, the dynamic economies of the Pacific rim and China are creating a distinctive zone which accounts for a quarter of the world's economy, including Japan (although just 5 per cent without Japan). Their growing strength shows that Majority World countries can break through the unequal pattern of development, although their very success is triggering a protectionist backlash which could entrench global apartheid.

These differences give hope that the world can overcome the depths of discrimination enforced in South Africa and find a just settlement before the millennium. There should be no illusions about the scale of the task nor the extent of inequality between the West and the Majority World.

WHY THIS ARGUMENT IS IMPORTANT NOW

The parallel between apartheid in South Africa and international relations is important today because the intensification of economic competition as a result of greater free trade is increasing political pressures for one-sided protectionism in the West. Small farmers, environmentalists, community activists, trade unionists and populist politicians are building new coalitions to protect what they hold most dear. Like it or not, they share a common cause with resurgent xenophobia and racism. Under the existing world order, one-sided protectionism will only increase inequality, injustice and conflict.

This is the most difficult part of the argument. There are justified fears that giving the Majority World equal access to Western markets will destroy jobs, undermine social security and erode environmental standards. The response to these concerns must be found within an equitable non-discriminatory framework of international law governing trade as well as security, environmental protection and human rights. The alternative is to entrench global inequality.

Apartheid was almost universally condemned. Left and right denounced it as evil. It was declared a crime in international law and made subject to boycotts by most countries of the world. Millions of individuals boycotted South African goods, demonstrated or donated money to the cause of freedom. Inequality between the West and the world's majority rarely arouses similar indignation or political action, although it is just as immoral and illegitimate. It deserves the same condemnation.

The battle against apartheid in South Africa was long and hard. It is not over yet, as the threads of inequality cling deep in the

fabric of society. Yet the ending of apartheid is a sign of hope.
After decades of international isolation, South Africa may lead the
way with a unique example of a privileged minority surrendering
power for its own long-term self-interest and the greater good.
South Africa's struggle to create a just and democratic system is of
global significance.

Further Reading

Global Governance

The Commission of Global Governance, *Our Global Neighbourhood*,
    Oxford University Press, 1955.
Dror, Yehezkel, *Ist die Erde noch regierbar?*, report to the Club of
    Rome, Bertelsmann, Munich, 1995.
McGrew, Anthony G., Lewis, Paul G., et al., *Global Politics*, Polity Press,
    Cambridge, 1992.
The South Commission, *The Challenge to the South*, Oxford University
    Press, 1990.
von Weizsäker, Ernst Ulrich, *Earth Politics*, Zed Books, 1994.

1

The World in One Country

Where in the world can you find a more just society than South Africa has?
P. W. Botha, 6 May 1976
South African Minister of defence

We remain the free-est, fairest, most just and most decent nation on the face of the earth.
President Bush, 10 May 1992, in Los Angeles after the race riots

In the family of Western nations, White South Africa was like a rich but boorish uncle whose brutal treatment of servants became embarrassing. The rest of the family had replaced live-in domestics with machines and contracted out their chores to migrants and the poor, but Uncle Apartheid stubbornly stuck to his Victorian ways. The question is, was apartheid in South Africa a cruder version of the West or an abhorrent aberration? The evidence suggests that the family resemblance deserves deeper investigation.

White South Africa was part of the West in terms of history, industry, infrastructure, living standards, culture, commerce and consumption. White suburbs of Cape Town and Pretoria rivalled the affluent outskirts of Los Angeles or Munich; central Johannesburg was like downtown Dallas or New York, a fast-moving cosmopolitan Western city. South Africa was a modern industrial state, its cities linked by motorways, railways, airlines and high-tech telecommunications. Out of sight, away from the centre, crowded black townships and hostels housed vast reserves of low-paid workers who served the homes, farms, factories and mines of white masters. Black people needed a pass and work permits to enter white areas, just as the West demands passports and work permits. 'Illegal immigrants' were detained and deported without trial or appeal, like many in the West.

White South Africa was one of the world's richest states in the midst of poor African peoples. Three-quarters of the land and all its natural resources could only be owned by whites, a sixth of the population. The West also has a sixth of the world's population and commands over three-quarters of global resources. Not only did Europeans colonize large parts of the world's arable land, particularly the Americas, but they control most of the rest through market forces. Large areas of the Majority World grow cash crops to supply the West, even where local people are malnourished. One study has estimated that 228,000 km^2 of agricultural land was needed to grow food imports for the twelve countries of the European Union in 1990, adding almost a fifth (17%) to the total amount of agricultural land it utilizes.[1]

Over half of this area was used to grow soya beans, coffee, cotton, grains and rubber in countries where many people do not have enough to eat. The concept of 'environmental space', sometimes called the ecological 'footprint' or 'rucksack', graphically describes the total resources used by a country. It includes land, raw materials, marine resources, energy and capacity for waste disposal. The West consumes a hugely disproportionate share of global resources, much of which is physically extracted from the Majority World or the global commons of air, sea and space. In terms of atmospheric pollution, the West causes over three-quarters of the carbon dioxide emissions which contribute to global warming. In this very real sense the West pre-empts the world's productive resources much as Europeans did those of South Africa.

South Africa's self-governing homelands were run by authoritarian black regimes and were highly dependent on aid, investment and support from white South Africa, like many former colonies of the West. Homeland tourism offered cheap, exotic holidays with a choice of gambling, sex, swimming, ethnic arts and adventure from the safety of modern hotels – a clear parallel with, for example, the Caribbean, Morocco or Thailand.

White South Africa was a parliamentary democracy, run on Western principles, with separate systems of administration for non-whites to run their 'own affairs'. Coloureds and Indians had separate parliaments and elected representatives to the President's Council, but the white minority had the final say over everything, just as Western leaders have the final say in the UN Security Council, IMF and World Bank.

South Africa had First World environmental problems such as acid rain and toxic waste alongside Third World problems of soil erosion, deforestation and desertification. Its white population suffered the ailments of affluence – heart disease, obesity, alcoholism – while the most common diseases among the black majority were those of poverty – malnutrition, tuberculosis, typhoid, cholera and leprosy. Its economic, social and environmental problems were a microcosm of the world's problems – and still are, although political power has now passed to the majority.

THE DEVELOPMENT GAP

In South Africa, inequality between the rich white 'First World' and poor black 'Third World' developed out of a long colonial history in which Europeans deliberately separated people on the basis of 'race'. Apartheid or 'separate development' was introduced by the National Party after the 1948 election to protect European interests and identity by enforcing separation between the 'races'. Apartheid was never static, but its aim was simple. Prime Minister Verwoerd bluntly told the House of Assembly in 1963:

> We want to keep South Africa White ... 'Keeping it White' can only mean one thing, namely White domination, not 'leadership', not 'guidance', but 'control', 'supremacy'. If we are agreed that it is the desire of the people that the White man should be able to continue to protect himself by retaining White domination, we say that it can be achieved by separate development.[2]

This was extraordinarily difficult in a country as ethnically diverse and intermingled as South Africa. The large Coloured population was a heritage of centuries of intimate liaisons between white and black. Prosperous and professional Africans lived alongside poor working-class whites. But the European minority had the political, judicial, military and economic power to impose its vision.

By contrast, the West claims to have pursued a policy of democratic development. After the Second World War, Western powers created the United Nations and other international institutions to develop a new world order of prosperity and peace. President Truman's inaugural speech in January 1949 consciously spoke for the West when he declared:

> We must embark on a bold new programme for making the benefits of our scientific advances and industrial progress available for the improvement and growth of underdeveloped areas. The old-fashioned imperialism – exploitation for foreign profit – has no place in our plans. What we envisage is a programme of development based on the concepts of democratic fair dealing.

The postwar settlement raised aspirations for independence, democracy and development throughout the Majority World,

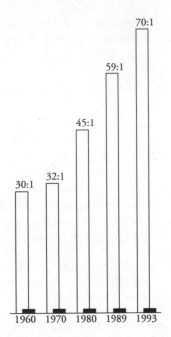

Fig. 1 Income disparity between the richest and poorest 20 per cent of the world's population
Source: UNDP/World Bank.

including the segregated southern United States. But the process of decolonization was not so much a liberation of the Majority World as a transfer of global hegemony from Europe to the United States. The new international institutions were far from democratic and US officials projected a 'Grand Area Strategy' for American global power, which I will describe later.

Western political leaders routinely reaffirm their commitment to 'developing countries': in the United Nations, at annual meetings of the G7, IMF, World Bank and other assemblies. Yet the gap between rich and poor has grown wider. Despite Truman's promise to share the benefits of progress, most 'development' has taken place in the West or on Western terms. As in South Africa, most people have experienced improvements in life expectancy, literacy, health and material conditions. Sections of the majority have grown significantly richer. Yet the overall picture is one of systematic inequality. For vast numbers of people, conditions have remained unchanged or got worse. Improvements have been precarious compared with the immense increase in Western affluence (see fig. 1).

The impressive improvement in material living standards among some Asian Pacific countries, as well as the growing middle classes of India and Latin America, are a sign that the global balance of power is shifting and a new settlement is in the making. But their very success in exporting low-cost manufactured goods to the West could become a new stimulus for global apartheid, just as the commercial success of African farmers and mineworkers during the first half of this century led to the entrenchment of inequality in South Africa. This dangerous possibility is a central concern of this book, developed more fully in chapters 3 to 5.

After over forty years, Truman's ambition to make 'the benefits of our scientific advances and industrial progress available for the improvement and growth of underdeveloped areas' has achieved less than separate development in South Africa during the same period, as is summarized below.

Summary of socio-economic parallels

The overall socio-economic fabric [of South Africa] is ... a unique mixture of First and Third World systems, values, cultures, practices, norms, and all other factors which make up the economic environment. There is a marked disparity in incomes, standards of living, lifestyles, education and work opportunities.
Republic of South Africa, *Official Yearbook 1988-9*

Across a wide range of socio-economic indicators, there is strong evidence for a profound parallel between South Africa and the world. Table 1 summarizes this evidence, together with historical and political parallels which are considered in later chapters. This chart also serves as a reminder of the development gap which must be closed to bring about greater global equality.

The many parallels between South Africa and the world do not necessarily have similar causes, but they raise profound questions which must be addressed. To answer them we first need to look at the origins of the Western dominance which established both South Africa and the Western Economic System.

Table 1 Political, social and economic parallels: South Africa and the rest of the world

South Africa	Global Apartheid
Common colonial history, religion, laws and customs, language, culture, economic system	

Political parallels

South Africa	Global Apartheid
Land Act	Grand Area Strategy/ecological footprint
Group Areas Act	Nation-states/regional groups
Independent homelands	Independent colonies
Race classification	Nationality laws
Pass laws/influx controls	Immigration laws
Job reservations, migrant labour	Trade tariffs, quotas, guest workers, wetbacks
Sun City	Cheap tourist resorts
Three-chambered parliament	UN System, IMF, World Bank
President's Council/State Security Council	Security Council
National Security Management System (NSMS)	NATO/ANZUS Pentagon treaties
Corrupt, undemocratic repressive homeland elites	Corrupt, undemocratic, repressive Third-World elites
Separate development	National sovereignty
White superiority	Western superiority
Christian faith	Christian faith
Secular Western values	Secular Western values

Social and economic parallels

Infant mortality (per 1,000 live births)

White	9	North	18
Indian	16		
Coloured	40	South (av)	121
African	80	LDCs	205

Life expectancy (years)

White	72	North	74
Indian	64	South	62
African	59	LDCs	50

Population growth (% per year)

African	2.80	Africa	2.8
Coloured	2.45	Latin America	2.4
Indian	1.98	Asia	2.0
White	0.95	OECD	0.8

Table 1 *(Cont.)*

South Africa		Global Apartheid	
Adult literacy (%)			
White	99	North	98
Black	70	South	60
		LDCs	35

Enrolment in education (% of all students in each group)

	White	Black	North	South
Primary	13	87	18	82
Secondary	30	70	31	69
Tertiary	67	23	53	47

Pupil–teacher ratios (no of pupils per teacher)

White	16	OECD	24
Indian	21		
Coloured	25	South	51
Black	40		

Sources: World Bank and UNDP Human Development annual reports; (1987/8 figures) South African Institute for Race Relations Survey, 1987/8 (1986/7 figures)

ORIGINS OF GLOBAL APARTHEID

> The discovery of America, and that of a passage to the East Indies by the Cape of Good Hope, are the two greatest and most important events recorded in the history of mankind. Their consequences already have been very great; but, in the short period of between two and three centuries, which has elapsed since these discoveries were made, it is impossible that the whole extent of their consequences can have been seen. What benefits, or what misfortunes to mankind may hereafter result from these great events, no human wisdom can foresee. By uniting, in some measure, the most distant parts of the world, by enabling them to relieve one another's wants, to increase one another's enjoyments, and to encourage one another's industry, their general tendency would seem to be beneficial. To the natives however ... all the commercial benefits which can have resulted from those events have been sunk and lost in the dreadful misfortunes which they have occasioned.
>
> Adam Smith, *The Wealth of Nations*, 1776[3]

When Europeans began to create a global economy in the fifteenth century, they also laid the foundations for separate development between themselves and other peoples. After three centuries of gradual expansion, Adam Smith extolled the potential of world trade to benefit all humanity and condemned the misfortune inflicted on the inhabitants of Africa, America and Asia. Smith's hopes for mutual enjoyment through trade were never fully realized, and the growing power of European commerce compounded misery for the majority almost everywhere it reached.

The roots of inequality between the West and the Majority World go deeper than the five centuries since Columbus set foot in the Americas and Bartolomeu Dias sailed round the Cape of Good Hope. While the institutions of global apartheid were created by Western powers after the First World War, their origins can be traced through the slow separation of society from nature. In order to overcome divisions which confront us now, we need to see the whole in which we have more in common than social distinctions of race, religion, culture or nationality and recognize ourselves as part of nature.

The West itself has deep roots in a common human history broader than any single people. The world today is not the product of fifty or even 500 years of development, but a dense fabric of human endeavour older than recorded history, woven into our emotions, beliefs, languages, landscapes and institutions. The components of today's global system evolved piecemeal over millennia as human societies acquired increasingly powerful ways of organizing themselves and using the world for their own ends.

Many of today's international institutions were built on the foundations of the Roman empire. Rome consolidated centuries of cultural, fiscal, legal, military, technological and organizational principles that provided a basis for five centuries of imperial rule over much of Europe, Asia Minor and North Africa. It established a vast economic area with a single currency and extensive trade between different regions. As the empire disintegrated under successive invasions by northern tribes, its accumulated experience continued through the church. Christianity spread by offering salvation to slaves, poor and oppressed people. After Emperor Constantine adopted Christianity for political reasons in 313, the church rapidly developed as an established, disciplined state religion, crushing heresy and imposing orthodoxy. Its administration, convictions and structure were modelled on those of the empire, but the church was not under direct imperial control. Dynamic tension between church and state enabled alternative centres of authority and belief to develop, paving the way for European pluralism.

The invading Germanic tribes imposed their rule over people whose religion, languages, laws and customs differed from their own. The common people were virtually slaves, tied to land they worked at the mercy of ruling families. Over time the conquerors intermarried, adopted Christianity and acquired elements of the Roman legacy. But there can be little doubt that the millennium of conquest and reconquest left deep traces in the habits of mind, institutions and social structures of the warring states that emerged as modern European history.

European expansion

By the late Middle Ages, different regions of the world were relatively equal in terms of economic development. Cities of Arabia, China, Europe, India and Sumatra had busy markets, linked by slow-moving chains of itinerant traders. The newer Islamic faith rivalled Christianity, propagated by holy war across three powerful empires which, at their peak, stretched from the Caliphate of Spain to the Philippines, Java and the Bay of Bengal. The Ottoman empire was the world's largest, most dynamic political force. Muslims were active merchants who developed many of the principles of today's economy, such as trading companies, double-entry bookkeeping, bills of exchange and the equivalent of stock exchanges.[4] The splendid cities of Baghdad, Mecca, Cairo, Seville and Granada were centres of civilization and a ferment of science, culture, trade and industry. Here the European renaissance discovered mathematics, philosophy, science, technology and knowledge of ancient Greece.

The reasons why European states eventually gained supremacy over the more sophisticated, extensive and commercial Islamic world are complex. Christendom was deeply divided between competing centres of faith and fractious kingdoms. Life was often harsh and violent, beset by famine, disease, peasant uprisings and war. Roman ruins, laws and literature reminded Europeans that life had once been better.

The nation-state was central to Western economic and political development. European states evolved out of ruling households and war councils of conquerors who imposed their will on subject peoples to exact tribute and allegiance. The state's main function was to prepare for war, protect the land from conquest and uphold the sovereign's rule. Justice, by all accounts, was swift and cruel. Most states were small, many little more than cities, competing for territory and trade in a kaleidoscope of alliances and wars. The fractured, complex geography of fortified city-states made it difficult for any one power to predominate, preserving a plurality of states. Military rivalry stimulated improvements in weaponry, technology, public administration and finance as states strove for superiority. Artillery and naval prowess eventually gave Europeans a decisive edge over other peoples.[5]

The need to raise money for arms, soldiers and fortifications gave European states an active interest in the economy, trade and finance. Direct taxes were unpopular and difficult to collect, so revenue was raised from taxes on the use of crown lands for hunting, fishing, mining or for other monopoly privileges. Since it was often easier to tax strangers, a wide range of tolls was levied on travellers and their goods. Local traders were granted exemption from these charges and paid an annual poll tax for protection instead. In England they became known as 'free traders' and in time whole towns became 'free-burghs'. Royal charters granted towns privileged rights to appoint magistrates, make by-laws, build defences and raise revenues for their own purposes. This freedom from arbitrary confiscation enabled cities to develop trade and industry as well as municipal services funded through taxation. In due course this marriage of privileged protection and free trade gave birth to the Western Economic System.

The growth of markets, trading companies, financial capital and banking during the Middle Ages created dynamic social forces which spurred Europeans to reach out beyond their local areas, while population pressures and recurrent famine provided a powerful push for agricultural improvement, technological innovation, military advances and colonization. These developments gave particular advantages to seafaring states like Portugal, Holland and Britain, which sent expeditions far beyond their borders. State surpluses were used to finance long-distance voyages, like that of Bartolomeu Dias (1487) and Christopher Columbus (1492–1504). Most English expeditions such as those of John Cabot (1481–97) or Francis Drake (1577–96) were financed by private subscription as speculative investments, backed by royal warrant.

Long-distance trade was expensive and risky but potentially very, very profitable. It demanded considerable investment which would not see a return until the cargo was delivered and sold. Trade with South-East Asia was carried out by specialist intermediaries who did not fully belong to the local networks of mutual obligation and tradition, but established relationships based purely on payment, in kind or cash, usually gold or silver. Long-distance trade developed the international financial system of credit, money transfers, marine insurance and shareholding. It helped to remove the taboo on charging interest – condemned by both Christianity and Islam – which made money cheaper and more readily available. Trade stimulated economic specialization in products such as cork and sugar in Portugal, wool in Spain, textiles in Holland and grain in Poland. Specialization spurred innovation, since more refined goods commanded higher prices in distant markets.

Royal privileges protected long-distance trade with monopoly rights and high tariffs to deter foreign competitors. Such privileges gave the state considerable benefits, since they often required payment in advance (a royalty) plus a share of the profit afterwards. The Dutch East India Company complained that 'The state ... derives three times as much profit from trade and navigation in the Indies as the shareholders.'[6]

The English East India Company was created by City merchants and granted monopoly rights in 1600, which were finally abolished only in 1865. The company expanded from trading in tea, spices and exotic goods to acquiring and administering the Indian subcontinent for the British government. The Dutch East India Company, founded in 1602, exploited Java, Sumatra and the Pacific, incidentally planting the first white settlement in South Africa as a staging-post on the way. The Dutch West India Company acquired the North American coast from Chesapeake Bay to Newfoundland, buying Manhattan for goods worth 60 guilders ($24) in 1624. It also pioneered trade with West Africa and conquered parts of northern Brazil from the Portuguese. Smaller companies, such as the African Lakes Company, Hudson Bay Company, Levant Company, Muscovy Company, National African Company, British South Africa Company and many others, staked out portions of the globe. Not all succeeded, but those that survived generated up to 500 per cent profits.[7]

European states competed against each other for trade routes. Their national interests were intimately linked with the fortunes of private companies as gold, raw materials, cheap food and slave labour from the rest of the world financed industrial development. Traders were gradually followed by colonizers, mainly private ventures backed by royal authority and, where necessary, warships. Most settlers were poor, escaping low wages, unemployment, religious turmoil and political conflict at home. They worked as servants, indentured labourers and craftspeople for merchants who financed their passage.

European expansion was resisted by indigenous people, who lacked weapons to withstand the onslaught. In the conquest of

America, Europeans wiped out over 85 per cent of the native population, estimated at between 50 and 100 million people in 1492, over a fifth of humanity. Today there are less than 35 million indigenous Americans, less than one hundredth of the world's population.[8] Slavery, slaughter, economic exclusion and European diseases completed this genocide. Hundreds of indigenous languages, cultures and civilizations were destroyed.

European expansion was driven by a massive population explosion – what biologists would call a 'breeding storm'. Between 1460 and 1620, its population doubled. Between 1800 and 1930 the world's white population increased by 350 per cent, from 200 million to 700 million people, growing from about 20 per cent of the human species in 1800 to about 35 per cent in 1930. Every year from 1846 to 1930 between 360,000 and 1 million people left Europe, more than 50 million in total. Most settled in North America, about 5 million colonized Latin America and more than 1 million went to Australia and South Africa.[9] Europeans took with them crops, livestock and agricultural methods which were critical in sustaining rapid population growth and freeing people from the chores of food production.[10]

This narrative oversimplifies the complex, chaotic history of European expansion and omits the many non-European empires. The fact is that by the twentieth century most of the world was controlled by descendants of the Nordic tribes who overran the Roman empire. Many factors contributed to this state of affairs, but the dynamic interaction between four distinctive types of institution – states, markets, trading companies and finance – seems crucial. This interaction stimulated improvements in agriculture, industry, technology and warfare as well as the pursuit of science, commerce, colonial expansion and civil liberties. At the same time, the once powerful institutions of church, feudal lord and monarch waned.

Emergence of global apartheid

Industrialization utterly transformed Europe, its colonies and America during the nineteenth century. The process was complex and different in every country, involving the extension of national markets, removal of feudal relationships, destruction of craft industries and creation of factories using wage labour and machines. In every country the state played a key role in removing legal, economic and institutional barriers to the expansion of markets and industrial development.

In Britain, the market system was promoted by conscious and often violent intervention by government to break up common lands, suppress combinations of workers and protect trade. Foreign policy was largely driven by economic interests. The textile industry, vanguard of the industrial revolution, was shielded from overseas competition between 1700 and 1813. Although Indian calicos and Chinese silks were superior to British textiles, state protection enabled cotton manufacture to become Britain's main export using raw material cultivated by African slaves on land taken from native Americans. Later the Indian textile industry was destroyed by Britain.

America, India, Africa, Australia and South-East Asia were a significant source of luxury goods as well as of raw materials for Europe's industrial development. They provided a safety-valve for capital and labour, relieving competitive pressures by absorbing surplus goods, people and money. Profits from industrialization and foreign trade generated huge sums for investment in Europe and abroad. Overseas investment had the sole purpose of producing wealth as cheaply as possible for the 'mother country'. Ports, railways, plantations, mines and cities were established to extract resources as efficiently as possible regardless of local needs.

Free trade became the dominant political faith among Britain's rulers. Markets helped to unify nation-states in Germany, Austria and Italy. Trade and industry contributed visibly to rising prosperity for growing numbers of people throughout Europe, who enjoyed a greater variety of goods and cheaper food. Industrialization also had a terrible social cost. Commercial agriculture forced people off the land into squalid, crowded cities, factories destroyed employment in traditional trades, and industrial work was hard, long and often poorly paid. Poverty, social discontent and political crisis were recurrent. Governments suppressed rural uprisings and working-class organizations which challenged market forces and state power.

Many social movements grappled with this transformation, from philanthropy and paternalism to social democracy and revolutionary socialism. Trade union action, national and local legislation, mutual societies, and charities gradually created minimum standards for health and safety, hours of work, levels of pay and social security. In Germany, Bismarck began the world's first welfare state to counteract revolution. Thus economic development was accompanied by political change as people attempted to control the powerful forces unleashed by industrialization. Since government had been used to widen markets, those who suffered their consequences demanded a say in government.

Between 1870 and 1914 the world economy became a single, interdependent whole, centred on Europe. In many respects the world economy was more globalized than it is today, with proportionately greater movement of people, goods and finance. The volume of world trade increased by over 50 per cent a decade after 1840, faster than increases in production. Almost every portion of the globe was connected by intricate webs of investment, trade, transport and telegraph cables. The gold standard facilitated economic growth and integration by providing a stable medium of exchange. The volume of gold production, particularly from South Africa, grew in line with trade, so that output could expand without running up against a shortage of a means of payment. Gold was essentially a sterling standard, but Britain's commitment to free trade, regardless of social cost, made sterling a reliable world currency.

Growing interdependence through trade contributed to peace between European states, and many people believed war was no longer possible. The Great Powers – Austria–Hungary, Britain, France, Germany, Italy and Russia – divided much of the non-European world between them and sought security through interlocking alliances. But the rise of Germany as an industrial and military power with imperial ambitions eventually erupted in the 1914 war, with catastrophic consequences for Europe and profound repercussions throughout the world.

The postwar settlement

The First World War ended the European world order and brought the rising powers of the US and Japan into the first attempt to create a global political settlement. The League of Nations was mainly a European body, although several Latin American countries, the British Dominions, British India and Japan were also members. The US decision to pull out in 1920 severely weakened the League's authority, but its achievements should not be underestimated. It resolved several disputes between member states, created the Court of International Justice in 1922 and addressed a wide range of social and economic problems. It founded the International Labour Organization to raise working conditions of 'civilized labour' and foster peaceful industrial relations. The World Health Organization was created to prevent epidemics and improve public health. It intervened to rehabilitate Austria, Hungary, Bulgaria, Greece and Estonia after their economic collapse and to avert the threat of Communist revolution. It assisted in massive transfers of peoples between Greece, Turkey, Armenia and other Balkan states to reduce ethnic conflict. Unfortunately the League's structure and powers were insufficient to halt rearmament or prevent the expansionist ambitions of Germany, Italy and Japan.

A major weakness of the new international settlement was the lack of any mechanism to manage the massive economic forces unleashed by unfettered finance and growing industrial capacity. Postwar reconstruction stimulated a worldwide economic boom, particularly in the US, which became the world's foremost industrial nation. A financial crisis in 1929 almost triggered the collapse of the capitalist economies. By 1931 industrial production had fallen by more than half in Germany and the US. World trade shrank by a third and over a quarter of workers lost their jobs in many countries. The crisis was the most severe in a series of increasingly volatile business cycles that had emerged with the industrial era, but the responses by governments made things worse. Only the Soviet Union, isolated from world markets, continued to increase production as the West reeled from crisis to crisis. Soviet stability won widespread admiration for central planning as a viable alternative to the chaos of free-market capitalism, although it concealed enforced collectivization in which millions died.

The West's prolonged crisis wrought a far-reaching transformation throughout the world. The sense of powerlessness, loss of identity and insecurity revitalized nationalism. In Africa, Asia and Latin America movements for national liberation and revolution gained strength as people were radicalized by the continuing crisis. Fascist movements sprang up throughout the West. The Ku Klux Klan revived in the United States. Populist authoritarian regimes replaced democratic institutions in Japan, Italy, Germany and Central Europe, rebuilding their economies through rearmament, public works and territorial expansion. Nationalism took its most extreme form in Germany with the industrialized genocide of Jews and other minorities.

Western governments abandoned *laissez-faire* for state intervention to overcome the continuing economic depression. Roosevelt's New Deal in 1933 included job creation schemes, employment

regulation, agricultural subsidies, financial regulations, social welfare programmes and massive public works, including dam-build-
ing and electrification. Coalition governments in Britain, France
and the Netherlands attempted to ameliorate the crisis through
different forms of intervention. In South Africa, the white coalition
government responded to the depression by reinforcing discriminatory labour policies, subsidizing commercial agriculture and
social welfare to deal with the 'poor whites problem'. High
unemployment persisted throughout the West until the Second
World War began in 1939. Karl Polanyi described the protracted
process of reasserting social control over the 'nineteenth century
utopia' of unregulated markets as 'the great transformation'[11]
which laid the foundation for Western peace and prosperity after
the war.

The cataclysmic upheaval of Western society during the Second
World War was accompanied by intense efforts to create a new
global settlement which would prevent war and economic collapse
from ever happening again. New international institutions were
built round the United Nations, drawing on the structures of and
lessons learnt from the League of Nations. The World Bank and
IMF were founded on the experience of coping with the Great
Depression through the US New Deal.

These institutions faced similar political and economic problems
to those of white South Africa, itself an active part of the Western
alliance. General Smuts, prime minister of South Africa, contributed extensively to proposals for the League of Nations and
United Nations. Most Majority World countries were European
colonies and not represented at the creation of these organizations.
But the United Nations and postwar institutions were greeted
with optimism within the Majority World as well as in the West.
The Second World War marked a dramatic shift of power from
Europe to the United States, which supported decolonization and
proclaimed a new world of freedom, equality and development,
notwithstanding the segregated southern states or its armed forces,
where racial discrimination was rife.

The postwar settlement was soon overshadowed by cold war
between the West and the Soviet Union, which permeated international relations. Since the collapse of the Soviet system it is clear
that continuing poverty and the struggle over resources in the
Majority World are still the major source of conflict.

Western peace was accompanied by almost continuous war in
the Majority World. National liberation movements against colonial rule did not bring economic freedom nor internal agreement

between peoples lumped together by European history. India, Pakistan, Bangladesh, Nigeria, Sudan and many other arbitrary states sacrificed millions of lives fighting over borders they did not make. Western military intervention in Algeria, Angola, Central America, Korea, Indonesia, the Middle East, Vietnam and over thirty other conflicts sought to protect its worldwide interests. For liberation movements in the Majority World these wars were an assertion of self-determination, chosen with their lives.

Thirty years of unprecedented economic growth gradually increased prosperity for most people in the West. But for many regions of the Majority World it brought continuing and some-times growing poverty. The coffee-growers of Latin America, Rwanda and Ethiopia, tea-pickers of Africa and Asia, tin-miners of Bolivia or copper-miners of Chile, Zambia and Zaire scarcely benefited from the growing affluence their produce helped create. Profits from their efforts were rarely reinvested in their own countries. Higher-value activities such as processing, manufacture and distribution were controlled and undertaken by Western companies.

The global economic system established by victorious Western powers after the war was very different from the nineteenth-century free market ideal. It explicitly set out to manage markets and protect people in the West from economic turbulence. The Majority World was outside the West's New Deal and served Western markets without the benefits of Western privileges. The settlement of South Africa was just one episode in Europe's worldwide expansion and its history followed similar stages to those seen in the world as a whole.

THE EMERGENCE OF SOUTH AFRICA

Only one race approached God's ideal type, his own Anglo-Saxon race: God's purpose then was to make the Anglo-Saxon race predominant, and the best way to help on God's work and fulfil His purpose in the world was to contribute to the predominance of the Anglo-Saxon race and so bring nearer the reign of justice, liberty and peace.

Cecil John Rhodes

South Africa's fate was deeply embedded in Europe's colonial history. Its development was dictated by European economic priorities. Its geo-political boundaries, institutions, laws, patterns of ownership and use of resources were designed to meet European needs. Apartheid emerged out of centuries of struggle between different European traditions transplanted into southern Africa. Each brought their own ways of seeing and of doing things, their laws and religious beliefs. They drew sharp boundaries between themselves and the unfamiliar, near-naked, dark-skinned inhabitants, who welcomed them, bartered with them and were betrayed by them again and again. Africans resisted the spreading white settlements on traditional grazing lands, but were repeatedly outgunned. The settlers were less numerous and less ruthless than the genocidal colonialists of North America, but similar forces were at work on both continents.

Like exiles everywhere, Europeans recreated the world they knew best, building little Holland or little England 6,000 miles and many months from home. Familiar place names, plants, buildings, institutions and customs marked out European enclaves on an alien continent. Each person was like a social gene, planting distinctive habits of thought, skills, aspirations and values. Each family and community reproduced and permutated its old culture in response to new circumstances. Over four centuries, they had fought Europe's wars and ideological battles between themselves to create their unique version of world history.

Private enterprise, sponsored and protected by European states, played a central role in appropriating and developing South Africa, starting with the Portuguese, who sought gold and a trade route to the East Indies from 1487. The Dutch East India Company destroyed Portugal's monopoly and in 1652 set up a refuelling station on the Cape. Soon the land became 'property of the Company by the sword and the laws of war.'[12] Britain acquired the Cape after 1795 to protect trade routes to India and controlled South Africa until 1910.

In Britain meanwhile, rising population, relentless industrialization and prolonged recession had caused severe impoverishment. Widespread social and political unrest gave rise to Luddite machine-breaking (1811–13), riots, the Peterloo Massacre (1819) and large-scale emigration to America. To relieve these pressures, Parliament offered assisted passages to the Cape, and 90,000 people applied for 5,000 places.

Conflict was inevitable. San bushmen were shot like vermin and virtually exterminated. The Khoikhoi perished as a result of European disease, abuse and social obliteration. The British attempted to Anglicize the 26,000 Dutch farmers (the Boers), seeding generations of resentment. They fought the Boers and the Xhosa people for over 100 years.[13] Africans were compelled to work for Europeans by economic pressures, vagrancy laws and the Masters and Servants Act which anticipated apartheid's labour laws a century later.

In 1834 the British freed slaves and granted black South Africans nominal equality with whites. As in America, they compensated the slave-owners, not the slaves, and limited the franchise through property qualifications. Abolition of slavery spurred Dutch settlers to leave the Cape *en masse* in what became known as the Great Trek (1836–8). Its leaders complained that slaves 'were placed on equal footing with Christians contrary to the laws of God and the natural distinction of race and colour ... therefore we rather withdrew in order to preserve our doctrines in purity.'[14] Fourteen thousand Boers loaded their ox waggons and headed north-east, creating two republics, the Orange Free State and Transvaal. They were a fractious lot and over twenty years the Transvaal trekkers fought each other ten times and established five separate republics. Even their church split three ways. Nationalism was a parochial thing. Their president, Paul Kruger, declared in 1875: 'May there no longer be talk of German or Englishmen, or Hollander or Afrikaner, but may they all be Free Staters, with one interest and one aim.'[15]

Britain, by contrast, ran a global economy in which goods, people and finance moved in response to market forces. In 1860, 100,000 indentured labourers were transported from India to work on sugar plantations in Natal. Africans were encouraged to stay in tribal reserves, run by indirect rule through local chiefs, which became the administrative foundations of the apartheid homelands a century later.[16]

The British attempted to withdraw from South Africa, but spectacular discoveries of diamonds in 1867 and gold in 1886 dramatically altered imperial interest. The Transvaal Republic was annexed in 1877, and African kingdoms were conquered or offered 'protection' within the British empire. Mining shattered this slow-moving rural backwater, wrenching South Africa into the world economy in a few hectic decades. The lure of wealth attracted poor workers and rich investors alike. Thousands of immigrants from America, Australia and Europe transformed sleepy Kimberley and Johannesburg into rough, cosmopolitan frontier cities. Entrepreneurs like Cecil Rhodes, financed by the London bankers Rothschild, bought up claims through De Beers Mining Company. The company concentrated ownership and mechanized production, replacing thousands of independent prospectors with waged labour. They built a convict station for prison labour, a precursor of the apartheid compound system, accommodating up to 3,000 black male workers. White workers pressed mine-owners and politicians to impose a colour bar in order to maintain wage differentials with black workers. The companies introduced passes for Africans, despite protests from the Colonial Office in London, thus laying a further foundation of apartheid. Cecil Rhodes made a fortune as chairman of De Beers and through his ownership of the gold industry through Consolidated Goldfields. He used the British South Africa Company to extend British interests into what became Rhodesia and presided over the Cape as prime minister. Rhodes was part of a network of financiers, imperial administrators and entrepreneurs who shaped southern Africa and had a profound influence on the Western world.[17]

The mines changed the balance of power and economic opportunity between black and white, Afrikaners and British, agricultural and urban workers, farmers and mine-owners. Many Africans prospered. They supplied food for the influx of foreigners, set up businesses and sent their children to multiracial church schools. This enterprise caused shortages of labour in the mines and on white farms, as well as anxieties about competition among white farmers and workers. They agitated for protection against 'unfair competition', as well as for laws to force blacks to work for whites. But the main conflict was between the expansionist British and the provincial, parochial, protectionist Boers.

Two centuries of cultural, political and economic domination by the British roused a bitter Afrikaner nationalism, which culminated in the empire's longest, costliest and bloodiest war, from 1899 to 1902. The Boer War had immense impact throughout the world. It cost Britain over £200 million, a huge sum at the time. Income tax was raised by two-thirds to pay for it, and the introduction of state pensions was postponed. It put a brake on imperial hubris and encouraged the Indian independence struggle. It influenced the seminal book *Imperialism*, by J. A. Hobson,[18] which informed Lenin's analysis of imperialism as the last stage of capitalism.[19] In South Africa itself it spurred Afrikaner nationalists to protect their political and economic independence in a world dominated by Britain.

Although economic factors drove the development of South Africa, the decisions which ultimately created apartheid were all made openly through the political system, through the British Parliament in Westminster as well as in Cape Town. The four most crucial decisions were to define the right to political participation in terms of property ownership and racial origin, to unite disparate republics under the Union of South Africa, to restrict land ownership by race and to legalize racial segregation, particularly in employment. Similar policies prevailed throughout Europe's empires and the segregationist southern United States at the time.

British public opinion had opposed the Boer War, and when the Liberal Party gained power in 1905 the former Afrikaner republics were quietly granted local autonomy under the British crown, following the model of Australia, Canada and New Zealand. The Cape and Natal had a limited non-racial franchise, which included a small black professional class of about 22,000 voters. The Boers were more numerous and maintained extensive segregation. The British rejected universal suffrage, but accepted the franchise for those who 'have really reached the average level of civilisation of the white man'.[20]

The political union of South Africa was driven by economic factors such as the cost of customs and tariffs. As in the formation of the United States over a century earlier and the European Union eighty years later, there were fierce debates about the loss of state sovereignty and the merits of federalism against a unitary constitution. Southern Rhodesia, Basutoland, Bechuanaland (now Botswana) and Swaziland were members of the customs union but did not join the Union of South Africa when it was formed in 1910. The black majority were not represented and the Liberal government in London accepted Afrikaner assurances on the fair treatment of 'natives'.

The apartheid solution

Apartheid evolved out of fierce economic struggles between different social groups. While mining companies eased competitive pressures through mergers, rationalization and political manoeuvring, workers were forced into intense competition for jobs. White workers used racial segregation to protect their privileges and higher wages from competition by lower-paid black workers. Mine-owners opposed racial restrictions and even imported 60,000 Chinese workers in 1904 to cut labour costs; these workers were repatriated at the end of their contracts in 1908. The Chamber of Mines accused British workers of being 'too expensive, too inefficient (in fact much worse than Kaffir labour) and too intermittent and discontinuous'.[21]

A severe economic depression from 1904 to 1909 forced Afrikaner small farmers off the land into the cities, where they were
unwilling to do the low-paid, unskilled heavy work in the mines
and industry. This created the 'poor white problem' and considerable unrest among whites. The Mine Workers Union leader put it
bluntly: 'if we have to compete against the native at the native's
standard it will be hopeless.'[22] Labour unrest in the mines was
recurrent and bitter. During violent strikes in 1911, trade-unionist
William Henry Andrews called on the government 'to protect
against the encroachment of coloured labour in the skilled trades
of South Africa', adding that 'the Government was guilty of a
crime not only against the white people, but against the "nigger"
himself in forcing him to go to the mines and work for the benefit
of the capitalist class'.[23]

Economic depression intensified industrial conflict. When the
price of gold fell by a quarter during 1921, mine-owners responded
by cutting white wages, laying off white workers and hiring black
workers, whose wages averaged one-tenth that of white. White
industrial workers called a general strike the following year in
what became known as the Red Revolt or Rand Rebellion. Twenty
thousand white miners marched through the streets of Johannesburg waving red banners, singing the Red Flag and chanting
'Workers of the World Unite for a White South Africa'. Martial
law was declared and massive force was used to crush the rebellion,
including aerial bombing and an artillery barrage on trade union
headquarters. Between 230 and 250 people were killed, hundreds
were wounded and imprisoned, and three strike leaders were
hanged. The strike was broken. Mine-owners employed more
black people and made record profits in 1924.[24]

The National Party formed an electoral pact with the Labour
Party (modelled on its British counterpart) and the Communists,
which enabled them to win the subsequent election on a platform
of socialism and nationalism. The new prime minister, General
Herzog, saw Bolshevism as 'The will of the people to be free' and
national freedom as 'death to capitalism and imperialism'.[25] The
alliance government introduced a Colour Bar Act, a Wages Board,
protection for domestic manufactures, nationalized industries, the
beginnings of a white welfare state, and the 'civilized labour'
policy, restricting government employment to whites. The mining
magnate Sir Ernest Oppenheimer declared 'it is an evil to impose
class legislation and the curse of such evil is that one must continue
to do evil.'[26] Afrikaner Nationalists opposed the destructive force
of free market capitalism. *Volkshandel*, a business paper, wrote:

Every sober minded, thinking Afrikaner is fed up to the top of his throat with so-called laissez-faire – let-it-be – capitalism, with its soul-destroying materialism and the spirit of 'every man for himself and the devil for us all'. We are sick of it because of its legacy of Afrikaner poor whiteism and the condition which makes the Afrikaner a spectator in the business of his own country.[27]

The essential pattern of apartheid was now firmly set, with a framework of Western parliamentary democracy, welfare state and protected private enterprise for the whites while the black majority were increasingly excluded. White women got the vote in 1930. In 1936 black people were removed from the common voters roll in the Cape. In 1951 Cape Coloureds were denied the vote.

The National Party won the 1948 white election with a manifesto that introduced the word 'apartheid', a policy 'which professes to safeguard the future of every race', but which emphasized that 'The fundamental guiding principle of National Party policy is preserving and safeguarding the White race.' It appealed to poor whites in the towns and small farmers in the countryside who feared that rich English-speakers would make concessions to blacks and ruin them. During the following decades White South Africa reinforced the policy of separate development with the Population Registration Act, Group Areas Act, pass laws, labour laws, separate amenities, separate education and separate systems of administration for Black, Indian, Coloured and White populations. As other African countries gained independence, 'native reservations' or Bantustans were turned into 'self-governing homelands', starting with Transkei in 1963 and KwaZulu in 1971. The ultimate aim was to divide the black majority into independent black nation-states, leaving whites as a majority in South Africa. By 1987, South Africa had created four 'independent' states and six 'self-governing' homelands, with a population of 10 million. The remaining 16 million blacks in sprawling townships like Soweto could, the National Party hoped, become independent city states. Apart from KwaZulu, the homelands were desperately poor and totally dependent on South African aid, expertise and military support. Most were ruled by dictators even more corrupt and repressive than the South African government itself.

With each intensification of apartheid, resistance grew. To enforce their inhumane separation of people, the white authorities required an increasingly complex and repressive security system. In the words of defence chief General Malan in 1977: 'South Africa is today ... involved in total war. The war is not only an area for

the soldier. Everyone is involved.'[28] Due to appalling poverty and
lack of opportunities for most black people, the institutions of
apartheid were largely run and enforced by black people. Like the
British empire, apartheid was a system of indirect rule, directed by
whites at the top but administered by blacks at the bottom. Half
the manpower of the South African police force was black,[29] and
about two-thirds of the African population earned their livelihoods directly or indirectly by working for Europeans.[30]

After 1940 South Africa experienced high economic growth-
rates and whites did very well. Farm prices were supported and
agriculture protected. A large nationalized sector and the fast-
growing arms industry created an engine for growth. An extensive
system of free public health, education and social security was
provided for the white population out of taxes. Gavin Relly of
Anglo-American complained that South Africa had become 'one
of the most socialist countries in the world, because the Afrikaners,
like any strong tribal group, have built it up to distribute the
wealth among themselves'.[31] The combination of cheap black non-
union labour and high standards of living, good infrastructure,
high consumption, a well-educated white professional class and
abundant low-paid servants was very attractive to Western companies. The high level of American and, above all, British investment was welcomed by Prime Minister John Vorster in 1972:
'Each trade agreement, each bank loan, each new investment is
another brick in the wall of our continued existence.'[32]

Economic growth strengthened apartheid, but also increased
black economic power. Shortages of white labour enabled black
workers to get more skilled jobs, organize trades unions, increase
their overall share of purchasing power, and press for economic
and political improvements. In response, white trade-unionists
demanded in 1983 'a specific, categoric and unambiguous under-
taking that the government will step in where necessary to protect
the rights of minority groups'. Tom Neethling of the Amalgamated
Engineers Union stated that 'On the shop floor it is the black,
who by virtue of his exploitability and his numbers, poses the
biggest long-term threat to the future of all workers ... We are
under a constant state of siege from employers.'[33]

The system eventually became unsustainable. Internal opposition and the cost of nine separate systems for each 'racial group'
as well as of security and international sanctions was becoming
too great. From the late 1970s the minority government modified
or repealed racist legislation on black business, mixed marriages,
sexual relationships and amenities, though without relinquishing

overall control. Apartheid's final chapter was the constitution of 1984, presented by President P. W. Botha as the 'end of apartheid'. It extended the vote to Indian and Coloured communities, but represented in separate chambers of parliament, with a President's Council drawn from all three groups. Africans were excluded on the grounds that they belonged to independent homelands and could vote for township councils. This constitution is the main point of comparison for global apartheid used in this book and is outlined in chapter 6.

Global apartheid arose out of similar economic pressures to those in South Africa, as Western states struggled to gain control over the powerful forces of free-market capitalism, although the ideology and specific historical details were quite different. The next chapter examines the underlying dynamics of the Western Economic System in order to identify the factors which separated the development of the West and the Majority World for most of the postwar period. Detailed parallels between the evolution of apartheid and the global system are covered in subsequent chapters.

Further Reading

World historical overview

Braudel, Fernand, *Civilization and Capitalism, 15th–18th Century*, Collins/Fontana: Vol. 1: *The Structures of Everyday Life*, 1981; Vol. 2: *The Wheels of Commerce*, 1985; Vol. 3: *The Perspective of the World*, 1985.

Cain, P. J., and Hopkins, A. G., *British Imperialism: Innovation and Expansion 1688–1914*, Longman, 1993.

Calvocoressi, Peter, *World Politics since 1945* (1968), Longman, 1982.

Carroll, Peter N., Noble, David W., *The Free and the Unfree: A New History of the United States*, Penguin, 1977.

Cipolla, Carlo M., *The Economic History of World Population* (1962), Pelican, 1974.

Crosby, Alfred W., *Ecological Imperialism: The Biological Expansion of Europe, 900–1900*, Cambridge University Press, 1986, Canto edn 1993.

Headrick, Daniel R., *The Tentacles of Progress: Technology Transfer in the Age of Imperialism, 1850–1940*, Oxford University Press, NY, 1988.

Hobsbawm, E. J., *Industry and Empire*, Weidenfeld & Nicolson, 1968, Pelican, 1969.

Kennedy, Paul, *The Rise and Fall of the Great Powers: Economic Change and Military Conflict from 1500 to 2000*, Fontana, 1989.

Nkrumah, Kwame, *Neo-colonialism: The Last Stage of Imperialism*, Panaf, 1965.

Polanyi, Karl, *The Great Transformation: The Political and Economic Origins of Our Time* (1944), Beacon, 1957.

Ponting, Clive, *A Green History of the World*, Sinclair-Stevenson, 1991, Penguin, 1992.

Stannard, David E., *American Holocaust: Columbus and the Conquest of the New World*, Oxford University Press, 1992.

Stone, Norman, ed., *The Times Atlas of World History* (1978), Times Books, 4th edn 1992.

South Africa and the origins of apartheid

Fage, J. D., *A History of Africa*, Hutchinson, 1978, 2nd edn 1988.

Greenberg, Stanley, *Race and State in Capitalist Development: South Africa in Comparative Perspective*, Ravan Press, Johannesburg/Yale University Press, 1980.

Lapping, Brian, *Apartheid: A History*, Paladin, 1986.

Lipton, Merle, *Capitalism and Apartheid*, Temple Gower Smith, 1985.

Meli, Francis, *South Africa Belongs to Us: A History of the ANC*, Zimbabwe Publishing House, Harare, 1988.

Mostert, Noël, *Frontiers: The Epic of South Africa's Creation and the Tragedy of the Xhosa People*, Pimlico, 1993.

Pheko, Motsoko, *Apartheid: The Story of a Dispossessed People*, Sharpeville Day Association, Dar es Salaam, 1972, 2nd edn, Marram Books, 1984.

Sampson, Anthony, *Black and Gold: Tycoons, Revolutionaries and Apartheid*, Coronet, 1987.

Serfontein, J. H. P., *Brotherhood of Power: An Expose of the Secret Afrikaner Broederbond*, Collins, 1979.

Sparks, Allister, *The Mind of South Africa*, Mandarin, 1990.

Wilkins, Ivor, and Strydom, Hans, *The Super-Afrikaners: Inside the Afrikaner Broederbond*, Jonathan Ball, Johannesburg, 1978.

Williams, Walter E., *South Africa's War against Capitalism*, Juta and Co., Kenwyn, South Africa, 1990.

2

The Dynamics of Separate Development

Whosoever commands the trade of the world commands the riches of the world and hence the world itself.

Sir Walter Ralegh, c. 1552–1618

Patriotism is easy to understand ... It means looking after yourself by looking out for your country.

Calvin Coolidge
US President, 1923–9

The Western Economic System is driven by ceaseless competition between companies, states and individuals buying or producing as cheaply as possible and selling for as much as possible. Writing at the start of what is often called the capitalist era, Adam Smith eloquently advocated free markets as a mechanism for universal prosperity in *The Wealth of Nations*, published in 1776. The industrial revolution was slowly transforming Europe's economy and Smith was optimistic that natural forces of competing self-interest would increase national power, wealth and greatness so 'that universal opulence ... and a general plenty diffuses itself through all the different ranks of society'.[1]

Fifty years later, Marx and Engels marvelled that over a period of scarcely 100 years this system had

> created more massive and more colossal productive forces than have all preceding generations together. Subjection of Nature's forces to man, machinery, application of chemistry to industry and agriculture, steam-navigation, railways, electric telegraphs, clearing of whole continents for cultivation, canalization of rivers, whole populations conjured out of the ground – what earlier century had ever a presentiment that such productive forces slumbered in the lap of social labour?[2]

Smith attributed constant improvement in productivity to the division of labour which he saw as a 'very slow and gradual consequence of ... the propensity to truck, barter, and exchange one thing for another'.[3] After 200 years this process is accelerating so fast that stallholders, wholesalers, advertisers, researchers, investors, accountants, engineers, factory workers, labourers and a myriad specialists are almost instantaneously integrated into an extremely flexible and fecund global system. The volume and variety of goods and services available today was unthinkable even fifty years ago, let alone at the time of Smith or Marx. There is no overall plan, yet this cornucopia is generated through an immensely complex organization of human effort and ingenuity as a result of people responding to others' wants as expressed through markets.

But market forces alone did not create this system. As indicated in the previous chapter, the postwar economy relied on powerful state institutions to manage and ameliorate markets. While there are significant differences between Western countries, all have a mixture of market-driven enterprises and extensive state intervention. This is explicit in Europe's 'social markets' and Japan's coordinated competition, but it is equally important in America's military–industrial–business complex. In each case, the state performs at least five functions:

1 *extending or protecting* markets, both internally and externally, through tariffs, trade agreements and other measures;
2 *laying down and enforcing rules* for conduct in markets, including company law, health and safety standards, consumer protection;
3 *providing services* which assist participants in markets, such as public education, training, infrastructure, research and development, trade missions, the gathering and dissemination of information;
4 *social protection* for individuals, communities, firms and the environment from the destructive consequences of market forces through social security, public services, agricultural support, regional assistance, national parks and other provisions;
5 *overall management* of the economic system by controlling the money supply and interest rates, ensuring stability of banks, averting large-scale market failure and influencing relationships between different interests such as workers, employers, investors, landowners, consumers or pressure groups.

The way in which a state pursues these roles is generally more important for economic development than the influence of individual firms or any other factor.[4] At a global level these functions are much less well developed, with the central banking system, G7, IMF, World Bank and GATT/WTO being the main institutions of economic governance; these will be discussed later. Political differences over the state's role in markets are central to most conflicts between trading nations, as they are to many conflicts within countries. These differences will become even more important as global economic integration increases through the World Trade Organization, European Union (EU), the North American Free Trade Agreement (NAFTA) and other regional trading blocs. Understanding the pivotal role of the state in market economies is essential for resolving these conflicts.

HOW THE WESTERN ECONOMIC SYSTEM WORKS

Profit-seeking is the guiding force which determines investment, productivity and pay in markets. Those who accumulate most profit gain power to set the pace of economic development. As a result, in Adam Smith's words, the 'plans and projects of the employers of stock regulate and direct all the most important operations of labour, and profit is the end proposed'.[5] Their power is amplified through the financial system, which creates new money in the form of credit. This multiplies the power to invest far beyond the surplus generated from savings and profit, giving those who control credit and investment immense power.

But competition inevitably squeezes profits. In genuine free markets, rates of profit fluctuate widely and tend to decline as more competitors enter the market. Adam Smith observed: 'When profit diminishes, merchants are very apt to complain that trade decays; though the diminution of profit is the natural effect of its prosperity.'[6] Faltering profits force firms to cut costs, diversify, innovate or seek new markets. This puts the entire system under constant pressure to improve efficiency and expand. Smith remarked that the 'natural diminution of profit' could be avoided by colonization, then taking place in North America and the Caribbean,[7] which partially explains the dramatic expansion of European empires as they developed capitalist economies. Profits have, on the whole, not declined in the mature markets of the West because of constant innovation and worldwide expansion as well as many subtle restrictions on competition.

Smith was optimistic that market forces would increase both prosperity and equality. He believed that the accumulation of capital would force down rates of interest and profits so that very few people could enjoy unearned incomes and almost everyone would work for a living.[8] He argued that, eventually, 'the advantages and disadvantages of different employments of labour and stock must, in the same neighbourhood, be either perfectly equal or continually tending to equality'.[9] Everyone would benefit from rising productivity and prosperity. 'The liberal reward of labour, therefore, as it is the necessary effect, so it is the natural symptom of increasing national wealth.'[10] Economics as well as morality confirmed Smith's view that 'No society can surely be flourishing and happy, in which the far greater part of its members are poor and miserable. It is but equity, besides, that they who feed, cloath [*sic*] and lodge the whole body of the people, should have such a share of the produce of their own labour as to be themselves tolerably well fed, cloathed and lodged.'[11]

In the relatively stable world of eighteenth-century Britain, Smith had little experience of the violent consequences of unrestrained competition and saw only the one-sided privileges which protected the powerful. These monopolistic practices, he believed, suppressed wages, inflated prices and denied liberty to the majority. Remove 'All systems either of preference or of restraint', he argued, and 'natural liberty establishes itself of its own accord. Every man, as long as he does not violate the laws of justice, is left perfectly free to pursue his own interest his own way.'[12] Smith's faith in British justice was fundamental to his view of the market economy:

> that equal and impartial administration of justice which renders the rights of the meanest British subject respectable to the greatest, and which, by securing to every man the fruits of his own industry, gives the greatest and most effectual encouragement to every sort of industry.[13]

As a professor of moral philosophy, Smith also believed competition would be restrained by 'the general fellow feeling which we have with every man merely because he is our fellow creature'.[14] He thought that 'rules of natural equity ... ought to be enforced by the positive laws of every country'[15] to protect 'every member of the society from the injustice or oppression of every other member'.[16] He condemned colonization as 'folly and injustice',[17] and regarded the East India Company as 'plunderers of India'.[18]

Adam Smith was an acute observer of the emerging market

system as well as an eloquent advocate of its power to evoke the industrial transformation of the world about him. He described how

> The exclusive privileges of corporations, statutes of apprenticeship, and all those laws which restrain, in particular employments, the competition to a smaller number than might otherwise go into them ... are a sort of enlarged monopolies, and may frequently, for ages together, and in whole classes of employments, keep up the market price of particular commodities above the natural price, and maintain both the wages of the labour and the profits of the stock employed about them somewhat above their natural price.[19]

Then, as now, the more powerful participants in the system had greater freedom to seek the highest return, so that corporation laws 'give less obstruction to the free circulation of stock [capital] from one place to another than to that of labour. It is everywhere much easier for a wealthy merchant to obtain the privilege of trading in a town corporate, than for a poor artificer to obtain that of working in it.'[20]

Urban corporations, craft guilds, local tariffs and regulations had evolved over centuries to protect townspeople from competition. The laws of settlement kept out itinerant labourers who worked for little more than food and shelter, much as did pass laws in South Africa, vagrancy laws in the American south and as do immigration laws throughout the West today.

In Smith's time, merchants had greater power to make the rules, so they naturally promoted their own interests. He warned that 'the clamour and sophistry of merchants and manufacturers easily persuade them that the private interest of a part, and of a subordinate part of the society, is the general interest of the whole.'[21] Since dealers 'have generally an interest to deceive and even to oppress the public', the 'proposals for any new law or regulation of commerce which comes from this order ought always to be listened to with greatest precaution'.[22] Smith described how 'Masters are always and everywhere in a sort of tacit, but constant and uniform combination, not to raise the wages of labour above their actual rate' or sometimes 'to sink the wages of labour even below this rate.'[23] On the other hand, he said that 'To widen the market and to narrow the competition, is always the interest of dealers.'[24]

Thus, when Smith saw markets as a means of establishing 'natural liberty', he did not see businessmen as custodians of the system. Here the state, identified as the 'sovereign, or common-wealth', had three responsibilities:

> first, the duty of protecting the society from the violence and invasion of other independent societies; secondly, the duty of protecting, as far as possible, every member of the society from injustice or oppression of every other member of it, or the duty of establishing an exact administration of justice; and thirdly, the duty of erecting and maintaining certain public works and certain public institutions.[25]
>
> In short, the state or commonwealth, not markets, should rule. The state had a duty to protect people, uphold justice and promote common interests by providing roads, bridges, canals and harbours as well as universal education.[26]

In the absence of fellow-feeling and a just, well-governed society, competition leads to oppression and exploitation. Child-labour, slavery, starvation wages, unemployment and despoliation of nature are inevitable as producers are driven to undercut each other. The brutal reality of unregulated markets is ruthless rivalry which creates winners and losers.

The losers include individuals made redundant, firms that go bust, whole industries wiped out by new products or processes and billions of people struggling for a living on the margins of the global economy. Entire countries decline when exports fall, exchange rates collapse or foreign debt soars. Nature is ransacked, polluted and wasted by the relentless drive to increase profit and production. Every advance in productivity, lower prices, new technology or new products compounds the process of accelerating change. Social bonds are dissolved under the corrosive tide of market forces. Ancient intimacy between communities and land is sundered through enclosure, foreclosure and auction. People are forced to move away from friends and relations to follow economic opportunities. Families disintegrate because the most cost-effective unit of labour is the single person, unencumbered by dependents or responsibilities. Hence the wretched conditions of early industrial Britain, the hostels for single men in South Africa and the barracks for young women assembly-workers in industrializing Asia.

Adam Smith provided the intellectual justification for commercial forces which propelled Western economies to expand across the globe. But *laissez-faire* was based on a selective and one-sided reading of his work, ignoring the need for fellow-feeling and justice. A hundred and sixty years after Smith, when the Western world was racked by high unemployment, poverty, falling production and a severe economic depression, John Maynard Keynes argued that the state had a central role in managing markets.[27] Throughout the West, governments developed strategies to deal with the terrible social and economic damage caused by free-market forces. Keynes, rather like Smith, believed that market forces balanced by state action would lead to 'a gradual disappearance of a rate of return on accumulated wealth'. Enterprise and skill would still yield a positive return but 'the rentier would disappear'[28] and it would no longer be possible for a few people to live on unearned income. Keynsian economics were also applied selectively in the West's favour so that destructive forces of trade still governed most of the Majority World. The following section analyses the basic principles of free trade in order to show how they become coercive in the absence of a just, well-governed world.

FROM FREE TRADE TO FORCED TRADE

The case for free trade is based on mutual advantage. Free trade, its supporters argue, encourages individuals, firms and countries to specialize in what they do best. Competition improves quality, efficiency and cost so that everyone prospers. Where a country has a *natural advantage*, such as resources not available elsewhere, the benefits are obvious. For example, grapes grow better in France than Scotland, so it makes sense for the French to produce wine and the Scots to specialize in whiskey, wool and other goods which can be sold abroad in exchange for wine. The government could subsidize vineyards and put a high tariff on wine imports to support Scottish viniculture, but it is more efficient to specialize in Scotland's natural advantages and import wine from countries where grapes grow easily.

Even if a country could produce everything it needed, international trade may still be worthwhile if different firms or countries develop a *comparative advantage*. Countries with few natural advantages can still specialize in specific skills and industries to earn sufficient income to buy what they need from other countries. The high priests of free markets, Milton and Rose Friedman, illustrate comparative advantage with the homely example of a lawyer who can type twice as fast as his secretary.

Although he has an absolute advantage in both law and typing, 'both he and the secretary are better off if he practices law and the secretary types letters'.[29] Because legal work is better paid than typing, both would be poorer if the lawyer did the typing. This example ignores the lawyer's privileged position in the labour market which enables him to command higher fees than typists. The legal profession runs a closed shop, fortified by arduous initiation rites and an elevated mystique, as well as local trading practices which give lawyers additional advantages. Even if the secretary were a better *lawyer* than her employer, she would not be allowed to do his job unless she passed specific exams. Without these, her legal work could be paid at secretarial rates. If the lawyer owned the firm, he could even hire trained young lawyers who were better than him to do the actual work and he would still benefit. Qualifications and ownership give the lawyer *privileged advantages* over the most expert typist. If the secretary were barred from taking legal exams on grounds of sex, race, religion, language or national origin, the lawyer would have an *exclusive advantage*. The persistent discrimination which prevents secretaries from becoming lawyers or personal assistants from becoming managers, even though many secretaries and personal assistants have the necessary abilities and may even do the job in practice, is one of the many ways in which exclusive practices preserve social inequality. Most trades and professions maintain some kind of closed shop to protect their collective reputation as well as their members' incomes.

On a national level comparative advantage has been utterly transformed by technological and political change. Classical economists like Adam Smith made at least four crucial assumptions about trade which no longer apply. One, that free trade would scarcely affect agriculture, since the cost of transport would make it uneconomic to import large amounts of food.[30] Two, that foreign trade mainly involved surplus produce left after domestic needs had been met, since it was cheaper to supply local consumers and 'every wholesale merchant naturally prefers the home-trade to the foreign trade'.[31] Three, that foreign trade would naturally balance, with the flow of exports and imports finding equilibrium. And four, that 'every individual naturally inclines to employ his capital in the manner in which it is likely to give revenue and employment to the greatest number of people in his own country'.[32] Classical economists assumed that capital was relatively immobile and that national sentiment would lead people with money to invest at home. David Ricardo wrote in 1817 that 'These feelings, which I should be sorry to see weakened, induce most men of property to be satisfied with a low rate of profits in their own country, rather than seek a more advantageous employment for their wealth in foreign nations.'[33]

None of these assumptions holds true today. Low-cost transport means that even the most bulky agricultural products can be sold anywhere in the world. Industrialization means that foreign trade is now essential for domestic production, since mass production dramatically cuts unit costs and demands bigger markets to justify investment. The combination of mass production and low-cost transport also means there is no reason for the balance of trade to be self-regulating, except in the extreme sense that a forest fire is eventually followed by new growth. As the world discovered during the 1930s, free trade causes violent fluctuations in production, employment and exchange rates that shake societies apart.

Underlying these changes is the fact that capital is international. Ricardo's men of property no longer invest in their home communities, but seek *absolute advantage* from the lowest-cost labour and latest technology anywhere in the world. For forty years after the war, competition between the West and the Majority World was restricted by a wide range of exclusive and privileged advantages, described in the next three chapters. German and Japanese investors still tend to be more nationalistic than their Anglo-Saxon counterparts, but investment capital today is essentially international. Where capital and goods are free to move, equilibrium can only be restored by equalizing labour costs, in other words, bringing wages and conditions in the West and in the Majority World closer together. As barriers to capital and goods are removed, particularly in Britain and the United States, wages and conditions have got worse, while average earnings in South Korea, Malaysia and a few other areas of the Majority World have risen. Now they too are under competitive pressures from China and Vietnam.

The only justification for trade is *mutual advantage*. When people specialize in what they do best and most enjoy, exchanging freely without coercion, then everyone benefits. Competition inevitably has an element of coercion, since it forces people to do better. If competitive pressures are roughly equal, and protective measures apply equally to all, then benefits would be shared more equally.

Any group or firm that has privileged protection or exclusive advantages over others will have greater power to set the terms of trade in their own favour. Monopoly suppliers can command systematically higher prices, as when oil-exporting countries raised prices in 1973. Where a firm, a country or a group of countries is the sole source of something everyone wants, then a shared monopoly or other privileges create *forced trade*. Monopoly suppliers can pick and choose among competitors, while setting their own terms. What applies to oil is equally true for the supply of money and purchasing power in the global economy, which are largely controlled by Western banks, governments, wealthy individuals and companies.

The 'exclusive privileges' protecting 'enlarged monopolies' identified by Adam Smith are as fundamental to the Western Economic System as the competitive forces which drive it. The many different forms of protection criticized by Smith were a natural response to the gradual increase in competition over previous centuries. Merchants and artisans created urban corporations and guilds to protect wages and profits from competition and keep the benefits of rising productivity to themselves. They enjoyed greater leisure and purchasing power, while improved roads and canals kept down the price of food by increasing competition between farmers. When innovation in agriculture and enclosures forced workers off the land they were excluded from towns, becoming paupers, vagrants, soldiers, sailors and colonial settlers. Municipal councils both regulated the privileges of the town and administered the Poor Law. As industrial productivity increased, merchants needed larger markets, so the exclusive privileges were gradually extended to national markets, as advocated in *The Wealth of Nations*.

Unregulated competition creates such unsustainable swings of boom and bust that no society can survive without protection. Since losers tend to be poorer, less powerful people, intensification of competition inevitably provokes political pressures for social control over the economy. Thus the extension of market forces inevitably creates public pressure for protection.

PROTECTION AND THE GROWTH OF POLITICS

Protection may be defined as any measure which restrains, mitigates or alters the effects of competition. Protection takes many forms, including regulation, prohibition, monopoly, cartels, copyright, insurance, tariffs, subsidy, minimum standards, qualifications, entry requirements, rights and social security. Broadly speaking, there are two types of protection:

- *universal*, applicable to all, such as regulations and rights that protect 'every member of society from injustice or oppression'; and

- *exclusive*, which gives privileged protection to one group, often to the detriment of another.

Universal protection is essentially about justice. Concepts of justice differ widely between societies and have changed considerably over time. States do not, of their own accord, create just laws or give fair treatment to those with conflicting interests. Most laws arise through conflict and reflect the balance of forces within society. Interests which are not represented in decision-making are much less likely to be taken into account.

Most systems of protection are exclusive, reflecting people's unequal power. The economic and political history of the West could be described as a dynamic interaction between pressure to extend or liberalize markets, followed by resistance to change and demands for increased protection from those most adversely affected by the resulting competition. Once a competitive advantage has been established, successful groups try to keep it to themselves. Almost every extension of competition creates losers, who in turn demand protection or challenge the new privileges established. And so the dynamic struggle continues, with groups both competing and seeking protection according to circumstances, often doing both in different spheres.

The need for protection is inescapable, and political battles by different groups to protect themselves from competition are as much part of the Western Economic System as the drive for profit. As markets grow, losers demand greater participation in government in order to protect themselves, win compensation or assert their own interests. Thus Western states have become a pivotal focus for struggles between different groups using the state's authority to promote or protect their interests. The need to reconcile conflicts of interests has forced Western societies to develop democratic assemblies and universal rights, guaranteed through the state. Political action has driven states to recognize ever-wider sections of society and become more even-handed. The advent of universal adult franchise – long resisted throughout the West – means that governments must at least appear to act on behalf of the whole nation and not just sectional interests. As a result every country has complex arrangements balancing protection and competition. Extensive legislation now provides health and safety at work, unemployment benefit, social security, consumer protection, environmental health, public libraries, education and welfare services.

Many of these measures were only won after fierce opposition from established vested interests. Yet without the pragmatic, piecemeal concessions in response to the horrendous social and environmental consequences of unregulated free markets during the nineteenth and early twentieth centuries, capitalism would have been overthrown, as it was by Fascism in Germany and Italy, and by Communism in Russia. The Soviet system was an extreme effort at protection, in which the state attempted to replace all competition by administrative decisions. Roosevelt's New Deal in the United States secured a permanent role for the state in economic management within even the most aggressive free-market economy. Apartheid in South Africa was a particular form of protection based on racial discrimination.

Few advocates of extending markets realize that this inevitably means extending political institutions as well, but all markets need to be managed to some extent, if only to reconcile different trading practices. For example, what one community regards as 'unfair trade' may be seen as a fundamental social and cultural tradition by another. Competitive differences between countries are directly affected by a wide range of factors including distribution systems, subsidies and public procurement policies as well as the use of child labour, slaves, prison labour or machines. Countries willing to sacrifice domestic consumption, home comforts and profit margins in order to increase exports will be able to win more markets and force competitors to choose between cutting domestic consumption, improving efficiency or quitting. These issues reach deep into people's social lives. Pressures of work, family arrangements, culture and personal relationships are profoundly influenced by markets and the rules under which they work. The only just way of resolving these differences is through political processes accepted and respected by all participants. This is the basis of the rule of law, which is almost universally accepted in the West as vested in the sovereignty of the people expressed through democratic institutions.

Struggles over the rules governing markets are central to Western history. The civil war between the northern and southern United States was due, to a large extent, to economic conflicts over import tariffs and slavery, which were resolved by establishing Federal authority above state sovereignty. The creation of a single European market required political agreement on social provision, agriculture, subsidies to industry, indirect taxation and exchange rates to avoid accusations of 'social dumping', unfair trade and competitive devaluations. This made the creation of a European Parliament or a political process of some kind unavoidable once the common market came into being. The World Trade Organization was likewise created to replace arbitrary decisions by powerful states with the rule of law in international trade. Although scarcely democratic, it is a legislative forum with supranational authority in the global economy.

Political battles over the rules of trade and protection also influence how the benefits of economic activity are allocated. Economic benefits are shared between companies through market shares, with consumers through prices, and within companies through wages, salaries, fees, royalties, profits, interest and rents. They are also divided between people involved at different stages of production – prospecting, raw materials, innovation, manufacture, distribution, servicing and waste disposal – as well as shared across society through taxation. Where any group establishes systematic, exclusive protection against others, it can gain permanent built-in advantages. One-sided protection is particularly powerful when it involves a degree of mutual dependence. In this case the more privileged, protected groups grow increasingly rich at the expense of those denied equivalent protection. This is often linked to geography or the division of labour, where it appears natural and is more easily justified. Thus divisions between town and country, unpaid domestic work and waged employment, manual and white-collar work are deeply rooted in most societies. The enforced division between black and white in apartheid South Africa and global inequality between the West and the rest can therefore be seen as particular examples of a more general process for the unjust division of economic benefit.

Universal franchise within the West has enabled people to protect themselves from the most damaging effects of outright competition and establish more equitable distribution between wages, profits, public spending and other forms of remuneration. The political process within the West put a floor on wages and conditions, which kept most of the benefits of economic improvement within the West, while greater competitive pressures suppressed prices, wages and conditions in the Majority World, often aided by political oppression.

The difference in average labour costs between the United States and Mexico, which are both part of the same continent, illustrate the powerful effect of protection. Wage differentials of 1 : 8 between markets in the US and Mexico are much greater than the ratio of 1 : 3 prevalent in South Africa in 1986, or the average of between 4 : 1 to 6 : 1 over the decades of apartheid. If the West had not systematically excluded the Majority World from direct competition, worldwide prices, wage levels and social security benefits would be much more comparable, as they are between Western economies, on the principle of factor price equalization.

Demands for exclusive protection are justified by the conviction that one group has more rights than another. Thus US citizens are entitled to social security whereas Mexicans are not, even when both do similar work serving the same markets. Instead of campaigning for US Federal resources to improve social and environmental protection in Mexico on equal terms, many US politicians want to exclude Mexican workers, restrict products covered by 'free trade' and reduce the rights of Mexicans living in the US. Similar pressures in Europe underlie the resurgence of discrimination against North Africans, Turks and others on the edge of European markets. These demands for protection are almost always argued for in terms of identity, which go to the heart of apartheid as an emotional and ideological force.

IDENTITY AND POLITICS

Most human beings have a sense of identity as part of a wider group. Belonging is part of being human. People have multiple identities. They belong to a family, nation, religious community, political party, trade union, football club, street gang, profession or company as well as having affiliations relating to gender, sexual orientation, caste, social class or their 'old school tie'. Group identities contribute to a sense of self, self-worth and even destiny. Group membership comes with rules, language, culture and ways of interpreting the world. It allocates social position, responsibilities or resources between group members. Shared identity has such a powerful psychological, social, cultural and economic function in people's lives that it is usually taken for granted, becoming visible only when threatened.

Group membership is particularly important for solidarity and protection. As a source of security greater than our individual self, we identify with that which represents our interests or aspirations. For most people over most of history there has been little question about which group one belonged to, or of the rules of allegiance and mutual obligation between members. But in times of change, when new social groups are forming or coming into competition with others, people feel a stronger need to assert their identity and defend the old or fight for the new. Then particular characteristics of the group become elevated into 'core criteria' which define who is 'in' and who is 'out'. The violent eruption of 'ethnic' conflict in the former Soviet Union and Yugoslavia, as well as the upsurge of religious fundamentalism throughout the world, are responses to increased insecurity as a result of wider political and economic change.

'Race' is only one of many possible sources of group identity, with skin colour or physical characteristics providing obvious criteria for inclusion or exclusion. The origin of most larger human groupings is in some way protective, to create a stronger defence against aggression and competition, or to gain competitive power over other groups. The extended family is almost certainly the oldest form of group identity. Beyond the family, the clan, tribe, class, caste or a shared language, accent, religion, history or nation offer people a larger group identity and basis for protection. Professional qualifications are a sophisticated and functional way of establishing 'core criteria' which include common values, codes of conduct and professional loyalties as well as technical skills.

Identity and discrimination

Group identity simultaneously creates a definition of those who do not belong, the Outsider or Other. Most groups have agreed ways of dealing with those who don't belong, whether hospitable or hostile. All groups use some forms of 'discriminator' to distinguish themselves from other groups. Most societies discriminate between human beings and other animals. Age and gender are the oldest and most widespread forms of systematic discrimination, arising from the temporal hierarchy of elders over youth and the subordination of women by men. Slavery is probably the next oldest form of systematic subordination, with the sign for 'slave girl' being much older than that for 'slave'. [34] Language, faith, citizenship, skin colour, membership of another village and many other characteristics have been used as 'discriminators' by various groups at different times. Catholics were legally barred from Parliament, public office and universities in England until 1829. Housing tenure in Britain is a subtle but significant discriminator linked to class. Qualifications for the vote have frequently been linked to property ownership, creating another class-based 'discriminator' which determines who has a right to have a say in government. Battles over the franchise are often about identity as much as political rights or economic benefits.

Fear is one of the most potent forces creating a sense of common identity. When a group or society has few real bonds left, fear unites people against the Other. In South Africa, fear of being swallowed up by the British empire united Afrikaner Nationalists against the Unionists. *Die swart gevaar* – the black danger – united the white minority after their savage conflict in the Boer War. The Communist Party's alliance with the African nationalist cause enabled the government to reinforce white unity through phantasmagoric fear of Communism, atheism and aliens. Fear of Communism was used to cement the Western Alliance after the Second World War.

A sense of common identity and belonging is like a powerful genie within the human spirit, which rises in rage against assaults on our security, self and community. When people face loss or an external threat, what they have in common grows in importance. For people dislocated by migration, atomized by modernization or unsettled by inexplicable events, a common language, religion and even the vaguest inklings of a common history may be their only connection with a larger whole. At such times, many people need to recreate a mythical past to strengthen their sense of self and solidarity, and find scapegoats to blame for their predicament.

Such feelings mobilize people in defence of perceived common identity. Feelings of loss are often linked to a sense of injustice, betrayal and anger that produces a defiant, assertive new identity capable of avenging the past and creating a future free of the shame and humiliation associated with loss. A renewed sense of identity often emerges with new leaders, prophets and social movements. These powerful feelings may be used by vested interests to protect their privileges as well as by excluded groups demanding justice. Many vigorous group identities were born or strengthened in opposition to oppression and injustice, including Afrikaner resistance to British imperialism and African resistance to apartheid. While oppression is frequently the crucible of an assertive identity, its ability to protect perceived common interests is more likely to come through an alliance with ruling groups. The creation of a common identity between ruler and ruled makes the nation-state a particularly powerful expression of common interests.

Nationalism and identity

Nationalism has been the world's most powerful unifier, because it is capable of reconciling and combining loyalties of family, faith, language, class, profession or other corporate identities under a single banner. The power of nationalism derives from its ability to provide a resilient basis for the state as a means of organizing duties, responsibilities and resources, with armies and officials to enforce its authority. Unlike religion, most nationalism is relatively free of ideological content and therefore more adaptable.

Nationalism and the nation-state are relatively new in human history. Their emergence was closely linked to the rise of capitalism and industrial society which integrated local and regional markets to create larger 'national' markets. States enforced order, protecting currency, property and communications. They provided a forum to reconcile conflicting interests and protected trade from excessive competition. The rise of representative democracy turned the nation-state into a powerful instrument for protecting people from the worst effects of economic competition and redistributed resources to provide common services beyond the means of most people.

Concepts of national identity are constantly reinforced and renegotiated through the media and national rituals, particularly sport, holidays and elections. Although nationalists often assert cultural or linguistic unity, these have often been imposed or invented. English national identity evolved to unite a French-speaking Norman aristocracy with its Anglo-Saxon subjects in the face of threats from France and Spain. American nationalism was deliberately promoted in order to knit together disparate groups of immigrants from England, Germany, Ireland, Italy, the Jewish diaspora and other peoples into a single state. The young Lincoln advocated a 'political religion of the nation'. Later, as president and commander-in-chief during the horrendous civil war, he expressed a divine mission to unite people into 'one national family' and 'let every American pledge his life, his property, and his sacred honour' to support 'the Constitution and Laws'.[35] Native Americans were entirely excluded from this new nationhood. African Americans were not part of the dream and were only granted citizenship after many fought and died on the side of the Union during the civil war. Even then, President Lincoln told a delegation of free blacks: 'On this broad continent, not a single man of your race is made the equal of a single man of ours.'[36] It was over 100 years before African Americans won constitutional equality throughout the United States.

'Nationality' is both a source of group identity and of discrimination, because it defines an 'in group' entitled to certain rights and support, and an 'out group', for whom assistance is discretionary. Coupled with statehood as a legitimate source of coercion, the concept of national interest and sovereignty justifies systematic discrimination against other groups by definition.

Apart from gender, no other form of group identity has quite such power to legitimate unequal treatment as nationalism. South Africa was an extreme example of the use of group identity to provide exclusive protection against competitive pressures. Apartheid wove together overlapping identities of family, language, history, faith, fear, nation and race to unite a divided minority against the world. Afrikaner racism was a particular form of nationalism which justified apartheid in terms of group sovereignty.

The link between group identity and a people or nation is largely arbitrary. Descendants of Europe's northern invaders are perhaps the most widespread and powerful in the world, but their original language has disappeared, their gods have become comic-book characters, their legal and political systems have changed beyond recognition, their identity has been subsumed under those of heterogeneous nations, and they have fought and killed each other on a larger scale than any other group. Their proliferation owes as much to promiscuous assimilation as ruthless expansion, and to adaptability and incorporation rather than any clinging to tradition or to Nordic identity. The reality is that there are many human identities but only one people, the human race. It is only justice that all deserve equal protection.

SUMMARY

The emergence of separate development can be seen as a consequence of a competitive economic system which creates winners and losers. Losers naturally seek protection by limiting or mitigating the worst effects of competition. People seek protection by establishing common interests with others through a shared identity, such as gender, clan, class, nation, religion or race. By definition, shared group membership excludes others to provide an 'objective' basis for discrimination and one-sided protection. Exclusive or privileged protection provides a double advantage to particular groups, because they suffer less from competitive pressures and take advantage of others denied the same level of protection.

Protection takes many forms, but the state is one of the most powerful means of both removing protective measures in order to increase competitive advantages for some groups and of enforcing protection through regulations and redistribution. Racial identity is only one of many means of justifying systematic discrimination and the creation of inequality. Nationalism is perhaps the most widespread, but cash is often the most powerful discriminator.

Chapters 3, 4 and 5 will analyse the interaction between competition and protection in the Western Economic System in more detail, illustrating how global apartheid works in practice. They will also outline steps towards a fairer economic system. Readers less interested in economics may prefer to read the first section of each chapter and then jump to chapter 6.

Further Reading

Economic fundamentals

Friedman, Milton and Rose, *Free to Choose*, Pelican Books, 1980.

Keynes, John Maynard, *The General Theory of Employment, Interest and Money* (1936), Macmillan, 1974.

Marx, Karl, and Engels, Friedrich, *Selected Works*, Lawrence & Wishart, 1968.

Polanyi, Karl, *The Great Transformation: The Political and Economic Origins of Our Time* (1944), Beacon paperback, 1957.

Ricardo, David, *Principles of Political Economy and Taxation* (1817), Staffa, Cambridge, 1951.

Smith, Adam, *Theory of Moral Sentiments* (1759), ed. J. C. Bryce, Oxford University Press, 1976.

Smith, Adam, *The Wealth of Nations* (1776): 5th edn, ed. Edwin Cannan (1904), University of Chicago Press, 1976; ed. and abridged Andrew Skinner, Penguin Classics, 1986.

3

The Economics of Global Apartheid

It is ordained that we [Afrikaners], insignificant as we are, should be amongst the first people to begin the struggle against the new world tyranny of capitalism.

> Jan Smuts, 1900
> South African prime minister, 1919–24/1939–48[1]

What is the market? It is the law of the jungle, the law of nature. And what is civilization? It is the struggle against nature.

> Edouard Balladur, 1993
> French prime minister 1992–5

Apartheid in South Africa was a political solution by the Afrikaner minority to the conflicts caused by unrestrained economic competition from low-paid black workers, who displaced white workers in the mines and farms. Poor white workers had the vote and were able to use political power to protect their interests by excluding the black majority, who could not vote. The political and legal system of apartheid was erected piecemeal by the white minority to protect themselves from the devastating consequences of economic competition. Decades of national liberation struggle, war, economic depression, strikes and political manœuvring established a political settlement between white workers, landowners and industrialists which excluded the non-white majority.

The white South African economy was part of the West in every respect. It was an affluent, modern industrial market economy, dominated by large firms and nationalized industries, with a high degree of state regulation and extensive public education, health and welfare services for whites. White people were protected from direct competition with the black majority by legal discrimination and benefited enormously from the low-waged work of black people. The key features of this two-tier economy were:

1 *imperial endowment*, which gave the minority total control over land, wealth, state, law and means of enforcement, while destroying indigenous patterns of production;
2 *natural heritage and low-cost resources* including fertile lands, abundant seas and, above all, rich mineral deposits of gold,

diamonds, platinum, uranium, chrome, manganese, copper, vanadium and asbestos, plus coal to provide cheap power;

3 *discriminatory labour policies* to maintain a large pool of low-paid workers, including:

   (a) total control over movement and supply of black workers;

   (b) hierarchical division of labour between black and white;

   (c) pay differentials between black and white ranging from 6 : 1 to 9 : 1;

   (d) powerful coercive back-up and ruthless suppression of black workers' organizations;

4 *access to Western markets* on equal terms with other Western countries;

5 *extensive state support* for economic development, largely benefiting the skilled technical, supervisory and managerial white minority who receive high-level education, social security and welfare provision;

6 *protected private enterprise* under concentrated minority ownership;

7 *favourable finance*, in the form of speculative international investment, reinvested earnings from gold and diamonds, and corporate investment attracted by cheap labour, industrial infrastructure and a supportive regime;

8 *managed domestic markets* under strategic state planning with;

   (a) a powerful corporate vision for the economy and country;

   (b) a well-developed infrastructure and primary industrial base in energy, steel and transport, supported by substantial state spending and nationalized industries;

   (c) a safe environment for investment and a flourishing stock exchange;

   (d) a stable and convertible currency supported by a wide range of fiscal, monetary and legal measures directing the economy;

   (e) import tariffs to create high consumption of home-produced goods;

   (f) tight state control over low-cost labour;

9 *political stability* and institutions through which powerful interests could reconcile their differences, usually at the expense of the majority;

10 *cultural unity* of the dominant minority with a common frame of aspirations and assumptions.

At a global level, the mechanisms of separate development are more subtle than racial discrimination, but in many respects the parallels with South Africa are striking. The West, too, enjoyed an immense imperial bequest after the war and controlled almost the entire resources of the planet. Western states vigorously supported 'their' transnational companies to increase international competitiveness. They actively fostered favourable finance for investment, carefully managing currencies, trade and industrial development. The particular reasons for uneven development between countries are complex, but for most of the postwar period the Majority World has been systematically excluded from the Western Economic System except as a supplier of raw material and workers. Far from presiding over global free markets, Western governments have protected private enterprise from outright competition with low-cost producers in the Majority World. The mechanisms of exclusion have acted at almost every level of the economy, year in, year out, to give the West stupendous advantages over the Majority World.

These advantages are being challenged by rapid industrialization in many areas of the Majority World, increasing competition and contributing to unemployment in the West. Further deregulation of global markets following the 1993 GATT Agreement will intensify competition at the turn of the century, increasing political pressures for exclusive protectionism throughout the West. These issues are complex and this chapter attempts to outline both the West's inheritance and its prospects for the future. Trade liberalization and protectionism are considered first because they represent the greatest challenges of the new global settlement and put other issues in context.

WORLD TRADE WARS

Now we must fight against world government – because that is what the WTO really means, my friends. It's anti-American.

Pat Buchanan, July 1994
Republican presidential contender

The World Trade Organization (WTO) is a multilateral political body regulating world trade with limited but explicit sovereignty over member governments. It was created through the Uruguay Round of GATT and started work in January 1995. Global management of trade was inevitable as the world economy became increasingly integrated. Without some form of regulation, most trade remains subject to private decisions by finance and the world's most powerful companies and states. The WTO will have some power to override domestic legislation, although much less than the European Commission has over EU states, and its powers of enforcement are even more limited.

The United States government sees the WTO/GATT as a way of forcing open foreign markets rather than regulating trade. It is likely to be vigorous when enforcing the GATT agreement against other countries while obstructing enforcement in its own markets. When Carla Hills was appointed US trade negotiator, President Bush presented her with a crow-bar, symbolizing America's determination to prise open foreign markets. President Clinton's trade negotiator Mickey Kantor was equally 'committed to building the strongest, most productive, most competitive economy in the world'.[2] The US does not accept that competition inevitably creates losers. *Fortune*, house magazine of corporate America, eloquently expressed this one-sided attitude to trade negotiations: 'Integration must reinforce U.S. economic and strategic needs, demanding, therefore, tough-minded plans to guard American influence and wealth. Integration is not the same as openness; America needs to build roads over which its commerce and conscience can travel to other lands...' It quotes the influential policy analyist Edward Luttwak to reinforce its case for economic warfare: 'In geoeconomics the firepower is capital, market penetration replaces foreign bases and garrisons... The equivalent of strategic nuclear weapons ... are things like industrial and investment policies. The everyday tool, powerful but enormously flexible, is market access.'[3] Within this creed real wars are conceived.

The West's main motivation in the GATT negotiations was to win increased market access to boost economic growth, jobs and profits. But many fear that GATT will be a jobs massacre and an environmental disaster. A much-quoted article in *Harper's Magazine* warned that GATT and NAFTA will create an overwhelmingly powerful, unaccountable free-trade regime 'ruled by the Bottom-Line', 'a global corporate utopia in which local citizens are toothless, worker's unions are tame or broken, environmentalists and consumer advocates outflanked.'[4]

Opposition to NAFTA and the WTO is creating an unlikely coalition of far-right conservatives, environmentalists, trade-unionists and industrialists. Pat Buchanan, former speech-writer for Richard Nixon and conservative contender for the presidency, denounced the WTO as 'an insult to everything for which our founding fathers launched the American revolution' and called it 'a UN of world trade, where America has no veto'. Consumer campaigner Ralph Nader demonstrated against 'this international autocratic regime that endangers our democracy ... dreamed up by global corporations that have no allegiance to our country, with faceless international bureaucrats cutting deals in secret'.[5] Wealthy businessmen turned populist politicians, like Ross Perot in the US and James Goldsmith in Europe, vigorously mobilized opposition to free trade. Goldsmith was elected to the European Parliament in June 1994, were he leads a new political group, L'Europe des Nations. His best-selling book *The Trap*[6] makes a powerful case against unfettered free trade. It argues that Majority World countries belong to a 'wholly different world' which cannot be integrated with the West. Goldsmith, like the dealers criticized by Adam Smith, wants free movement of capital but opposes free movement of people and goods.

These unholy alliances have a haunting echo in the coalition between white trade-unionists and nationalists which constructed apartheid in South Africa. The Majority World has long been integrated into the world economy, but few champions of fair trade protest at the supply of low-cost raw materials. Now that the Majority World is competing successfully for higher-value work, it is being made a scapegoat for the consequences of competition. Both Ross Perot and James Goldsmith know that competitive markets create constant pressures to cut costs. Changes in technology, production methods and consumer demand cause more job losses than competition from the Majority World.

The key issues are how change is managed, how benefits and losses are distributed, how losers are compensated, how communities and the environment are protected, and how benefits from investment and increased productivity are shared. Until now, these decisions were made through industrial and political struggles within the West. By excluding the Majority World from this struggle, Western workers, businesses, consumers and states all benefited from their low-cost labour and lack of social protection.

Realization that genuine free trade could wipe out swathes of Western industry and take the West's tax base to the Majority World is making strange converts to the cause of workers' rights and environmental protection. President Bush's GATT delegation raised the issue early in the negotiations, acknowledging that:

> the denial of workers' rights can prevent the attainment of the objectives of GATT, and can bring about distortions of trade which then lead to protectionist pressures. Consequently, negotiations

should ... consider ways of tackling the problem of workers' rights in the context of GATT, in such a way as to ensure that the growth of trade relations benefits all workers in all countries.[7]

Bush pulled back from inserting social clauses into the GATT agreement, but the reality of free trade in an unequal world makes them an urgent item on the trade agenda. The president of the European Commission, Jacques Delors, argued for an extension of the 'social chapter' through GATT. President Clinton saw 'the question of workers' rights very much as a global issue', suggesting that the WTO should be responsible for global antitrust and competition policy.[8] In 1994 the G7 summit welcomed 'work on the relation between trade and the environment in the new WTO' and called for 'intensified efforts to improve our understanding of new issues including employment and labour standards and their implications for trade policies'.[9] Such proposals are increasingly likely as the West feels the impact of competition from the Majority World. They are to be welcomed, provided the world's poorest can ensure that their concerns are addressed equitably. This also means taking account of the legacy of appropriation and discrimination through which the West created the modern world.

IMPERIAL ENDOWMENT, NATURAL HERITAGE AND LOW-COST RESOURCES

Big territories were conquered ... with small forces. Income, first of all from plunder, then from direct taxes and lastly from trade, capital invest-ments and long-term exploitation, covered with incredible speed the expenditure for military operations. This arithmetic represented a great temptation to strong countries.

Owen Lattimore
US adviser to Chiang Kai-shek[10]

Western development was built on a vast accumulation of wealth which endowed it with enormous economic advantages. The sheer scale of Europe's imperial booty is immense beyond comprehension or calculation:

- By 1800 Western Europeans had added 790,000 square miles of overseas territories to their homelands of under 2 million square miles. By 1900, they had added another 9 million square miles, including the world's most valuable lands. Ninety years later the West still occupies a quarter of the earth's most productive land. Russia and the countries of former Soviet bloc have over a fifth, leaving the Majority World less than half.

- Enslavement and transportation of 10 to 20 million Africans deprived that continent while providing the West with unpaid labour during the formative century of the industrial revolution.

- Millions of indentured workers from Asia did backbreaking menial work for empire and industry.

- Taxes and other payments from imperial possessions flowed into Europe's state treasuries, funding public spending and investment, financing armed forces, and keeping domestic taxes low.

- Stupendous mineral wealth extracted from the Majority World, including over 200 tons of gold and 18,000 tons of silver from Latin America alone, laid the foundation of Europe's capital markets.

- Extensive biological resources provided staple foods, industrial materials and medicines, including cotton, maize, potatoes, rubber, tomatoes, turkeys and countless other products, which have been valued at over $70 billion. The West's pharmaceutical industry is estimated to benefit from tropical biodiversity to the tune of $5 billion a year now, rising to $47 billion by the year 2000.[11]

- Over 200 years' supply of underpriced raw materials and food sustained Europe's balance of payments deficits during the nineteenth century and similar supplies continue to give the West an annual bonus worth billions of dollars.

- Western goods were forced on local markets; examples include the destruction of India's textile industry after 1814, the wars to make China permit the sale of opium in 1841/2 and 1856, the opening up of Japan in 1854, and countless occasions in the twentieth century when Western governments have pressurized Majority World countries to sell Western cigarettes, chemicals, computers, pharmaceuticals and other products in violation of local needs and wishes. This trade war continues with the GATT battering-ram driving Western services, television and advertising into every country of the world.

- Almost every economy in the world has been reconstructed to serve Western markets: this has created an infrastructural incentive for Majority World countries to produce goods for export rather than local consumption.

The imperial endowment includes one item which is almost invisible but worth more than all of the above, namely:

- Unrestrained use of land, sea and air as a dump for toxic wastes, carbon dioxide and noxious by-products of industrial development. This poisonous legacy bequeaths the whole world a debt of billions of dollars to clear up land-fill and incalculable sums to dispose of nuclear and other industrial wastes. Emissions of CO_2 represent a debt of billions or even trillions of dollars by the West to the Majority World.[12]

This inconceivably large subsidy from the Majority World gave the West the investment and incentives to develop its agriculture, finance, manufacturing and technology. It was used to build dikes, harbours, roads, railways, canals, housing, and telegraph, public administration and social services systems. Many monuments of Western civilization were created from wealth brought from the Majority World, such as the Tate Gallery in London, financed from the sugar trade and slavery.

Europe's empires left the Majority World in a severely depleted, distorted and debilitated condition. Most local systems of government and economy were destroyed or restructured to serve European needs. The colonial experience was not universally bad and sometimes replaced even greater tyranny, but even the most benign imperial administration put European priorities before local people.

The division between 'developed' and 'developing' countries largely follows the contours of empire. It is institutionalized in the hierarchical classification of countries by international organizations and treaties. Like racial classification in South Africa, these divisions defy the diversity of peoples, but reflect political realities. 'Developed' and 'developing' worlds are not separated by race, although race plays a part, so much as by economic discrimination. In particular, one-sided control over the movement of people and goods systematically prevents people in the Majority

World from participating equally in the global economy. These barriers create highly unequal labour markets, separated by national boundaries rather than racial classification. In effect, immigration and import controls perform a similar function to the pass laws, influx controls, and job reservation policies in South Africa.

DISCRIMINATORY LABOUR POLICIES

Western prosperity owes much to millions of workers transported long distances to meet demands for labour in the plantations, mines and industries of the emerging global economy. Slaves from Africa, economic refugees and bonded workers from Europe, indentured labour from Asia – whoever was most cost-effective was used. Employers played off different groups against each other to keep labour costs as low as possible while workers organized to improve their bargaining power. European settlers in Australia, America and South Africa frequently excluded non-white workers on racial grounds and demanded segregation, immigration controls and other forms of protection from employers and the state. In 1885 the Socialist Party of the United States demanded a ban on Chinese and Japanese immigration, while agreeing that European immigration should continue. The German Social Democrat Otto Bauer wrote in 1906 that 'the proletariat feels threatened when workers of foreign extraction and from alien civilizations enter the international labour market as competitors' and that it should 'therefore seek to exclude' them. Although Kautsky and others warned against replacing 'the class struggle with racial conflict',[13] discriminatory labour controls were introduced in most countries. Western governments began to regulate global labour markets after the First World War, entrenching inequality in law. The first general meeting of what is now the International Labour Office (ILO) voted in favour of an eight-hour day and forty-eight-hour week for Europe and the USA in 1919. China, Persia (Iran) and Siam (Thailand) were explicitly excluded, while the working week in British India was fixed at sixty hours.[14] These unequal standards reflected both the greater influence of working-class organizations in the West and the commercial pressure for cheap labour in the colonies.

Economic growth after the Second World War enabled most Western workers to secure a steady increase in real incomes.

Employers recruited workers from the Majority World to do lower-paid jobs which white workers abandoned for better-paid skilled work. US industries hired from Puerto Rico, Mexico, the segregated southern states, and inner-city ghettos. During the boom years of the 1960s, over 30 million migrant workers were given temporary status in Europe. Britain enticed people from the Commonwealth. Germany recruited from Italy, Turkey and Yugoslavia. A seventh of all manual workers in Germany and Britain came as migrants. In France, Belgium and Switzerland a quarter of industrial workers were foreigners.[15] In 1992 the West imported over $50 billion-worth of labour services, mainly from the Majority World. Saudi Arabia, which is closely tied to the West through its oil exports as well as through arms and other imports, is the world's largest user of migrant labour in cash terms, importing over $25 billion-worth.[16] Like the South African homelands, Mexico and Europe's former colonies have acted as reserves of cheap labour which are drawn in or pushed out according to demand. As the postwar boom faded, restrictions tightened and pressure grew to repatriate workers like disposable raw materials. Hostility towards people from the Majority World grew during the 1980s and 1990s throughout Western Europe and the United States.

In theory, free market competition should lead to greater equality in wages for similar work in different countries, after taking account of differences in productivity, transport and trading costs. People would move to better-paid areas and learn the necessary skills to earn more, thus reducing differentials between countries. At the same time, investment would move to low-waged areas, raising productivity and wages. While wages have risen rapidly in some countries, for example South Korea, differences are still wide. Where people are paid widely different amounts for similar work serving the same markets, some form of discrimination is almost certainly taking place.

Wage differences between the West and the Majority World are steep, with hourly pay for comparable occupations ten to twenty times lower in most Majority World countries. Work that earns $19 an hour in Tokyo or $13 an hour in Chicago only brings $5 in Seoul and less than $1 in Bombay (see table 2).[17]

The higher cost of social insurance and of providing suitable working conditions in the West mean that differences in labour costs are even greater. Average labour costs are 50 per cent higher in Norway and Germany than in the United States, but twelve times lower than the US in Mexico.[18] These differences between

Table 2 Hourly pay for equivalent work ($ US)

Place	$US per hour
Tokyo	19.3
Chicago	13.0
Frankfurt	11.3
Seoul	5.0
São Paulo	2.7
Bangkok	2.0
Budapest	1.2
Bombay	0.8

the West and the Majority World are much greater than between white and black in South Africa during the heyday of apartheid.

For twenty years after the postwar settlement, most workers in the West experienced improvements in wages, conditions of employment and social protection. Countries with the highest wages, such as Germany, Holland and Switzerland, also had the best conditions of work, longest holidays, most extensive public services and best welfare provision. At the same time, they were among the most productive and prosperous in the world. This strongly suggests that wage costs were not the main factor in economic competition.

By excluding workers from the Majority World, except during boom years, the West maintained relatively high wages which generated higher taxes, higher public spending, higher savings, higher levels of investment and greater purchasing power. Average labour productivity in manufacturing grew more rapidly in the West than in the Majority World as a result of greater investment. Between 1960 and 1970, annual average growth in labour productivity in manufacturing grew by 4.1 per cent in the West, compared with 2.3 per cent in the Majority World. During the following decade productivity growth slowed to 2.8 per cent in the West and 0.4 per cent in the Majority World.[19]

This pattern changed in the 1970s for a variety of reasons, including Nixon's devaluation of the dollar, OPEC's oil-price rise, increased Japanese competition in specific markets and the introduction of new technology. During the 1980s increased competition and the use of microelectronics affected employment throughout the West. In the US, real average earnings remained stagnant, while the bottom 10 per cent of incomes fell by over a fifth. In Europe average earnings continued to rise, although they fell slightly for the lowest-paid, while the level of unemployment rose dramatically, particularly for unskilled workers.

As in South Africa, so in the global economy, low-paid competition is used by employers to exert a downward pressure on labour costs, within limits of local economic and political conditions. The impact of low-waged competition is complex. Many Western firms have cut costs by relocating production to the Majority World and reducing pay, conditions of employment or union privileges in the West. One closely argued study suggests that, between 1960 and 1990, competition from the Majority World cost the equivalent of 12 per cent of manufacturing jobs in the West, most of them unskilled.[20] But there is also evidence that trade with the Majority World has prevented unemployment falling even faster than it actually has in most Western countries. Majority World countries which increased exports also imported more, creating a positive balance of trade and employment for the West. Although the West's share of world trade in manufactured goods fell from 84 to 78 per cent between 1975 and 1992, total trade in manufactured goods increased by a quarter, so that Western exports still rose by a sixth. The picture is complicated further because most low-priced products from the Majority World did not exist twenty years ago. New technology has created new jobs and destroyed old ones. The falling price of manufactured goods has meant that distribution, retail and other services take a rising share of the value of production. Lower prices have also given people in the West greater disposable income, thus increasing domestic spending. Both these factors mean that even imports from the Majority World add to Western economic growth and employment. However, significant differences in economic policies between Western states mean that changes in the balance of trade have affected countries in very different ways. While Europe and Japan have increased their net balance of trade with the Majority World, US exports have fallen substantially, largely as a result of the debt crisis. Countries like Taiwan, South Korea and then China have run up substantial surpluses with the US while importing goods from Japan and Europe. Thus rapid growth in a few Majority World countries has probably had a positive effect on Western employment overall, while exacerbating imbalances between Western economies and depressing wages, conditions and employment for unskilled workers.

Countries with relatively high levels of social solidarity, like Germany and Japan, have been better able to keep high value employment within their borders, while governments in the more polarized countries such as Britain and the USA have encouraged competition to drive down labour costs. The British government has vigorously opposed European laws on social protection and equal treatment of migrant workers in order to suppress employment costs and attract investment. However, even the British government does not suggest that companies should import large numbers of very low-paid workers from the Majority World on short contracts, something which would be logical in a free market and which actually happened during the nineteenth century.

Controls on immigration give exclusive advantages to workers within a country to enjoy its economic opportunities and social benefits. Such controls violate free-market principles, but are necessary for both economic management and social stability. The West manages the global economy in such a way that the best-paid and most value-adding activities take place in the West while low-waged work is done in the Majority World or by migrants, as in South Africa. The parallel is not exact, because employment and wage levels for unskilled workers have been allowed to fall further in the Anglo-Saxon West than white South Africans would have tolerated. But the wide differences in pay and conditions between the West and the Majority World are sufficiently striking to expose labour controls as a pillar of global apartheid.

TARIFF TYRANNY AND UNEQUAL TRADE

In theory, dramatically lower labour costs in the Majority World should have attracted investment and raised productivity and wages to Western levels. This did not happen because discriminatory trade policies inhibited Majority World countries from making and exporting manufactured goods. The West discriminates against manufactured goods made by workers in the Majority World through tariffs and a wide range of exclusive trade practices.

All three of the West's trading blocs – Europe, the USA and Japan – developed behind protective tariffs against external competition. Britain led the industrial revolution by imposing a 100 per cent tariff on Indian textiles and destroying the Bengali cotton industry through competition from cheap machine-made fabrics from England. Tariff barriers were largely beneficial for Western industrial development. Although domestic prices were marginally higher, wages and purchasing power were also higher, stimulating demand. The cost of bankruptcies, unemployment and economic restructuring caused by foreign competition was lower. As an added bonus, tariffs tax foreign workers to pay for domestic spending – they are effectively taxation without representation. US income from tariffs was so high during the last decades of the nineteenth century that the government ran large budget surpluses which paid for bridges, canals, harbours and railways. Abraham Lincoln neatly summed up the case for tariffs: 'when we buy manufactured goods abroad we get the goods and the foreigner gets the money. When we buy the manufactured goods at home we get both the goods and the money.'[21] Japan, South Korea and other countries also achieved industrial take-off behind tariff barriers.

As economies become more diverse, the benefits of tariffs become less clear-cut. Many imports are also used by industries which benefit from greater competition among suppliers, thus contributing to lower consumer prices. The removal of tolls and internal tariff barriers within countries like the UK, France and the United States, as well as the European Union stimulated economic growth through trade, industrialization, and political integration.

Since the Second World War, Western industrial countries have gradually reduced tariff barriers between themselves through GATT negotiations (described later), but kept high tariffs on many products from the Majority World. Tariff reduction is rarely undertaken lightly by the West. The European customs union has been being painstakingly negotiated over four decades since 1952, and it is still not complete, as governments haggle over quotas, subsidies and standards in agriculture, fishing, steel and other industries. This protracted process contrasts starkly with the rapid market liberalization demanded by the West from the Majority World and former Soviet economies.

The most unfair tariffs are those which increase with each stage of processing, selectively excluding goods with higher added value while permitting tariff-free imports of raw materials. This inhibits Majority World countries from investing in skills and equipment to produce manufactured products from their own raw materials. They therefore have no option but to supply the West with raw materials at low cost. Western companies enjoy a double benefit because the Majority World cannot compete with their products in international markets. Before the Uruguay Round of GATT, the EU had a tariff of 9 per cent on raw coffee, but 16.5 per cent on roasted ground coffee. Oilseeds had zero tariff, but vegetable oils carried over 7 per cent and margarine had 25 per cent. On average, Western tariffs on raw materials were under 1 per cent, on semi-manufactured goods they were about 4 per cent and on finished goods over 6 per cent. The cost of Western tariffs to the Majority World has been estimated at over 10 per cent of its trade, at least $50 billion a year, during the 1980s.[22] Western tariff cuts as a result of the Uruguay Round mainly benefit the West, since over a fifth of Majority World trade will still face tariffs of above 7 per cent.

Rich countries also exclude exports from the Majority World through non-tariff barriers. The most important of these is the Multi-fibre Arrangement (MFA) which allows importing countries to set quotas on imports of textiles and clothing from countries like Bangladesh, Hong Kong, India and the Philippines. The MFA started as a 'short-term arrangement' for cotton in 1962, then became a 'temporary measure' in 1974, and has since been renewed five times. UNCTAD has estimated that it has cost the Majority World $31 billion in lost trade, more than half the value of the aid received by these countries.[23] For example, in 1985 the US, Britain, Canada and France suddenly imposed textile quotas on Bangladesh, forcing 500 factories to close and putting tens of thousands of people out of work. Less than 2 per cent of US clothing imports came from Bangladesh.[24] Jamaica, Mexico, Pakistan, Tanzania and many other countries have suffered similarly from the imposition of textile quotas. While the MFA is due to be phased out slowly over the ten years following the Uruguay Round, half the restrictions will remain until the very end of this period.

Cars, consumer electronics, machinery, shoes, steel and other manufactured products from the Majority World are often subject to 'voluntary restraint'. About a fifth of all exports from the Majority World face non-tariff barriers. These barriers have grown since 1970. About a third of US manufacturers enjoyed some protection against foreign competition by the end of the 1980s. Even the much-vaunted NAFTA includes special protection clauses for US sugar- and citrus-growers and other vested interests, illustrating the highly selective nature of free enterprise doctrine in practice.

Discriminatory trade policies have concentrated the more valuable processing and finishing stages of production in the West. Instead of goods being produced close to sources of raw materials, as advocated by classical economics, bulky materials are transported to the West or its satellites for production. One side-effect of this is that many people in the Majority World migrate to work abroad, with paradoxical consequences. Cotton grown in Egypt, Turkey and Mexico is exported to be made into fabric and garments in the West. These three countries are also the world's largest exporters of labour, while the textiles industry is a major employer of low-waged immigrant workers in the West. In Germany, Turkish workers employed in Turkish-owned textile factories produce clothes from raw material grown in Turkey. Some of these clothes are even exported to Turkey and bought with money remitted from Turkish workers in Germany.

Discrimination against manufactured products has forced most Majority World countries to export raw materials in an unprocessed form. Many countries still depend on exports of a few primary commodities, particularly in Africa. Zambia is totally dependent on copper exports. Niger relies on uranium for 85 per cent of earnings. Burundi and Rwanda derive almost all of their earnings from coffee. This leaves them extremely vulnerable to price fluctuations in just one commodity. Unlike Western countries, where production shifts between a wide range of products, it is difficult for most Majority World countries to diversify. Even successful manufacturing exporters like Malaysia rely on primary products like palm oil for 45 per cent of export earnings. The combination of low investment, tariff barriers, lack of domestic purchasing power and internal economic organization historically geared to just a few export products makes it difficult for most countries to develop new industries. Although Majority World countries increased manufactured goods as a proportion of exports from 15 per cent in 1975 to 60 per cent in 1992, their total share of world trade remained stagnant due to increased competition.

While most Majority World producers have a limited range of outlets in the West, Western purchasers can usually choose between many competing suppliers as well as having access to synthetic substitutes. Competition for access to restricted markets between raw material producers lowers prices, creating buyers' markets in which transnational corporations strike hard bargains. In addition, a high level of investment in education, research and development, and infrastructure enables the West to produce goods not available elsewhere. As Majority World countries have industrialized the price of manufactured goods has fallen, and Western companies and countries have tried to maintain their exclusive advantages by tightening control over intellectual property rights and the sale of software, insurance, advertising, entertainment and other services. Even this is changing as many Majority World countries have invested heavily in education and are increasingly competing over higher-value goods and services as well.

Import controls are an essential pillar of global apartheid that is both being challenged through competition and partially dismantled through trade negotiations, but is still largely in place. Its effect is starkly reflected in the terms of trade for goods from the Majority World, which I will now go on to consider.

Terms of trade

The West has almost three-quarters of world trade and production in cash terms. The Majority World and countries of the former Soviet Union account for less than 4 per cent of manufactured goods bought in the West. The Majority World's share of manufacturing trade is increasing, but it is still less than 15 per cent of all imports into Western countries and just over a fifth of world trade. Almost half of all trade from the Majority World is in relatively low-value commodities and raw materials. In financial terms, the West's entire imports from the Majority World are worth less than 3 per cent of Western production. This means the total imports from the Majority World, including oil, raw materials, agriculture and manufactured products, are paid for with less than 6 per cent of monetized labour-time worked in the West. This implies a massive, systematic undervaluing of the resources, labour and production of the Majority World. On the other hand, the West takes 60 per cent of exports from the Majority World, making Western markets extremely important to the Majority World. This systematic trade imbalance means that the Majority World has relatively low purchasing power in the West, creating systematic balance of payments difficulties.

The cumulative effect of this unequal trading regime is that average export prices of primary commodities from the Majority World fell by half during the 1980s while prices of imports from the West rose. As a result, terms of trade deteriorated by 22 per cent. Rwanda, which depends on coffee for three-quarters of export earnings, was worst affected as its terms of trade fell by 47 per cent. This meant it had to export twice as much coffee to buy the same amount of imports. In cash terms, it has been estimated that the Majority World lost $553 billion between 1981 and 1985,

122 per cent of the total value of commodity exports in 1980. Excluding oil, the accumulated loss was $57 billion. This amounts to a massive subsidy from the world's poorest people to its richest societies. The West, by contrast, enjoyed a 12 per cent improvement in terms of trade during the 1980s, increasing its purchasing power in the Majority World.[25]

Terms of trade for manufactured goods from the Majority World declined by an average of 1 per cent a year between 1970 and 1987, with a cumulative drop of about 20 per cent. Spectacular growth in the sheer quantity of manufactured exports meant that total income of the Majority World grew by an average annual rate of 10 per cent. Allowing for different rates of population growth and other factors, this means that average annual increase in purchasing power per head in the Majority World rose by 3 per cent a year. Most of this growth was in a relatively small number of countries, particularly South Korea, Taiwan, Hong Kong and Singapore, and to a lesser extent in Argentina, Brazil, Malaysia, Morocco, Pakistan, the Philippines and Thailand.

The cumulative effect of immigration controls, selective import controls and unequal terms of trade has meant that the rich world has paid less and less for imports, while the majority were forced to serve the wealthy minority in order to survive – much as most black South Africans had little choice but to work for whites. The dynamic growth of the Asian–Pacific region as an independent economic centre has reduced the West's importance for the Majority World while increasing conflict and demands for one-sided protectionism. This is most visible in the fierce controversies over NAFTA, GATT and other trade negotiations.

WORLD TRADE RULES

> The interest of dealers ... is always in some respects different from, and even opposite to, that of the public... The proposal of any new law or regulation of commerce which comes from this order ought always to be listened to with great precaution [since they] have generally an interest to deceive and even to oppress the public.
>
> Adam Smith, *The Wealth of Nations*, 1776[26]

The rules of international trade determine how economic opportunities, production and income are shared between participants in the world economy. Just as domestic politics establish patterns of income distribution between workers, employers, investors and public spending within nation-states, so trade negotiations influence how the value of production is shared on a global scale. International regulations for finance, transport and tariffs influence every economic transaction, permeating society and culture throughout the world. For example, imports of subsidized maize from the West may undercut a staple commodity in the Majority World like rice, forcing growers off the land, villages to decline and society to change. A fall in food crop prices can lead, for example, to increased cultivation of coca leaves or heroin poppies.

The main forum through which the international rules of trade are agreed is GATT, the General Agreement on Tariffs and Trade. It was the last of the major institutions of the post war settlement to be established and the first to be renegotiated, through its transformation into the World Trading Organization from January 1995.

Britain and the US agreed to set up an international trading organization alongside the IMF and World Bank at Bretton Woods in 1944. Its charter was signed by fifty-six countries in Havana in 1948. This outlined guiding principles for regulating restrictive practices, creating full employment and stabilizing prices of staple commodities, among other things. It would have protected Majority World countries from the violent price fluctuations which made them so vulnerable. This was too much for the US Congress, which refused to ratify the treaty. Instead, the US and twenty-two other countries used chapter 4 of the charter to create GATT. Ironically, now that the balance of international trade is shifting to the industrializing countries of the Majority World, the US has begun to see advantages in linking trade regulations with employment conditions to protect itself.

The General Agreement on Tariffs and Trade had the much narrower aim of creating free trade by removing tariff barriers and restrictive practices. It remained a provisional treaty between contracting parties and was not formally within the UN framework. By 1993 GATT had 128 'contracting parties', most of whom have now become members of the World Trade Organization. Its main principles are that:

- trade should not discriminate and all member countries should have equal status as 'most favoured nation';

- protectionist measures should take the form of tariffs rather than import quotas or other barriers, in order to promote transparency;

- tariff barriers should be reciprocal;

- all members commit themselves to periodic negotiations to reduce tariffs, known as 'rounds'.

In the thirty years after 1947, average tariffs on manufactured goods were cut from 40 per cent to 5 per cent. This largely benefited trade between industrialized countries, since agriculture, textiles and key industries for the Majority World were excluded. Since the Tokyo Round in 1973, the West has stealthily increased trade barriers, contrary to the rhetoric of its leaders and its legal obligations under GATT. The Majority World countries were promised 'a substantial improvement' in access for exports, but almost immediately industrial countries pushed through the Multi-fibre Arrangement to protect textile companies. The MFA was presented as a measure for 'the reduction of [textile] trade barriers and the liberalization of world trade'.[27] Like many of South Africa's laws, its purpose was the opposite of its stated aims. This was the first of many 'safeguard' measures to shield domestic industries from the tough reality of free trade, in contempt of GATT. Privately, the Majority World was advised to accept 'political realities' as the price of greater transparency.[28] In reality, the West increased trade barriers since 1973, while the Majority World liberalized trade.[29]

The United States in particular has used GATT to prise open foreign markets while shielding its own markets with anti-dumping laws and other measures. By 1990, almost a third of standard goods made in the United States, by value, were protected from international competition.[30] When Bangladesh tried to put health restrictions on cigarettes, the US trade representative, Carla Hills, said: 'We want to abolish the right of nations to impose health and safety standards more stringent than a minimal uniform world standard.' As countries of the Majority World have become more competitive with the West, it has used the excuse of higher standards to exclude imports. Thus Western trade policy is steeped in double standards and is an essential pillar of global apartheid.

Decision-making in GATT

GATT works by consensus and in secret. In practice, there is a lot of tough bargaining between the OECD countries before proposals are brought forward for a decision. All member states have one vote in annual sessions of Contracting Parties. Between sessions, decisions are taken by the Council of Representatives and Standing Committees. Although two-thirds of GATT's members are now from the Majority World, its agenda is dominated by the concerns of the rich world. This is justified by the US on the grounds that 'trade weight' gives it the largest stake in the trading system. Western power is enhanced through regular discussions between the US, EU, Japan and Canada at so-called quadrilateral meetings as well as other internal forums, such as the G7 and the OECD. Countries of the Majority World have been less able to develop a common approach or resolve their differences. The G77 and UNCTAD are unwieldy, representing interests too diverse for concerted action. ASEAN has become increasingly useful as a forum for Asian and South-East Asian nations to develop a common approach, increasing their collective bargaining power. On the other hand, Western business interests have the money, contacts, skills and experience to lobby governments directly, using the politically sensitive issues of jobs, national sovereignty and even the environment to make a persuasive case for their particular industry.

Even when the Majority World wins favourable agreements through GATT, they cannot be enforced against economic super-powers. Western countries simply take unilateral action and ignore decisions they dislike. In 1969, the West agreed to cut customs duties on manufactured goods from the Majority World so that they could increase export earnings and boost their economies under a 'Generalised System of Preferences' (GSP). This was introduced very, very slowly – in contrast with the speed with which the West responds to alleged dumping. The West decided which goods would be covered, excluding agriculture, textiles and metals that would be of most interest to the Majority World. And it ensured that the system could be set aside at such short notice that cargo in transit could be turned away on arrival – not conditions to encourage long-term investment. Twenty years later less than a fifth of imports from the Majority World were covered by the system. Only a few countries benefited, mainly Hong Kong, South Korea, Taiwan, and of course the transnational corporations which control most of their trade.[31]

The West is quick to act when its perceived interests are threatened. Under Section 301 of the Trade and Tariff Act of 1984, the US is legislator, prosecutor, judge and jury in deciding cases of unfair competition. These powers were first enacted in 1962, revised in 1974 and greatly strengthened by the 1988 Trade and Competitiveness Act, since when they have been known as 'super

301'. Countries which are too successful in exporting to the US are threatened with unilateral retaliation. This enables domestic manufacturers to lobby for selective protection against particular imports or to force countries to change domestic law, often in contravention of GATT rules.[32] These powers have been used against patent laws in Brazil (at the behest of the US Pharmaceutical Manufacturers Association), against copyright law in Brazil and South Korea, and on over fifty other occasions since 1975. When Majority World countries challenged the US for taking unilateral action, the US reply was: 'There is no article in the GATT that prohibits GATT-inconsistent laws, neither is there a requirement that GATT rules be incorporated into domestic laws.' This is like saying that there is no law which says you must obey the law.

In theory, the World Trade Organization will replace unilateral action with agreed procedures supervised by independent international arbitration. Peter Sutherland, GATT's last general secretary, has argued that the WTO would establish an objective, rule-based trading order in which 'the big guy' does not push round small states,[33] replacing 'the rule of law for the rule of the jungle'.[34] In practice, it could be as powerless over the West as the World Court and as one-sided in its dealings with the Majority World as the IMF/World Bank. Demands by the EU and US for two seats each on the WTO's seven-member appeals tribunal gives the rest of the world little confidence in their commitment to fairness in international law. Moreover, implementation and enforcement of WTO rules depends largely on the interpretation and goodwill of national trade officials and politicians. Many fundamental issues in relation to the environment, labour laws and finance have yet to be addressed.

The Uruguay Round

The world's most momentous trade negotiations formally began in Uruguay in 1986. They consisted of fifteen parallel discussions and twenty-eight 'dossiers' covering almost everything from agriculture to services, textiles and television programmes. The agreement was due to be completed in 1990, but dragged on until December 1993 due to the intense sensitivity of the issues. Four hundred pages long, with 18,000 pages of details, it was finally signed by ministers from 125 countries in Marrakesh, Morocco.

Under the treaty average import duties will be cut by a third and non-tariff barriers against imports from the Majority World will be slashed by three-quarters. Restrictions against agriculture and textiles will be phased out over ten years. GATT itself was to be superseded by the World Trade Organization.

The treaty was returned to national parliaments for ratification, where it faced widespread opposition. In the United States a broad coalition from labour unions to the conservative right and environmentalists won a proviso that the US would overrule WTO adjudications in certain circumstances. Members of the European Union delegated ratification to the Council of Ministers, thus avoiding democratic debate.

It was finally ratified in December 1994. Within a few months the US threatened unilateral action against Japan, bypassing the painfully negotiated disputes machinery. Thus the United States demonstrated yet again that there is one rule for the powerful West and another for the rest. Like the drug barons of Medellín, US trade barons cut their own deals with international law enforcement agencies. The farmers of India or manufacturers of Brazil will have no such privileges when US companies demand market access or a cut for patent rights.

Most Majority World governments supported the Uruguay Round as a lesser evil in the face of Western protectionism. They believe that export-led growth will bring prosperity, as it did for Singapore, South Korea and Taiwan. Above all, they see the WTO as a way of preventing the United States from imposing unilateral punitive tariffs. Many Majority World countries had already reduced trade restrictions as a result of pressure from the World Bank, IMF and transnational corporations or regional trade agreements even before the Uruguay Round concluded.

Opponents in the Majority World fear that removing national control over foreign investment and market access will amount to a transfer of sovereignty to transnational corporations. Local cultures and national sovereignty will be undermined by free trade in services, particularly press, television, telecommunications and transport. Technology transfer will be entirely on Western terms, entrenching inequality. The extension of property rights to seed varieties and breeds of animal could force farmers to pay royalties on seeds for replanting which have been harvested from their own crops. Finally, they see a danger that energy-intensive Western agriculture will undercut small-scale, labour-intensive farms, destroying rural economies and driving people into overcrowded cities.[35] The Uruguay Round was almost entirely a battle between

Table 3 Who gains what from the Uruguay Round of GATT? Official estimates of annual increase in trade by the year 2002 ($bn by region)

Region	$bn	% GDP (1992)
European Union	61.3	0.9
China	37.0	12.0
United States	36.4	0.6
Japan	27.0	0.7
Asia (excl. India)	25.9	—
South America	8.0	—
India	4.6	2.0
Eastern Europe	2.1	—
Australia/New Zealand	2.0	0.6
Africa (excl. Egypt, Libya)	(2.6) loss	—

the European Union, Japan and the US. For the Americans, GATT will open up European and Japanese markets in agriculture, while removing competition with subsidized food dumped on world markets. GATT will also open more markets to Western goods and services and increase earnings from copyright and patents.

Western supporters argue that reduced trade barriers will increase world income by $235 billion by the year 2005, stimulating growth, jobs and prosperity. This is highly speculative and is anyway less than 1 per cent of world GDP in 1992. Even so, official estimates show that the European Union is likely to be the biggest winner, with the West as a whole taking 60 per cent of the gains. The world's thirty-five poorest countries, mainly African, are expected to be net losers. Although they have 30 per cent of the world's population, they account for only 3 per cent of output in cash terms, and are treated as insignificant in trade terms – much as they were in South Africa. China and Asia (excluding India) are expected to make the biggest percentage gains (see table 3). None of these estimates takes account of social or political costs which will inevitably follow trade liberalization.

GATT is a colossal gamble for the West. Its effect on investment, jobs and competition is already being felt, as companies switch accounting, data-processing, typesetting and software engineering, as well as manufacturing, to low-waged areas. The most far-reaching measures will only come into force at the turn of the millennium, which could raise a worldwide economic and political whirlwind. Scenario-planners at Shell Oil anticipate economic growth and rising living standards, but they fear an equally plausible scenario in which 'Global trade liberalization triggers unrelenting job cuts and downward pressure on wages in industrialized nations.'[36] It is also a high-risk strategy for the Majority World. As traditional agriculture is thrown on to the mercy of global markets, over 2 billion people could be forced off the land to find work in cities and in the countries of the West. Long-established social and economic patterns could be shaken by a hurricane of market forces. The potential for conflict is immense. These very real dangers mobilized millions of Indian farmers in massive demonstrations against GATT and raised new political spectres in the West.

The contrast between the response to farmers' protests against GATT in France and India provides a vivid illustration of global apartheid in action. French government ministers shuttled frantically across the Atlantic, holding up the GATT agreement until they won concessions and financial aid from the European Union at the very last minute. In India, where most of the population live on the land, millions of farmers held massive demonstrations. Yet the government pressed ahead, confident that industrial trade will recoup losses on the land. In India the rural poor will pay for free trade through the loss of land and livelihood.

In the West, many of the consequences of competition will be taken care of by the state or private insurance, which provide an extensive support system to individuals and industry – as in white South Africa.

WESTERN AID FOR MARKET MECHANISMS

Competitive markets, as argued in chapter 2, cannot survive without social protection. The child carpet-weavers of Pakistan, cotton-pickers of Egypt, copper-miners of Zambia, assembly-workers of Indonesia and software engineers of Bombay are as much part of the global economy as Hollywood film-makers or French farmers. Yet they are conspicuously excluded from most of the world's welfare provision. Europe and the US have the world's largest aid programmes, redistributing resources between citizens through social security, public services, agricultural subsidies and industrial support. Minute amounts of discretionary aid are allocated for the Majority World, mostly on the basis of Western political interests rather than need.

The replacement of charity and discretionary aid with entitlement programmes is central to the Western Economic System. Social security and services such as education, health, child protection and public safety are provided as a right to citizens by redistributing income through the state. Inadequate as it may be in particular areas, this massive intervention in the market is essential for social stability and cohesion. The West spends, on average, over 30 per cent of its combined Gross Domestic Product (GDP) on internal aid, about $4,900 per head in 1990, ranging from under 20 per cent of GDP in Japan to almost 50 per cent of GDP in Sweden. This compares with an average of 0.33 per cent of Western GDP spent on aid for the Majority World, about $75 per person in the West, ranging from 0.17 per cent of GDP ($44 per head) in the US to 1.4 per cent of GDP ($282 per head) in Norway. Even then, most aid is not spent on the world's poorest people, but on projects which support Western interests.

By contrast, states in the Majority World spend, on average, less than 10 per cent of national income on social provision, or about $30 a head, ranging from under $12 a head in Somalia, Mozambique or Ethiopia, to over $1,500 in Singapore and Hong Kong.[37]

The richest Western countries also provide substantial aid to poorer states within the West. The US provides military assistance through NATO. The European Union has a well-developed system of automatic international aid through the Common Agricultural Policy, Structural Funds and smaller schemes. Structural Funds allocated some $170 billion (142 billion ECU at 1992 prices) for 1994–9, almost $30 billion a year.[38] This is slightly more than the total aid from all European countries to the Majority World. Over half (68%) of European aid is allocated to regions where GDP per head is less than the Community average (this was about $13,000 in 1990). This was sixteen times the average GDP per head in the Majority World, and fifteen times more than the threshold for interest-free loans from the World Bank. European structural funds provide a quarter of public investment in Greece, Portugal and Ireland, increasing GDP by up to 7 per cent. Agricultural subsidies can add a further 5–8 per cent of GDP. By contrast, structural adjustment for the Majority World means cuts in living standards and a reduction in public investment. The world's poorest countries receive, on average, 3 per cent of their GDP in aid. Europe gives more aid to its cows than to people in the Majority World.

Aid for agriculture

All Western countries protect their agriculture to some extent. The combination of tariffs on agricultural imports and subsidies protects the livelihoods of millions of farmers in the West, but can be doubly damaging for the Majority World. Dumping subsidized surplus on world markets undercuts producers in the Majority World, damaging their own agricultural development as well as denying them equal access to Western markets. For example, in the early 1970s, the US and Europe imported large amounts of sugar from the Caribbean, Latin America and the Philippines. A combination of subsidies and tariffs increased income from sugar for Western producers, who dramatically raised production so that by the mid-1980s they became net exporters. The price of sugar in world markets fell to 3 cents a pound, about a quarter of the production costs in the Philippines, while European and North American producers enjoyed prices of about 20 cents a pound. Twelve million sugar producers in the Majority World were plunged deeper into poverty. In the Philippines a quarter of a million people became unemployed, without social security or even land on which to grow food, causing widespread starvation on the fertile island of Negros.[39] In the Dominican Republic, one of the world's most efficient cane sugar producers, production had plunged 40 per cent by 1990, causing sugar mills to close, incomes to collapse and 20,000 Haitian cane-cutters to lose their jobs. Rural incomes fell by 40 per cent, infant mortality and malnutrition rose, and the impoverishment of the Dominican Republic deepened.[40] Meanwhile the loss of export revenues added to the mounting international debt of sugar-producing countries. Similar stories could be told about edible oils, pulses, grains and other crops.

Agriculture needs some form of protection from the vagaries of the weather and markets. Food security is fundamental for all human communities. Completely free trade in agriculture might make it more profitable to turn farms in Western Europe into theme parks, golf courses or nature areas and import food from the rest of the world, but this would leave Europeans extremely vulnerable. The issue is not the existence of farm protection, but the way in which it is applied by the West. This is a complex topic, but three criticisms of the present system are that:

● current policies discriminate against Majority World producers. Western agricultural support contrasts starkly with its opposition to commodity agreements for staple crops produced in the Majority World;

- Western agricultural subsidies tend to support larger, wealthier farmers, the agrochemical and equipment industries at the expense of small farmers, consumers and the environment;

- Western economic policies substitute human labour with chemicals, energy and machines, transfering costs onto the environment. This is aggravated by artificially low transport costs and aid for industry.

Aid for industry

All Western countries support selected manufacturing industries through direct subsidies, research and development, and assistance with restructuring. Britain, France and the US pour vast sums into arms industries. Aerospace enjoys extensive, mostly hidden, subsidies for development and production of aircraft, air traffic control, airports and national carriers, as well as tax-free fuel. The Japanese Ministry of International Trade and Industry (MITI) sponsors strategic sectors to develop internal infrastructure and exports abroad. Throughout the West industrial decline and overcapacity have been made more bearable through redundancy payments, retraining and stimulus for new industries. Painful as the process was for workers and communities who lost their livelihoods in coal, steel, shipbuilding and many other industries, their suffering bears little comparison with the wretched conditions created in the Majority World by Western protectionism. Concern over unemployment has also prompted most Western states to develop regional programmes and investment incentives to attract large employers. States within the US, for example, have spent between $120 million and $325 million to attract investment from the car industry.[41] Britain has spent over $1 billion on sustaining and restructuring its car industry, and continues to provide grants for foreign investors.

Energy subsidies in the West include support for the nuclear power, coal mining and electricity industries; indirect aid through tax allowances, particularly for new plant, oil and gas prospecting; and the uncounted costs of environmental damage, increased health care and unemployment. Estimates of the cost of US energy sector range from $100 to $300 billion a year.[42] The British nuclear

Table 4   Top recipients per capita of Western aid

Rank by aid per head	Aid per head ($)	GNP per head ($)	GDP per head
1 Israel	295	11,000	103
2 Jordan	283	1,240	60
3 Gabon	123	3,330	93
4 Botswana	118	2,040	71
5 Jamaica	115	1,500	64
6 Egypt	108	600	37
7 Mauritania	107	500	33
8 Senegal	100	710	46
9 Papua New Guinea	96	860	50
10 Congo	92	1,010	56

Source: World Bank, *World Development Report 1992*, pp. 256–7.

industry receives a subsidy of $2 billion a year. Although low energy prices appear to boost economic growth by stimulating industry, GDP and profits, they cause long-term damage to both domestic and global economies as well as to the environment. Low energy costs enable firms to substitute people with machines, increasing unemployment. Subsidized energy also encourages unnecessary transport of goods and people, distorting land use and industrial development by undermining local economies. They also discourage investment in energy efficiency and conservation, create the permanent hazard of nuclear waste and produce CO_2 emissions which increase global warming.

Indirect aid

'Official Development Assistance' – foreign aid – is an extension of Western industrial policy and diplomacy, and very often a form of indirect aid for the West. In order to defend itself from political pressure in the US, the World Bank itself has advertised that its aid for the Majority World increases spending in the West. Bilateral aid is frequently tied to specific policy conditions, such as market liberalization and privatization, or to the purchase of Western goods, or is a sweetener for commercial deals. In 1989 the British government granted Malaysia $350 million to build the

Table 5 Bottom recipient per capita of Western aid

Country	Aid per head	GDP per head
1 Mozambique	60	80
2 Tanzania	47	110
3 Ethiopia	17	120
4 Somalia	55	120
5 Nepal	23	170
6 Chad	56	190
7 Bhutan	33	190
8 Laos	37	200
9 Malawi	56	200
10 Bangladesh	20	210
17 Nigeria	2	290
21 India	2	350
23 China	2	370

Source: World Bank, *World Development Report 1992*, pp. 256–7.

controversial Pergau dam on the understanding that the Malaysian government would buy $2 billion worth of arms. This was ruled illegal by the British High Court in November 1994. Indonesia received over $100 million in soft loans in 1993 in connection with a similar arms deal. Jordan, Oman and Thailand are other major arms purchasers which have similarly benefited from questionable largesse. Britain is far from alone in using aid in this way.

Most of Europe's foreign aid programme is governed by the Lomé convention, a long-term binding legal agreement between the EU and the seventy African–Caribbean–Pacific (ACP) countries, mainly former colonies. The programme includes humanitarian aid as well as automatic allocations determined by objective criteria and the funds to compensate for falls in world prices of commodities and minerals. These are a form of common agricultural policy, in which ACP countries are second- or even third-class members of the human community, much less deserving of assistance than the much richer European citizens.

The biggest *per capita* recipients of development aid were not the world's poorest, but those whose political support was most important to the West (see table 4). It is as if unemployment benefit and social security were paid according the political complexion of the parish or county rather than according to need.

People in some of the world's forty-three poorest countries

received an average of $10 dollars each in 'official development assistance'. Amounts received by the world's very poorest countries are shown in table 5.

By comparison, approximate European Union support per person in Ireland was over $1,200 and in Greece over $850, between 20 and 600 times more than the entire West gave to the world's very poorest people. This is not to argue against transfers from poor to rich within the West, simply to highlight double standards. The solution is not to cut aid for the poor in the West, but to develop fair and sustainable social protection worldwide.

Further Reading

Global political economy

Barratt Brown, Michael, *Fair Trade: Reform and Realities in the International Trading System*, Zed, 1993.

Beenstock, Michael, *The World Economy in Transition*, Allen & Unwin, 1983.

Bovard, James, *The Fair Trade Fraud*, St Martin's Press, NY, 1991.

Coote, Belinda, *The Trade Trap*, Oxfam, Oxford, 1992.

Goldsmith, James, *The Trap*, Macmillan, 1994.

Hart, Jeffrey A., *Rival Capitalists: International Competitiveness in the United States, Japan and Western Europe*, Cornell, Ithaca and London, 1992.

Hines, Colin, and Lang, Tim, *The New Protectionism*, Earthscan, 1993.

Page, Sheila, *How Developing Countries Trade: The Institutional Constraints*, Routledge, 1994.

Perot, Ross, *Save Your Job, Save Our Country: Why NAFTA must be Stopped – Now!*, Hyperion, NY, 1993.

Porter, M. E., *The Competitiveness of Nationals*, Macmillan, 1990.

Potts, Lydia, *The World Labour Market: A History of Migration*, Zed, 1990.

Raghavan, Chakravarthi, *Recolonization: GATT, the Uruguay Round and the Third World*, Zed, 1990.

Reich, Robert B., *The Works of Nations: A Blueprint for the Future*, Simon & Schuster, 1991.

Thurow, Lester, *Head to Head: The Coming Economic Battle among Japan, Europe and America*, Nicholas Brealey, 1993.

Wood, Adrian, *North-South Trade, Employment and Inequality: Changing Fortunes in a Skill-Driven World*, Oxford University Press, 1994.

4

Global Privileges of Private Enterprise

A merchant ... is not necessarily a citizen of any particular country ... a very trifling disgust will make him remove his capital, and together with it all the industry which it supports, from one country to another.

Adam Smith, *Wealth of Nations*, 1776[1]

Free trade is an article of faith for Western business, but nowhere is it practised. Most large-scale private companies owe their existence to state intervention and privileged protection from competition. Most are quasi-command economies, harnessing corporate loyalty and administration to create economies of scale which cannot be sustained under unrestrained competition. Corporations, no less than societies, cannot withstand the instability of totally free markets and do everything within their power to minimize competition. This chapter explores the powerful and often paradoxical role of private corporations and finance as unwitting agents of global apartheid.

The global economy, like that of South Africa, was created by transnational trading corporations driven by the pursuit of profit. These vast organizations are successors of the mercantile trading companies which led Europe's global expansion from the fifteenth century. They opened national and international markets, set up colonies, created empires, built infrastructure and invented the institutional and legal framework which propelled Western economic growth. Today they integrate worldwide investment, production, technology transfer, marketing and financial flows, dominating the global economy. They control over $2 trillion of foreign direct investment, generating almost half of world income in sales, and own over $31 trillion in assets worldwide. This immense economic power is highly concentrated, with the top 100 firms controlling over 60 per cent of sales and assets.

Global corporations came into being as a result of decisions by

Western governments. British manufacturing flourished under imperial preference, while American business was fostered behind protective tariffs of almost 50 per cent, or more in the case of iron, steel and textiles. In the nineteenth century, the governments of Germany, France, Italy, Japan and Russia challenged British and US dominance by creating their own conglomerates.[2] During the second half of the century Japan, South Korea and other South-East Asian states have likewise established competitive advantages through state intervention to support big business.

Global corporations are incredibly diverse in their ownership, purpose, structures, strategies and impact, with significant national and individual differences. While some companies plan production on a global scale, many are loose conglomerates linked mainly by financial controls. The ultimate strength of a company is its trading ability and control over markets. Brand names, production, technology and almost every aspect of a company may be sold, subcontracted out or even run as a joint venture with commercial rivals. What matters is revenue from trade. If income falters, management loses control and the company may be bought up, broken up or even disappear. In many respects it would be more accurate to call them transnational trading cartels (TTCs) than the more usual transnational corporations (TNCs). In this book they are called global companies to emphasize their global role, although other terms will occasionally be used.

Global corporations are the modern equivalent of the Vikings and feudal barons combined, but bigger, wealthier and more powerful than most modern states. Robert Monks, who twice stood as a Republican candidate for the American Senate and held top positions in the Reagan administration, described the corporation as 'so powerful that it has outstripped the limitations of accountability, becoming something of an externalizing machine, in the same way that a shark is a killing machine – no malevolence, no intentional harm, just something designed with sublime efficiency for self-preservation. And when companies are not held accountable for the power they exercise, we all pay the price.'[3]

This vast concentration of corporate power was a direct result of privileges granted by Western states, including infrastructure, research and development, free-trade zones, export credit guarantees and a wide range of subsidies and support to promote 'their' industries. Above all, governments have provided a framework of regulation and law which protects companies as almost autonomous economic agents. These privileges have helped to create a corporate command economy at the heart of the Western Economic System.

CORPORATE COMMAND ECONOMY

Limited liability is perhaps the most powerful privilege of private companies. It establishes them as distinct legal entities, independent of the individuals which make them up. It encourages enterprise and greater risk-taking because management and owners are protected from ruin if they fail, but it also limits corporate responsibility. Outsiders dealing with the corporation can assume that everything is done properly. Limited liability virtually absolves investors, management and customers from personal responsibility, upon which accountability depends. Members of the corporation are not personally answerable for its actions and the cost of mistakes is passed on to the customer, taxpayer or shareholder. All companies are of course subject to national laws. Publicly quoted companies are also supervised by the stock exchange, but this is only concerned with financial probity.

Corporate law gives management potentially autocratic powers. Staff have almost no rights to influence policy or conduct. Although many companies have learnt that tyranny is counter-productive, business bullies are often glamorized as corporate heroes so long as they deliver the bottom line. In theory, management is accountable to the shareholders, but ownership is often fragmented among institutional investors whose only concern is a reliable return.

Bankruptcy law is another bastion of corporate privilege, particularly in the US. In principle, modern bankruptcy law offers a positive approach to business failure. It should provide creditors with an orderly way of dealing with default, make it possible to salvage something from failure, and wipe the slate clean so that people can learn from mistakes and start again. In practice, it has become a shield for corporate irresponsibility. A leading US bankruptcy lawyer described the US Section 11 bankruptcy proceedings as 'a form of corporate welfare' for megacorporations to escape 'the effects of their arrogance, greed and illegal conduct'.[4]

Trade marks, patent protection and intellectual property rights create further layers of protection for Western companies by granting monopoly rights over names and inventions. These measures serve some useful functions. But they also permit monopolistic profits, particularly in the pharmaceutical, electronics and entertainment industries where rewards are out of all proportion to risks. Although these privileges are granted in law by the state on behalf of the public, there is no duty on private companies to account for how they are used. Patent rights are arguably less important than human rights, yet they are enforced more vigorously by Western governments, particularly the United States.

The privileges of business incorporation contrast greatly with other forms of incorporation to protect people from the vicissitudes of market forces. Trade unions were persecuted as conspiracies during the nineteenth century and are still harassed in many countries. Charities and non-profit organizations work under tighter legal limits than private enterprise. Local government is controlled and supervised even more closely, with precise and limited powers. Even the legitimacy of elected governments to determine a country's political and economic framework is increasingly under attack from supporters of private enterprise.

The internal environment of many corporations is relatively free from the intense competition of the marketplace, since long-term survival depends on cooperation and loyalty to common goals. Left to themselves, large corporations develop bureaucratic sclerosis. Like many people, they prefer predictable, safe sources of income to the relentless innovation, restructuring and relocation demanded by competition. During the 1960s and 1970s commentators spoke about 'convergence' between Soviet state bureaucracies and Western corporate bureaucracies. This ended with the intensification of competition even before the Soviet Union collapsed. Now many companies use internal competition to pitch managers, plants and branches of the same company against each other. But the boundaries of internal competition are carefully managed so that subsidiaries do not compete against each other.

Global companies run a private 'welfare state' of perks, health care, insurance and other facilities for senior employees, largely at the expense of the customer, taxpayer and shareholder. The privileges of the Soviet nomenclature were insignificant compared with the expense account existence and 'compensation packages' of top executives. Most company boards are a self-selecting, self-perpetuating group who decide what to pay each other and do very well for themselves in good times and bad. Although their decisions may have more impact on people's lives than those of most politicians, they complain when subject to public scrutiny. They are public servants who pay themselves like princes.

Corporate privileges are reinforced by the fact that global companies have no formal existence in international law, but are governed only by the national laws of each country. Since corporations have coopted or neutralized almost all regulatory bodies affecting their activities,[5] they are virtually above the law, free to create their own rules for global conduct.

Managed competition

Global corporations manage competition between themselves according to a robust etiquette that is most visible when it breaks down, in price wars and takeover battles. Even these contain large elements of ritual jousting, since outright competition is extremely damaging. The unspoken rules governing corporate competition ensure a reasonable return for all by maximizing the benefits of shared monopoly. Competition rarely drives down costs to such an extent that global companies are forced out of business. Most competition is for additional profit or market share over and above the 'going rate' of corporate costs and shareholder dividends. These 'rules' are contrary to anti-trust laws and free-market principles, but are essential aspects of the Western Economic System.

- *Sheer size* enables global corporations to maintain their dominance through advertising, economies of scale, cross-subsidies, transfer pricing and innovation as well as giving them influence over regulators, retailers and suppliers.

- *Product demarcation* enables companies to target distinct sectors of particular markets. Much apparent competition between different brands or shops is within the same company, so that a range of products gives consumers choice while reducing competition with rival producers.

- *Price leadership* acknowledges certain brand goods like Heinz, Marlboro or Mercedes as 'price leaders' which sell for as much as the market will bear. Large differences in prices between the similar goods in different countries shows how different market conditions affect prices.

- *Strategic alliances* or partnerships between global companies based in different countries allows them to develop new advantages, spread risks and benefit from the economies of

cooperation, scale and synergy. Sharing development, marketing and production of new technology is widespread.

- *Corporate conquest* enables large firms to buy out, undercut,
intimidate or otherwise exclude smaller competitors. Standard
Oil virtually created the global oil business by subsuming small
US producers.[6] Control of the computer industry,[7] telecommunications,[8] entertainment, media, cars and many other sectors are similarly concentrated into a few hands.

- *Cartels*: Companies continue to form open or secret agreements to share out markets between them. Perhaps the most
successful is the Anglo-American Group of companies which
controls a large part of South African gold mining as well as
the world's diamond market.[9]

As well as unwritten rules, global corporations maintain industrial pressure groups to protect their interests. American and
British producers made several agreements to stabilize the oil
market before OPEC seized the initiative in 1960.[10] In every
industry, international associations, trade fairs, chambers of commerce, policy forums and industrial organizations enable global
companies to promote a mutually beneficial framework for international trade, to defeat perceived threats and, more often than
not, form a tacit understanding about market shares, profit margins
and trading conditions.

Bursts of competition can trigger upheaval within the commercial world. US and European car markets have been severely
shaken by Japanese companies from the 1970s onwards, causing
huge losses, redundancies, state intervention and massive restructuring. Japanese imports were restricted by 'voluntary restraint
agreements' and local production of Japanese models. During the
1980s computer and micro-electronic industries were radically
transformed by upstart companies such as Apple and Microsoft as
well as by South-East Asian firms. Such challenges are usually
assimilated. As in the Football League, top teams buy new players,
hire new managers and overlook the occasional professional foul
to stay on top. One company may take over another and monopoly power is strengthened. Deregulation of world trade is
increasing both the rate of upheaval and concentration of control.

Most governments collude with tacit corporate conspiracies in
what they believe is the national interest. During and after the
First World War most Western countries initiated various forms
of industrial planning, which continued long after the war was

over. After the catastrophic crash of free-market capitalism in the United States after 1929, a council of senior business leaders was formed to liaise with the Department of Commerce under the Roosevelt administration. This continued until the Kennedy era when it became the Business Round Table. In every industry, private corporations work intimately with 'their' government department, far more closely than consumers, workers or other interest groups. As a result, governments sponsor particular industries, and even particular companies, 'in the national interest'. Government procurement is often done with agreed profit margins on a 'cost plus' basis, to provide the most comfortable protection against competition.

Western global corporations have been even more successful in controlling international trade negotiations such as GATT. Its trade advisory committees consist almost entirely of representatives of large corporations and industry associations, not workers or consumers. Out of 111 members of three key advisory committees, 108 represented twenty-four of the fifty largest producers of toxic pollutants in the United States.[11] Similarly, the UN's Codex Alimentarious Commission, responsible for additives, labelling, pesticides and other food standards, is dominated by global companies and industry federations, with delegates from the West heavily outnumbering those from the Majority World.[12] The US film industry was deeply involved in the negotiations over intellectual property laws and narrowly failed to stop other countries from supporting domestic film production and distribution. In almost every industrial sector representatives of global companies set the pace. They provide officials with the technical information, draft legislation and hospitality which secure business interests in international affairs.

Cooperation between business and government is inevitable and necessary. No company or country could survive the ravages of unrestrained free enterprise. But the present system gives powerful corporations extensive privileges with little social or environmental responsibility in return.

EMPIRES OF THE ECONOMY

Western states have enabled giant global corporations to become the largest and most powerful organizations in the world, more powerful than even the state. They control 70 per cent of world trade and 40 per cent of the world's total Gross Domestic Product, double the cash value of the entire production of the Majority World. Global sales of the top 500 companies were $10 trillion in 1994,[13] compared with global GDP of about $25 trillion. Many global companies are bigger than most countries. In dollar terms, over fifteen (30%) of the world's fifty largest economic entities are global companies. The 500 largest corporations are financially bigger than 60 per cent (110) of UN member states together. In economic terms the world belongs to private corporations.

In 1992 there were over 37,000 global industrial companies worldwide, of which 34,280 (91%) were based in the West, with over 170,000 foreign affiliates, almost half of these in the Majority World. Over half of all global companies are based in just five countries – Germany, Japan, Sweden, Switzerland and the US.[14] The activity of global companies is highly concentrated. The top 100 companies, excluding banking and finance, owned $3.4 trillion in assets in 1991, about a third of foreign direct investment worldwide.[15] The top ten companies controlled a quarter of these assets. The top 500 companies owned $31 trillion in assets in 1994.

Figures for company revenues and assets are deceptive. Most lists, like the *Fortune 500*, do not include private companies like Mars or the giant grain merchants Cargill. Banks and service companies were only added in 1995. Most figures cannot fully take account of franchising, licensing, out-sourcing and subcontracting. They do not show cross-linkages whereby companies share the same strategic direction through overlapping directorships, shareholdings and shareholders. The real value of most assets and production in the Majority World is seriously underrepresented due to exchange rate distortions. Figures are also based on published accounts submitted for tax purposes rather than on independent investigation.

As organizations, corporations have more flexibility than any state. They choose their own purpose, design their own structure, pick their own geography and, to a large extent, select – or sack – their workers (or constituents). They have much narrower responsibilities than do governments, and can dump social and environmental costs of production onto host countries. Unlike elected governments, decision-making is in secret and not accountable to the public except through sales. Corporations' first and final responsibility is to make a profit. Profitability of publicly quoted companies is under constant scrutiny by shareholders, investment analysts and the financial press. Any slackening of profitability reduces their asset value, which limits their ability to borrow and makes them vulnerable to takeover. Armed with the rod of profit, top executives wield immense power to protect their own interests within the corporation. An investor coup or takeover can unseat them only at considerable cost.

Companies can pick and choose the national regimes which offer the greatest advantages in terms of tax, labour laws, legal restrictions and disclosure, pitching states into competition against each other for investment and employment. They demand preferential treatment for planning permission, infrastructure, tax breaks, grants and flexible, low-cost labour. They shamelessly threaten to close down plants, move investment and cut jobs if states do not comply. And these tactics work.

Mobile industries have left countries unwilling to lower standards to 'competitive levels'. Thirty years ago 80 per cent of the world's shipping was owned by Western maritime nations. Now 70 per cent sails under flags of convenience, registered in countries with weak regulations. Private companies are registered in small statelets like Liechtenstein, Luxemburg or the Cayman Islands, whose main commodities are secrecy, discretion, the absence of supervision and low taxes. Large sections of the finance industry have gone 'offshore', out of reach of regulators. Chemical companies transfer their most dangerous plants to countries like India, Mexico and Africa. Toxic wastes are shipped from the West to be dumped in less vigilant areas of the Majority World.

The 'race to the bottom' for the lowest possible regulation has measurably increased human suffering. In the shipping industry, marine safety, working conditions and the pay of seafarers has been eroded, with the result that 121 ships were lost at sea in 1993, 9 per cent up on the previous year. The loss of life jumped by 35 per cent, to 592.[16] Inadequate banking supervision allowed the Bank of Credit and Commerce International (BCCI) to launder billions of dollars from crime and illegal drugs trade over nineteen years, defrauding savers of $20 billion before it was raided in 1991.[17] Lack of transparency in Robert Maxwell's corporate affairs meant that thousands of people lost their pensions when his private empire collapsed. Britain's oldest merchant bank, Barings, folded in 1995 as a result of unregulated and highly speculative trade in derivatives, almost destroying the highly respected Barings Charitable Trust in its wake.

Governments continue to value the contribution of global companies for many material reasons. Their single-minded economic purpose generally makes them more innovative and efficient in delivering goods, services and revenue than state agencies.

Although this may have social and environmental costs, experience shows that these are often better dealt with through regulation than by state ownership.

Employment is frequently given as the main reason for favouring global companies. They employ about 73 million people directly, more than two-thirds in the West and 12 million in the Majority World. Although this is less than 3 per cent of the labour force worldwide, they account for about a fifth of paid employment in non-agricultural activities,[18] usually the more skilled, better-paid sector of the economy. At a conservative estimate about 80 million more people are employed indirectly through subcontractors, suppliers, services and distribution. Spending by employees and tax contributions probably doubles the number again. Yet, as major users of new technology, global companies are more likely to cut their workforces. Numbers employed by industrial companies fell by 3.8 per cent in 1992 and by over 1 per cent in 1994, although service companies increased their employment levels slightly.

Global companies are often able to pay higher wages, rents and other charges than smaller local companies in the Majority World because of their greater investment and productivity as well as unequal exchange rates. They are also the main source of hard currency, technology, investment and access to Western markets. For these reasons most Majority World countries became less suspicious of global companies during the 1980s, preferring direct investment to borrowing from Western banks. At least corporations invest in productive capacity and only take a profit if they make one, whereas banks demand interest payments regardless of how the money is used.

Global companies are a significant source of government revenue, directly and indirectly through their employees, suppliers, purchases and sales. The US government has estimated that American-based corporations paid about $100 billion in direct taxes to foreign governments in 1989, about 10 per cent of foreign sales.[19] If all corporations pay a similar proportion in tax revenues, this would amount to about 10 per cent of government revenues in direct taxes alone (see table 6). Income from indirect and employment taxes is almost certainly higher, adding perhaps a further 10 per cent. Although global companies are extremely skilful in minimizing tax bills, they cannot avoid being a paymaster of national governments, particularly in the Majority World. In corporate terms they hold a significant stake that skilful executives are not slow to exploit.

Table 6 Tax payments by US global companies as a percentage of government revenue (1989)

Country	%
Guatemala	15.5
Trinidad & Tobago	13.0
Peru	12.0
Thailand	7.4
Malaysia	6.8
Philippines	5.4
Indonesia	5.3

Source: UN, *World Investment Report 1992: Transnational Corporations as Engines of Growth*, 1992, p. 15.

Some countries are virtual clients of major companies, which provide the elite with luxury cars, executive jets and the trappings of privilege which the poor country itself can hardly afford. They provide jobs for favoured citizens and relatives, bestow grants for students to study abroad, establish research institutes, build prestige projects, host conferences, sponsor publications and pay government officials to participate in international conferences.

As the major source of foreign earnings, global companies bind every country into the international trading network, a world they created and dominate. They determine investment, jobs and economic infrastructure like few other organizations. They have unprecedented influence over communications, sport and cultural life through advertising, sponsorship and media ownership. They buy political influence by lobbying, campaign contributions and sometimes corruption. Their sheer size makes them appear indispensable for economic growth and jobs – a litmus test of political success – and they exert a pervasive influence on economic, financial and foreign policy in almost every country of the world. The creation of the single European market, GATT and NAFTA was largely driven by global companies. The Rio Earth Summit in 1992 was sponsored by global companies, so criticism of their role was muted and its published report gave more prominence to corporate advertising than the agreements. Western financial markets were almost totally deregulated in response to demands from global corporations for a more competitive environment. Corporate influence can take extreme forms. United Fruit persuaded the US to topple the democratic government of Guatemala in 1954.

ITT encouraged the Chilean coup in 1973. More recently, President Clinton set aside human rights and foreign policy considerations over trade with China in favour of Boeing and other US commercial interests.

A growing number of global companies recognize the value of good citizenship and a few are developing social and environmental policies.[20] But these issues are subject to much less scrutiny than profitability, which ultimately determines corporate destiny. The greatest rewards come to those who drive a hard bargain and deliver the highest returns. Until now, the division of the world into two unequal parts has been immensely profitable for corporations and their shareholders.

The profitable divide

Profits from investments in the Majority World are generally higher in the West. Investments in the Majority World brought an average rate of return of at least 8 per cent a year over the period 1983–90, compared with 5 per cent in the West (based on the returns of non-bank US firms).[21] At this rate of return, the total investment stock of $266 billion in 1990 would have brought the West $18 billion a year, of which about a fifth was reinvested in the Majority World. On this estimate, roughly $160 billion was earned over ten years and about $100–$130 billion returned to the West.[22] US banks made much higher profits, from 28 to 42 per cent a year between 1979 and 1984, compared with a range of 6 to 17 per cent profits from manufacturing during the same period.[23]

Income from investment by global companies is hard to calculate, and declared rates of return vary widely between sectors, countries and years. Declared profits are only a small proportion of the income from the Majority World. Transfer pricing, royalties on copyright, patents, licences, trade marks and fees for services as well as unequal exchange rates all contribute to financial streams flowing into the West through global companies. For example, US income from royalties and licences alone was $16 billion in 1990, up from $8 billion in 1986. Although less than 5 per cent of this was from the Majority World ($690 million), the total was up from 4 per cent in 1986 ($296 million)[24] and the proportion is rising.

These rates of return benefit enormously from the division of the world into two unequal parts:

- the high-spending, high-consuming, affluent West, which has relatively protected, regulated markets offering reliable profit margins;

- the low-waged Majority World, which supplies low-cost raw materials and manufactured goods for Western markets. It also provides markets for high-value capital goods, such as machine tools, and low-cost premium goods with high margins, such as cigarettes, pharmaceuticals or soft drinks.

This division is the economic basis of global apartheid. From a commercial point of view, the ability to buy raw materials or produce in low-cost areas for sale in high-income areas is ideal. The driving forces behind the pressure for profits are investors and financial institutions, represented as the City, whether this is in London, Wall Street, Tokyo, or elsewhere.

FINANCE RULES: MONETARY MONARCHS OF THE SOVEREIGN CITY

I lived in a world where reality and moral values became warped, where a million dollars seemed like a paltry sum, where right and wrong became blurred.

Dennis B. Levine, 1992
Managing director, Drexel Burnham Lambert[25]

South Africa has always been regarded by foreign investors as a gold mine, one of those rare and refreshing places where profits are great and problems are small. Capital is not threatened by political instability or nationalization. Labor is cheap, the market is booming, the currency hard and convertible.

Fortune, July 1972[26]

Western finance propels global economic expansion through the simple mechanism of maximizing returns on investment. Every day vast sums pour into the financial system from savings, pension funds, insurance premiums, dividends and other sources. The Majority World contributes to this cash stream through fees, interest payments and profits from trade as well as illegal capital flight, corruption, drug-dealing and the arms trade. Like an elaborate suction pump, the financial system siphons cash through a worldwide network of capillaries into vast reservoirs of capital which allocate funds for dams, car plants, films, oil wells, power stations, roads, rockets, satellites, steel mills, tunnels and other large-scale projects. Most money is not not even invested in any real sense, but put into 'financial assets' like shares, futures, currency and derivatives. Yet this paper power exerts huge pressure on managers in the real economy to extract revenue from sales and production to feed the City – milking money rather than making it.

Investment finance is highly mobile. About $1,000 billion cross national borders every day, more than twenty times the level of world trade. Of this 10 to 15 per cent is investment and international share dealing. The remaining amount is merely trade in money. So-called investment fund wizards deal in financial futures, options, virtual securities, junk bonds and derivatives several removes from the real economy. Only a fraction of the financial system is based on direct profits from trade and industry. Barely 2 per cent of the $800 billion traded on the London Stock Exchange accrues to companies; 98 per cent is made up of paper transactions in second-hand capital. The entire financial system is a derivative of the real economy, and like the derivatives trading which bankrupted Orange County and Barings Bank in 1995, it could bankrupt the earth. Like a gigantic global chain letter, money keeps pouring in to the City, confident that money makes money. The power of the City to skim profits from all trade, through loans, shares and insurance, means that however inefficient, incompetent or corrupt it may be, the system continues. As in the story of the emperor's new clothes, the rich world invests in shared illusions.

The City concentrates immense power in a few hands. George Soros controls funds worth over $11 billion and won over $1 billion gambling against the Bank of England. Young Nick Leeson was earning six-figure bonuses until it was discovered he had lost over $450 million and brought down Barings Bank. Arbitrageurs like Dennis Levine, Michael Milken and Joseph Boesky became billionaire celebrities fulfilling the creed that 'greed is good', until they too were caught.[27] Anonymous pension fund managers are no less influential, although they are less conspicuous and more likely to follow trends than create them.

This is not to deny that there is an important and useful role for financial services, that much of the City may be both honourable and efficient, and that these services generate real wealth by stimulating greater efficiency. But most of the apparent wealth produced by the financial sector is a mirage, recycled rents derived through exclusive privileges granted by the state. These privileges include limited liability, the protective role of central banks, the relatively 'hard' status of Western currency, capital mobility, the liquidity of finance compared with real assets, investors' narrow duty to maximize returns above all other considerations, and the practice of pricing money in percentages.

The privileges of finance are neither uniform nor consistent across the world. For a long time the United States restricted interstate banking, and still restricts foreign investment for national security reasons. Continental Europe requires companies to show greater responsibility towards employees and maintains higher takeover barriers than Britain or the US. Until the 1980s most Western governments controlled capital movements to some extent. These policy differences are significant, but deregulation of global financial markets during the 1980s strengthened worldwide privileges of finance, forcing national economic policies to converge.

Money and merchants, as Adam Smith observed, enjoy privileged freedom of movement denied other participants in the economy. Workers cannot easily cross national boundaries to high-waged areas, while their produce faces import controls. Most landowners and manufacturers in the Majority World cannot move productive assets to areas which offer higher rates of return. But if they deposit savings in the Western financial system, legally or illegally, they can share in the highest returns available anywhere in the world. This flexibility gives the financial sector a competitive advantage over more productive ways of earning a living. So long as it attracts savings, it generates an income. Ultimately it too depends on real earnings in the productive economy, but most of the City's income is from fees, savings, insurance premiums, interest payments and rents rather than dividends from improved productivity.

Two other significant features give finance a competitive advantage, with damaging side-effects. First, as Keynes pointed out, the ease with which money can be exchanged for goods gives it a 'liquidity premium'. In other words, people with resources they do not need for immediate consumption are willing to pay for the convenience of getting it at short notice rather than tying it up in longer-term investment. Unlike real resources, money has no storage costs and can even earn income (interest) while not in use. This creates incentives to put money into short-term deposits or 'financial assets' which can have the effect of withdrawing money from the real economy, destroying purchasing power and contributing to economic depression. During most of the postwar period Western governments avoided this danger by issuing bonds for public investment. In many Majority World countries liquidity preference diverts resources from local investment into safe havens abroad or inert assets such as gold.

Second, liquidity preference is closely linked to the role of interest rates, the price of money. As Keynes pointed out, if people were willing to pay a premium for money, then 'it was almost inevitable that the rate of interest ... would rise too high to permit of an adequate inducement to invest'.[28] The ability to charge compound interest for money gives the wealthy exclusive advantages, with disastrous implications for the productive economy. This subtle sabotage through interest rates deserves deeper investigation.

THE PERCENTAGE RATE RACKET

Interest rates are a hidden distribution mechanism, taking from people who work for a living and giving to those who own wealth. Paying interest is now so deeply engrained that it is taken for granted, much as slavery was 300 years ago. Charging interest was prohibited by the church until 1545 in England and then capped by law. Adam Smith argued that maximum interest rates should be legally fixed at about 5 per cent.[29]

Taboos on charging interest were based on the sound ethical principle that lenders should share the risks, rewards and responsibility of investment. This reinforced the idea that money should only be borrowed for a useful purpose, for investment rather than consumption. If investment failed, borrowers would not suffer additional misfortune by losing their property or being forced into bondage to pay off debts. Charging interest implied an impersonal relationship, in which lender and sharer did not belong to the same community and therefore had no mutual obligation. This suggests an explanation why moneylenders often belonged to a different faith to those who borrowed.[30]

Lending money serves a necessary and useful function. It makes sense to give people an incentive to invest spare money rather than squander or hoard it. Interest and profits provide that incentive. Even when usury was forbidden people usually paid something to borrow money. Outright prohibition often added to the cost of borrowing. The development of interest was an important step in the creation of the Western Economic System by making money more cheaply and easily available, thus stimulating productive investment. Having an obvious way of showing the cost of money also provides a useful measure of the relative merits of different investments in financial terms. But the accumulation of money through compound interest can be dangerously deceptive.

Money and interest are like powerful drugs which are incredibly useful for a wide range of purposes but have dangerous side-effects outside a prescribed field. Like certain drugs, they can create euphoria and addictions which distort the entire system. Compound interest in particular generates illusions of economic growth which eventually cause severe hangovers or life-threatening cold turkey.

Both Adam Smith[31] and John Maynard Keynes[32] point out that market forces ought to bring down the cost of money (interest), thus stimulating productive investment, full employment and higher wages while eliminating unearned income as a source of wealth. Keynes recognized that this does not happen because people who control the price and quantity of money have a vested interest in raising its price and protecting its value through government intervention. This leads to the paradox that, instead of letting market forces drive down the cost of borrowing as the quantity of money increases, Western governments are more likely to raise interest rates in order to control inflation and exchange rates. This increases the income of people with money and cuts spending by people who are forced to pay interest, directly or indirectly. As Keynes argued in the 1920s, monetary policy is 'simply a campaign against the standard of life of the working classes' through the 'deliberate intensification of unemployment'.[33]

Interest rates are a key weapon in the struggle over how the benefits of economic activity are shared. When governments raise interest rates in order to stop savings from seeking higher rates of return abroad, they are responding to the power of financial institutions to withhold investment until profitability is restored. Because 'strikes' by capital do not stop production or the trains from running they are less visible than industrial action by workers, but a lot more effective. The concerted action by currency speculators to bring down the price of the UK pound in September 1992 was a rare display of raw power that sleeplessly stalks the City and which no mere state dare defy. Normally the everyday tugs at currency rates and bond prices keep governments on their knees.

All Western governments try to manage the internal (interest rates) and external (exchange rates) price of money to promote domestic economic priorities. A 'strong' exchange rate helps keep down inflation by making imports cheaper. While most attention is on the exchange rate between Western countries, it also suppresses prices from the Majority World. High interest rates have an even more devastating effect on the Majority World, as in the debt crisis, described below (pp. 113–15).

State regulation of interest rates through the central banking system creates a floor which effectively sets a minimum income for investors. Curiously, this rouses less opposition from conservatives than the idea of a minimum wage, although productive industry is often harmed more by the former than the latter, since higher wages are more likely to be translated into purchasing power while excess interest stifles it.

A paradox of the financial system is that Western leaders are worried about too much money causing inflation, so they raise interest rates to reduce the money supply. Meanwhile most people in the Majority World have too little money to buy what they need or to invest in even small-scale improvements. What money is available usually costs more than in the West, although the marginal productivity of poor people is often higher because they start from such a low base.

Profit is also a charge for the use of money, based on sharing risks in investment. In principle this is a more responsible way of rewarding saving, but in practice the Western Economic System grants a wide range of privileges to investment finance while passing much of the risk on to workers, consumers and the public sector. Investors expect a premium above the rate of interest, so that the level of real interest rates determines whether people with spare money are willing to invest in productive projects rather than lend at interest. This creates a direct link between interest rates and competitive pressures on the economy, since investors demand greater productivity to raise profits above the prevailing rates of interest.

Both interest and profit margins are calculated as a percentage of the money loaned. The practice of compounding interest and profits multiplies the power and profitability of the financial sector out of all proportion to its utility. The process is invisible and pernicious. Profit is added as a percentage at each stage of production, so that the total share of profit multiplies as the product is transformed between primary producer, merchant, manufacturer, wholesaler, retailer and any other stage in between. Interest charges are likewise added as a percentage at each stage. Western wages also include a significant element to pay for interest charges on housing and investment for pensions. When insurance charges are added, finance becomes a relatively high proportion of the final price of most Western goods, even when profit margins appear low. Thus the financial component in the cost of every product multiplies exponentially during production, while labour and other costs are added arithmetically. As a result, a growing proportion of the price of all goods is paid to those who own and manage money. Even people who never borrow any money pay an invisible amount of interest with everything they buy.

This mechanism automatically redistributes wealth from poor to rich – the opposite effect of competitive markets as described by Adam Smith. Charging a percentage for money makes it more attractive to earn a living from owning or managing money than running a business or working for a wage. This gives capital systematic advantages over labour, since it is always more attractive to invest in money than people or even equipment. As a result, cash is sucked into the Western financial system from the entire world, building up a great wall of capital.

Compound interest means that the amount of money tends to grow exponentially, creating enormous pressure for economic activity to keep up with monetary growth. In other words, higher sales, more production and new investment opportunities are constantly demanded to pay for the use of money, either as interest or profits. This fuels inflation, speculative bubbles and debt as well as unnecessary production. Speculative binges are inevitable in a system driven by the exponential growth of money. Past excesses include tulip mania in 1637, when coveted bulbs changed hands in Holland for more than the price of a house, the South Sea Bubble of 1720 and the US stock exchange boom before 1929. Periodic crashes, like the UK secondary banking crisis of 1974, the 20 per cent drop in stock exchange values in October 1987, or the US Savings and Loan fiasco of 1990, which cost between $500 billion and $1 trillion, are a stark reminder of the system's inherent instability. The vast sums of money surging through today's financial markets have been called 'great destabilizers' and a 'pathological phenomenon' by business guru Professor Peter Drucker,[34] but they are an inevitable consequence of fiscal privileges and pricing money in percentages.

The impact on the real economy can be devastating. Excess amounts of money build up into speculative storms which inflate asset values and shake the entire economic system. Meanwhile insufficient money in the Majority World creates a vacuum of debt that sucks up money and goods like a financial tornado wrecking the land and people while showering exports, profits and interest payments into the West, where the torrential downpour of under-priced goods erodes jobs, conditions of employment and social security systems.

Western economies have developed elaborate mechanisms to protect themselves from the most damaging effects of monetary escalation, such as interest rate relief, tax credits, loan guarantees, deposit insurance and secondary markets. In a crisis, financial establishments are frequently bailed out by governments equally terrified by loss of confidence in the system. These measures make interest charges more bearable, but the cumulative effect is to subsidize the cost of borrowing. While selective support for productive or social investment can be highly beneficial, most fiscal support increases the cost and supply of money, thus fuelling inflation.

The solution lies in transforming the financial system itself. Keynes quotes 'the strange, unduly neglected prophet Silvio Gesell (1862–1930)' and commends his arguments for fee-based financing as a way of overcoming the damaging effects of interest.[35] The failure to control finance has created one of the greatest catastrophes for much of the Majority World this century, namely the international debt crisis.

FOREIGN DIRECT INTERVENTION

> In the art of acquiring riches its end has no limits, for its object is money and possessions; but economy has a boundary, for acquiring riches is not its real end ... For the getting of money differs from natural wealth and the latter is the true object of the economy.
>
> Aristotle, *Politics*, Bk 1 (384–32 BC)

Money does not work, whatever the adverts say. It enables people to work. The main utility of financial markets is that resources not needed for immediate consumption can be directed towards productive investment. The grotesque effect of the Western Economic System is that investment is poured into the most privileged sections of the economy while money drains away from places where it is most needed.

The people who most need money for investment are the poor. For a woman who has to get up before dawn to grind grain, gather firewood and fetch water, small investments such as a well, a good stove and a hand-grinder could make a big difference. Investment in appropriate irrigation, plants that fix nitrogen and improved seed varieties can help a village grow more food. Better tools, workshops, a sewage system and potable water can help people in shanty towns improve their own housing, and produce more for their own use and for sale in local markets. Appropriate infrastructure can create a 'productivity platform' through which people make better use of available resources. Relatively small investments enable very poor people make large improvements in their lives. Measured in terms of money it may not be much, but in real terms it could mean enormous increases in productivity and quality of life. But little investment reaches the very poorest, because they are frequently outside or on the edge of the cash economy and are treated as bad risks. State agencies such as the World Bank and national governments often provide inappropriate aid which undermines self-reliance and impoverishes them further. Credit unions in the Caribbean, the Grameen (village) Bank in Bangladesh, the Six S Association in Africa, or the South Shore Bank in inner-city Chicago show that it is possible to run highly successful community-based financial services.[36] The World Bank announced in 1995 that it would follow their example and increase provision for small-scale loans, a welcome shift in policy.

Almost all investment since the Second World War has been in the West, including Japan. During the 1980s over 80 per cent of global investment poured into the West, increasing productivity per worker and competitive advantage over the Majority World in high-value-added goods. In 1990, total investment worldwide was almost $4 trillion, of which $232 billion (5%) was foreign direct investment (FDI). Only 14 per cent of foreign investment was in the Majority World, and two-thirds went into just ten countries (see table 6). Since then the buoyant markets of the Far East have continued to attract growing amounts of foreign investment, rising to 52 per cent of the total invested in 1993 and 40 per cent in 1994. A few Majority World countries, such as South Korea and Hong Kong, have also become a source of foreign investment in other countries, although still representing less than 6 per cent of the total FDI. Reinvested earnings are a considerably larger component of FDI in developing countries than in developed countries.[37]

During the 1980s many Majority World governments changed their views about foreign direct investment. Earlier restrictions on foreign ownership had simply led foreign firms to buy cooperation from local people, called 'name lenders' in Mexico. Direct investment can have many positive benefits, but foreign investment still means foreign control. In the words of the World Bank, 'the

Table 7 Foreign Direct Investment (1991): Major recipients in the Majority World and the West

Area	$ millions	$ per head
Majority World		
China	4,366	4
Mexico	4,762	56
Malaysia	4,073	219
Africa	2,514	4
India	1,116	1
Singapore	3,584	1,280
Taiwan	1,271	71
Thailand	2,014	35
Bangladesh	1	—
Latin America/Caribbean	15,235	34
West		
Western Europe	84,065	242
United States	11,500	45

investor's purpose being an effective voice in the management of the enterprise'.[38] The international financial system ensures that, however successful firms and countries of the Majority World are, Western investors take a cut through shares, bank loans, exchange rates and financial services. The cut is a big one, sucking vast amounts of money from the Majority World into the West.

Relatively high levels of investment in the West have created recurrent bouts of over-capacity, so that it produces more than people can buy. The causes are complex, but one key factor is the privileged position of finance which redistributes income from the majority to a wealthy minority. Since they cannot spend it all, they invest. But if people cannot afford or do not want to buy what is produced, the result is over-production.

Rapid industrial development by a few countries, particularly in South-East Asia, is transforming the global economy, so that by the end of the century more investment may go into the Majority World than into the West. The causes of this transformation are complex, but the combination of relatively high domestic savings, a vigorous private sector and strategic, often autocratic intervention by the state is a very different model from the pure free-market orthodoxy advocated by most Western institutions. This 'Asian model of development', as it has been called by the World

Bank demonstrates a different combination of competition and protection than in the West.

As the scale of global investment increases, Western governments, under strong US pressure, are demanding global rules to protect foreign investors' rights. These include freedom to establish operations, repatriate profits and conduct foreign exchange transactions, as well as safeguards against nationalization, with disputes mechanisms to enforce agreements. A key demand is equal treatment, giving foreign investors rights to participate in government research programmes and national support schemes on the same basis as local business. US companies like IBM want 'an aggressive agenda', with commitments to open up state monopolies, lower takeover barriers and freedom to employ expatriate managers. These proposals pose key questions about global governance and communities' rights to determine their own affairs. The US itself does not give outside investors equal rights. Many US states have restrictions such as contract compliance for equal opportunities, job creation targets and preferential procurement policies. The federal government prevents foreign companies, such as British Airways, from controlling US airlines. Many government grants for industry were set up in response to foreign competition, so that making them available to foreign firms would be bizarre. There is a case for a system of international regulation of investment, which would apply equally to conditions of work, social provision and environmental protection, factors which also affect competitiveness. Moreover, democratic principles mean that such rights and rules should be vested in the people, not undemocratic institutions like the OECD or WTO. As is so often the case, participants in a competitive economy seek exclusive advantages over others – the essence of separate development and global apartheid.

PURCHASING POWER IMPERIALISM: CURRENCY COLOUR BARS

Further evidence for systematic economic discrimination can be seen in the privileged role of hard currencies like the Deutschmark, dollar and yen. When people from the West travel or trade in the Majority World, their money usually goes much further than in the West. Meals in restaurants, and the cost of things like taxis and food in local markets often seem ridiculously cheap. Countries with well-developed tourist industries usually have parallel markets, with much higher prices in Western hotels and tourist areas. Many shops even have two sets of prices, Western and local, enabling enterprising tourists to bargain. Until 1995 China attempted to manage this difference between local and international prices by having two currencies in circulation.

This distinction between 'local' and 'international' prices forms an intangible 'currency bar' between the West and the Majority World. It is not imposed by the West, but arises from unequal trading relations and exclusive privileges maintained by it. Countries with relatively little trade, or who export goods that fetch low prices on international markets (like most Majority World commodities), have weak or volatile currencies in international markets.

An entirely self-sufficient economy would not even have a foreign exchange rate, because it would not need to trade. In the international economic system its currency would be worthless, its gross domestic product zero and its goods free of charge. Of course, an exchange rate would be created as soon as anyone visited that country and bought goods. If local people were unwilling to sell or did not want to buy foreign goods, the exchange rate could be very high. Global markets were created over the five centuries by Western countries forcing the Majority World to open their self-sufficient economies to Western traders, for example through textiles in India, opium in China or coal and other provisions from Japan. Once begun, trade has its own momentum, generating irreversible change. This may be beneficial or harmful depending on circumstances, but most people have little choice. For much of the Majority World, Western purchasing power is an economic force that continued conquering when the guns ceased firing.

The distinction between local and international currency values is vividly illustrated by comparing the value of currencies on the basis of how much they buy in their home market using a standard basket of goods and services. This provides a conversion factor known as purchasing power parity (PPP), defined by the World Bank as 'the number of units of a country's currency required to buy the same amount of goods and services in the domestic market as one dollar would buy in the United States',[39] and known as the International Dollar, I$. Estimates of purchasing power parities are far from exact.[40] There are many issues raised by using the US as the universal reference-point and questions about the comparability of any 'standard basket' for countries as diverse as Kenya and Iceland, but PPPs offer a better basis of comparison than market exchange rates. IMF economists admit that 'market exchange rates may be distorted by speculative bubbles, exchange market intervention, asymmetric speed of adjustment in goods and asset markets, or macroeconomic shocks'. In the case of 'developing' countries, they are also affected by 'differences in the relative price of traded versus non-traded output'. This leads to 'highly volatile and potentially misleading exchange-rate-based weights'.[41] In other words, conventional financial comparisons between countries are virtually nonsense. It is as if the West traded litres for gallons and grams for ounces, one for one.

Differences between exchange rates and PPP rates are due to the non-traded sector, that is, goods and services like haircuts, hospital treatment and subsistence crops which are not sold abroad. Yet these goods contribute indirectly to the value of traded goods. Farms and factories which produce goods for export pay workers in local currency, which they spend in local markets. Lower prices mean they can survive on lower pay in foreign currency terms than workers in the West. In effect, the non-traded sector provides a hidden subsidy to export markets.

The difference between exchange rates and purchasing power parities explains why over 3 billion people appear able to survive on unimaginably low average incomes of $390. In 1990 the average annual income in India was $300 at international prices, while the PPP rate was I$1,150. This meant $300 could buy goods in India which would cost $1,150 in the United States. It also meant that every US dollar could buy goods worth $3.83 in India. In other words, the dollar was almost four times stronger than the rupee, giving people in the West four times as much purchasing power in India as Indians themselves. This additional purchasing power is over and above the factor of higher incomes in the West. The multiplier between the two rates is a measure of the separation between the international traded economy and non-traded sectors, something which deserves deeper investigation (see table 8).

The gap between domestic and external currency values automatically gives Western buyers greater purchasing power in the Majority World than the people who live there. In world markets the Indian rupee is worth a quarter of what it can buy at home, so that it cannot compete equally with hard currencies, effectively undervaluing Indian purchasing power. On the other hand, the same amount of foreign currency goes four times as far in India as in the United States. This gives Indian workers a formidable competitive advantage over Western workers. As global trade

Table 8 Per capita income at relative currency values, 1990

Country	Market rate (1)	PPP rate (2)	Multiplier (2/1)
India	300	1,150	3.8
Pakistan	316	1,770	5.6
China	322	1,950	6.0
Sri Lanka	426	2,370	5.6
Egypt	637	3,100	4.9
Philippines	713	2,320	3.3
Thailand	1,437	4,610	3.2
Turkey	1,720	5,020	2.9
Brazil	2,753	4,780	1.7
Mexico	2,758	5,080	1.8
S. Korea	5,523	7,190	1.3
UK	17,006	14,960	0.9
Canada	21,515	19,650	0.9
Japan	23,829	16,950	0.7

Sources: **GDP**: IMF, *World Economic Output*, 1993, p. 117; **population**: UN, *Human Development Report*, and World Bank.

barriers come down this difference is attracting a growing amount of investment and intensifying competition with the West.

In classical theory, a free market would eliminate differences between internal and external prices of traded goods, while internal market mechanisms would bring prices of non-traded goods closer to international levels. Thus low internal prices would lead to increased purchases of Indian goods until supply and demand brought foreign exchange rates into line with domestic purchasing power. Differences between internal and external prices would then become smaller, as they are between Western economies. But Western controls over the movement of people and goods from the Majority World mean that their prices are suppressed, much as the colour bar suppressed black South Africans' income as they worked for the white economy. In both cases purchasing power is transferred from poor to rich as a result of systemic discrimination. Countries which have been able to join the Western Economic System, such as Japan during the 1960s and South Korea in the 1990s, have seen internal and external purchasing power move closer together.

The calculation of purchasing power parities is a controversial issue, with extensive debate over equilibrium exchange rates and appropriate policy responses.[42] Whatever the standpoint, it is clear

Table 9 National economic comparisons by PPPs and market exchange rates (1990 figures)

Country and rank	Market exchange rates GDP ($m.)	Country and rank	PPP (I$m.)
1 United States	5,392,000	1 United States	5,392,000
2 Japan	2,943,000	2 China	2,388,000
3 Germany	1,488,000	3 Japan	2,176,000
4 France	1,191,000	4 Germany	1,448,000
5 Italy	1,091,000	5 Russian Fed.	1,187,000
6 United Kingdom	975,000	6 France	982,000
7 Canada	570,000	7 Italy	917,000
8 Spain	491,000	8 India	914,000
9 Brazil	414,000	9 United Kingdom	907,000
10 China	365,000	10 Brazil	710,000
11 Australia	296,000	11 Canada	510,000
12 Netherlands	279,000	12 Mexico	491,000
13 India	254,000	13 Spain	457,000
14 Mexico	238,000	14 Indonesia	389,000
15 South Korea	236,000	15 South Korea	290,000

Source: World Bank.

that international market exchange rates are not a reliable indicator for most Majority World economies. Comparing countries on the basis of purchasing power parities rather than market exchange rates shows dramatic differences in relative wealth and productive capacity (see table 9). China leaps from tenth to second or third place in international league tables. In 1990 the Russian Federation rose out of the non-league rouble zone to fifth place, although it has since fallen in real terms. India nudges past the UK while Spain and Canada are pushed out of the top ten. This is equivalent to discovering that the Western economy has been on steroids for forty years. In sport, all past records would be disallowed, the cheating teams relegated and steroids banned. Instead, PPP records are relegated to footnotes and everyone is told to take Western economic medicine.

Relative shares of global production also appear less unequal when expressed in PPPs. The West's share of world production falls from two-thirds to about a half, while the Majority World's share rises from one-fifth to a third (see table 10). Average GDP per head also appears to be more equal when expressed in terms of PPP rather than market exchange rates, with a ratio of 1 : 16

Table 10 Global inequality in exchange rates and purchasing power parities (1987–9)

Area	% of world GDP		% of world population
	Exchange rate (%)	PPP-based (%)	
West	73	54	15
US	26	23	5
Japan	15	8	3
EU	25	19	6
Majority World	18	34	77
Africa	2	4	13
Asia	7	18	54

Source: Rangit Sau, *Economic and Political Weekly*, 11 Sept. 1993, New Delhi.

rather than 1 : 72. This is still grossly unequal – and much more unequal than between black and white in South Africa – but it means that global inequality may not be quite as great as it appears from exchange rate comparisons. Even in PPP terms inequality between Africa and the West is still immense.

It is essential to be wary of all numbers in economics, since even purchasing power parities are a poor representation of real differences in wealth and well-being between countries.

Economists have known about the limitations of market exchange rates and the need for better comparison since Ricardo in the nineteenth century. The UN started calculating PPPs in 1968 and the World Bank/IMF began publishing data in the 1980s. This has influenced policy decisions at many levels and could have very far-reaching implications. There are many reasons why both the West and the Majority World are reluctant to use this knowledge. For the West, this reflects deeply rooted prejudices in favour of international trade as the basis of economic development. Unequal exchange rates are extremely advantageous to the West and widespread use of PPPs would weaken its political power. Purchasing power parities could be used to recalculate quotas and voting power in the IMF/World Bank, giving the Majority World a 50 per cent stake. On the other hand, Majority World governments are concerned that PPPs could reduce their eligibility for aid and increase payments to the United Nations. These issues are only likely to be resolved as part of an equitable restructuring of global governance.

GROSSLY DECEPTIVE PRODUCT

At a more profound level, the use of the PPP draws attention to the fact that conventional economics is a poor measure of real wealth. As well as non-traded goods, it does not take account of non-monetary values, including unpaid work, mostly done by women. According to one estimate, as much as 80 per cent of world production is not monetized.[43] In addition, conventional GDP ignores or undervalues environmental assets. This means that in real terms conventional economic figures are wildly inaccurate. Developing alternative indicators for the economy is now a major task for many governments and international agencies.[44] Even the United States is working on a 'Green GDP', although it is unlikely to be adopted without an effective campaign.

Purchasing power parities reveal the real economic strength of the Majority World which is already asserting itself. While Western politicians and economists delude themselves with distorted statistics, they are already being overtaken by events in the real economy. The Majority World could speed up this process by creating its own currency based on a basket of commodities to bypass Western currencies when trading between themselves. Counter-trade, a form of international barter, has been widely used to overcome the inherent inequity of Western currencies. It has been estimated that about 15 per cent of trade in the Majority World included some element of counter-trade at some stage.[45] A well-regulated purchasing power-based currency could overcome the difficulties of counter-trade swaps and undermine Western currency privileges.

Most figures in this book are based on market exchange rates, because they express the real power of the West over the Majority World. They determine a country's credit rating, income and investment as well as voting power in the IMF/World Bank and the assumptions which inform decisions by those who run the system.

THE INTERNATIONAL DEBT TRAP

The combination of unequal trade, unequal access to finance, unequal exchange rates, soaring interest rate charges and other factors plunged many countries of the Majority World into debt during the 1970s. Like the scramble for Africa after the 1873 economic depression, the debt crisis began as a solution to the West's problem of over-production and too much money chasing too few investment opportunities following the oil price rise and recession in 1973. Majority World states were able to borrow money at low or even negative rates of interest, in real terms. This money was used to import from the West, increasing exports by about 5 per cent, equivalent to over 2 million jobs in the West.[46] The debt crisis was caused by several interrelated factors,[47] many of which were due to the systematic inequality between the West and the Majority World. Beryl Sprinkel, Under-Secretary in the US Treasury, confirmed that 'The debt crisis is, to a large extent, an indirect result of our success in curing inflation and revitalizing the American economy'.[48]

The sudden change in Western economic policy after 1979 raised interest rates dramatically, making repayments impossible for many large debtors. The crisis broke in August 1982 when Mexico declared it could no longer pay interest on its $60 billion foreign debt. One country after another followed, revealing over $250 billion-worth of debt, mostly to Western banks (74%) or to multilateral agencies like the IMF and World Bank (14%). But the debt continued to grow. By 1993 it was five times higher, at $1,300 billion. Between 1982 and 1990, the Majority World paid $1,345 billion on debt servicing, both interest and principle. This was 30 per cent *more* than the total aid, private investment, new loans and trade credits, so that a net flow of $418 billion was paid to the West, an average of $4 billion a month or $46 billion a year.[49] Over eight years this massive transfer of resources from poor to rich financed the equivalent of six Marshall Plans for the West.[50] This form of debt bondage enables the West to extract resources from the Majority World at virtually no net cost. In fact the debt crisis has also imposed costs on the West, including a fall in exports to debtor countries, higher unemployment, drug-trafficking, increased migration and political instability worldwide.

Debt is a powerful and legal way of maintaining slavery. When people are too poor to buy, they are forced to borrow. People can also be beguiled into debt by smooth-talking salesmen promising instant gratification and easy terms. They can be foolish and take on more than they can repay. In most cases, however, people get into debt beyond their means when circumstances go against them – income falls, interest rates rise, work is hard to find and goods difficult to sell. The crisis would never have happened if Western lenders had observed two elementary ethical principles of lending

– to lend only or mainly for investment which will bring about an improvement in productivity capable of paying back the loan, and to share in the risk for which the loan is ventured, for good or ill. To achieve this we need to establish a new international regime for finance and transnational corporations.

TAMING THE TITANS

There can be no real change until business takes the side of freedom.
Winnie Mandela, 1986[51]

The best global corporations provide excellent goods and services. They are well run, and are good employers who support local communities wherever they work. They actively develop sound environmental and ethical practices, including accountability to local communities. They enable the most effective, efficient and environmentally friendly technologies to be introduced quickly, sensitively and equitably. They provide excellent staff training and promote equal opportunities for people to develop themselves personally and professionally. The best companies are often more progressive than national governments, local authorities and voluntary organizations. But they are also far and few between. While good ethics can mean good business, ethical companies are constantly challenged by cost-cutting competitors. Inevitably they tend to serve high-income customers in affluent markets who can afford higher standards, leaving the poor at the mercy of unscrupulous employers and producers.

Concern about ethical, environmental and social issues needs to be underpinned by government, community, worker and shareholder action. Few governments are sufficiently powerful to control global companies on their own. Only states like Japan, Germany and California or regional authorities like China, the European Union and United States are powerful enough to enforce corporate ethics. These big markets inevitably set standards for the world. There is a danger that high standards may be used to exclude the Majority World, so that high quality and safe and attractive jobs and products are restricted to the West while unsafe, second-rate cheap goods and low-paid jobs are left for the poor worldwide. But there is nothing inevitable about this. Public pressure can make a difference.

Global corporations had a central role in creating and sustaining apartheid in South Africa. They also played a significant role in its demise. Decades of public pressure in the West forced companies to improve their business practices in South Africa or pull out. Boycotts, demands for disinvestment and codes of conduct all have a place in the campaign against global apartheid, but they need to be even more focused on specific objectives. Global corporations are extremely experienced at getting round the most sophisticated laws and regulations. They are not even defeated by nationalization. When Nicaragua nationalized its gold mines, it lacked expertise to run them effectively and employed the former owners as consultants. Similarly, oil companies quickly found other ways of making profits following nationalization of oilfields in Iran and Mexico. Taming corporate titans needs fundamental change in the rules under which they operate, amounting to a democratic transformation greater than that of the nation-state over the past 150 years.

This is not the place to provide a detailed programme, but the following seven basic principles suggest a starting-point:

- *Accountable governance*: requiring a strict legal duty of care and responsibility of investors and managers; board-level representation of all stakeholders (investors, workers, consumers, community); explicit economic, environmental and social objectives, evaluated according to universal basic standards of financial, environmental and social accounting which are monitored by independent auditors and regulatory bodies; transparency of ownership and decision-making; and public accountability for all expenditure, remuneration and actions within the company.

- *Fair competition*: abolition of tax havens and offshore privileges, strict rules to prevent cartels, monopolies, restrictive business practices, predatory pricing and subsidies, except under public supervision for specific social and environmental objectives.

- *Fair employment*: rights to agreed standards of health and safety, employment conditions, independent trade unions, and worker participation in decision-making worldwide.

- *Sustainable production*: full-cost pricing to cover social and environmental costs, future risk for product life-cycle and sustainable use of resources.

- *Corporate citizenship*: so that companies pay their fair share of taxes, support the rights of democratic governments to govern, obey the law, develop genuine accountability to local communities wherever they work and entrench public responsibilities in the company purpose.

- *Enforceability*: violations of a corporate trading framework should be equally enforceable in every country, so that the people of Bhopal are entitled to similar protection as the residents of Boston.

- *Equity*: ensuring that companies apply consistently fair practices worldwide. International law should take best corporate practice as the basis for 'common law' governing corporate conduct.

These seven principles should apply to private, publicly quoted and state corporations equally. They need to become as basic as the ballot-box and civil liberties are to political democracy. Where these principles are insufficient, as they may be for natural monopolies, public utilities and strategic sectors such as essential drugs, pensions, public transport, broadcasting or arms production, it would be desirable to have publicly owned controlling shares or to create *public interest corporations* as a new form of non-profit public ownership. As low rates of profit are likely to be the norm in mature market economies, customer service and public purpose should assume a greater role in all enterprise.

A great deal of work on regulating transnational corporations has been done by the United Nations, UNCTAD, the European Union, state governments, trade unions and voluntary organizations and this needs to be used in applying these principles. A few companies are voluntarily seeking to apply higher standards to their own business practices, but most will resist any increase in external accountability. It is therefore necessary to organize on several levels, and not rely on government action alone:

- People working for companies as employees, or those who provide professional services to companies, such as accountants, lawyers and fund managers, can shift the agenda by raising questions about accounting practices, ethics, environment, pricing policy and corporate responsibility.

- Company sensitivity about corporate image gives scope for public campaigns on specific products or practices, such as wages and conditions in the Majority World.

- Shareholder action, particularly through pension funds, local authorities, churches and other corporate investment institutions.

- At a local and national level, people need to develop a strategic view about what *they* want in terms of economic activity, which involves monitoring and debating economic activity by sector in order to create opportunities for local participation.

- Elected representatives at state and regional level (ASEAN, EU, OAU, USA) can act to replace the corporate welfare state with systems of public scrutiny, accountability and appropriate regulation.

- At a global level, there is a need for international law on incorporation, disclosure of information, regulation and liquidation.

Corporations will squeal that regulations stifle enterprise and economic development. The truth is, current corporate practice stifles enterprise and distorts economic development. These principles would offer more opportunities for enterprise, but with greater protection for those who need it. Companies are already subject to scrutiny from the City, which gives them huge incentives to disregard the needs of workers, communities and the environment.

Democratic reform of the City itself needs to follow similar principles to those for proposed transnational trading cartels, with the significant proviso that the price of money should be regulated in the interests of people instead of regulating interest at people's cost. The price of money is one of many aspects of the economy which Western governments actively manage, as I will describe in the next chapter.

Further Reading

Global corporations

Barnet, Richard J., and Cavanagh, John, *Global Dreams: Imperial Corporations and the New World Order*, Simon & Schuster, NY, 1994.
Carroll, Paul, *Big Blues, The Unmaking of IBM*, Orion/Weidenfeld, 1994.

The Global Fortune 500, *Fortune*, annual, July/August.

Innes, Duncan, *Anglo American and the Rise of Modern South Africa*, Heinemann Education, 1984.

Kallen, Laurence, *Corporate Welfare: The Mega Bankruptcies of the 80s and 90s*, Lyle Stuart, NY, 1991.

Keay, John, *The Honourable Company: A History of the English East India Company*, HarperCollins, 1991.

Korten, David C., *When Corporations Rule the World*, Earthscan, 1996.

Monks, Robert A. G., and Minow, Nell, *Power and Accountability*, HarperCollins, 1991.

Sampson, Anthony, *The Sovereign State: The Secret History of ITT*, Hodder & Stoughton, 1973.

United Nations Transnational Corporations and Management Division, *World Investment Reports*, NY, annual.

Yergin, Daniel, *The Prize: The Epic Quest for Oil, Money and Power*, Simon & Schuster, 1991.

Global finance

Anders, George, *Merchants of Debt: KKR and the Mortgaging of American Business*, Jonathan Cape, 1992.

Levine, B. D., *Inside Out*, Century, 1992.

Nelson, Benjamin, *The Idea of Usury: From Tribal Brotherhood to Universal Otherhood*, Princeton University Press, 1949.

Robert, John, *$1000 Billion a Day: Inside the Foreign Exchange Markets*, HarperCollins, 1995.

Stewart, James B., *Den of Thieves*, Simon & Schuster, 1992.

Taylor, Russell, *Going for Broke: How Banking Mismanagement in the Eighties Lost £ Thousands of Billions*, Simon & Schuster.

5

Managed Markets of Global Apartheid

The capitalist system which is based on self-interest and the right of the strongest is in any case doomed.

D. F. Malan, Oct. 1934
South African National Party leader; prime minister, 1951–4

Laissez-faire is as dead as the slave trade.

Stanley Baldwin
British Conservative prime minister, 1923–4, 1924–9, 1935–7

The IMF and World Bank were the hub of the postwar settlement, launched at Bretton Woods in 1944 as a New Deal for the world. US Treasury Secretary Henry Morgenthau recalled how the 'bewilderment and bitterness' of the Depression had bred Fascism and war. These new institutions would create 'a dynamic world economy in which the peoples of every nation will be able to realize their potentialities in peace ... and enjoy, increasingly, the fruits of material progress on an earth infinitely blessed with natural riches'.[1] Since then we have learnt that natural riches are not infinite and that these two institutions served the West better than they did the majority of the world's people.

The political, cultural and institutional roots of the IMF and World Bank are in the national treasuries and central banking system of the West. This invisible *éminence grise* protects Western economic superiority with hard currency pass laws, fiscal discipline and supranational oversight of the financial system.

CENTRAL BANKERS INTERNATIONAL

Central banks are the guardians of national currencies and financial stability. They seek to protect national economies from both violent fluctuations of international currency markets and from what they regard as profligate government spending. They have been described as 'a sort of world House of Lords, an international screen for the monetary excesses of heady democracy',[2] to which most governments ultimately defer. The reason is simple: the financial community exerts more power over domestic economic decision-making than do elected governments. International financial credibility depends on the standing and decisions of central banks, so governments learn to listen to central bankers. Even Western governments, like Britain in 1976 or France in 1983, are brought to heel if they stray from central banking orthodoxy. Only the United States is big enough to flout the faith and change the rules, as it did under Nixon in 1971, Reagan during the 1980s and under Clinton in the 1990s.

Relationships between central banks and governments are subtle and deeply rooted in the institutional experience of each country. Most central banks are responsible for issuing currency, controlling the money supply and interest rates, managing foreign exchange, holding national reserves, regulating the banking system, for government borrowing, and for sharing overall economic management with the government. In practice, central banks have a high degree of independence from political oversight while maintaining close working relationships with national treasuries and the financial sector.

Western central bankers share a common purpose in maintaining their currencies as a flexible and reliable medium of international exchange through turbulent currents of speculation and trade. Behind the scenes, this international brotherhood strives to manage international money markets through the Bank for International Settlements (BIS). Founded in Basle in 1931, this was created by European central bankers, not governments, to take finance out of politics. It still performs a crucial role in maintaining financial stability, counteracting currency speculation, providing emergency loans to central banks, coordinating the actions and policies of central banks, clearing international payments, acting as a watchdog over international banking and maintaining bankers' collective solidarity in defence of 'sound money'. Although some of its functions have been superseded or supplemented by the IMF and the European Exchange Rate Mechanism, the BIS remains a substantial player in the global financial system, beyond public scrutiny or political supervision.

Central bank intervention in currency markets developed because international capital flows and trade do not automatically balance. At any particular moment the value of exports does not match that of imports, while capital flows can disrupt finance for trade. Since demand for foreign currency fluctuates widely, foreign exchange rates rise and fall. These fluctuations are amplified by speculators, who can make very large profits (and losses) by gambling on currency movements. Sharp swings in currency values are devastating for industry, since it is impossible to invest or plan ahead without knowing how much goods will fetch. A rise in exchange rates makes it harder to sell goods in foreign markets, leading to loss of income, while a fall raises costs of imported materials. Firms hit by exchange rate fluctuations may respond by cutting costs or laying off workers, which deflates the economy.

Central banks act as a buffer between domestic and foreign trade by working closely together to even out everyday fluctuations in exchange rates. As a rule, they do not compete against each other and, with rare exceptions, such as the Nixon devaluation of 1971, cooperate to keep exchange rates within a predictable range. Since 1971 Western currencies have been more volatile, but they have remained fully convertible into other currencies and relatively 'hard' compared with Majority World money. Central banks buy currency by the billion on behalf of governments to support their own and other Western exchange rates. These transactions cancel out over time when exchange rates are stable, but occasionally speculative runs on a currency force governments to devalue, causing real financial losses. In September 1992 Britain spent several billion dollars in just one day before being forced to devalue. US intervention to support the Mexican peso after its dramatic devaluation in December 1994 was a rare example of support for the Majority World, demonstrating the partial political integration that followed economic integration under NAFTA. When underlying economic trends require a major realignment of Western currencies, these are usually agreed at a political level and managed by central banks. The European exchange rate mechanism (ERM) is a more formal and tightly controlled version of this system.

Thus Western central banks run the oldest and most effective commodity stabilization fund in the world, and one of the most systematic, sophisticated forms of government intervention in the market. This is tacit recognition that money is not a commodity, but a powerful social and economic tool which must be kept under control and in good repair.

The effectiveness of Western central banking depends crucially on cooperation and trust between Western governments. As the pre-eminent economic power after the war, the United States held the ring. The US Treasury acted as a world central bank and the dollar was used as an international reserve currency. Most countries still hold dollar balances for transaction purposes, although the Deutschmark and ECU are replacing it in Europe while the yen has grown in importance in Asia. Thus the dollar accounted for 80 per cent of foreign exchange held by central banks in 1976, but less than 60 per cent in 1991, with almost 20 per cent being held in DM. These vast overseas dollar balances amount to an interest-free loan to the US, which it used to acquire goods, services and assets from other countries. In theory, they represent a claim on US goods and services, but so long as they circulate elsewhere this 'loan' is evaporating. The US also has a very large international debt, on which it pays interest, and a persistent balance of payments deficit. Gradual devaluation of the dollar means that the US is effectively writing off its debts. Thus the US government uses its privileged position as a global central bank and reserve currency manager to avoid the balance of payments constraints and financial disciplines which restrict all other governments. This has enabled the US to maintain a huge military presence worldwide, to wage a long, expensive and illegal war against Vietnam and Cambodia, run several other covert wars and consume a disproportionate share of global resources. US profligacy facilitated global economic growth by increasing the amount of money in circulation, but it also contributed to world-wide inflation. US fiscal delinquency represents a massive betrayal of financial trust that is tolerated by other Western governments because they all share some benefits.

Stable exchange rates contributed to high economic growth in the West between 1950 and 1973, when average GNP grew by almost 5 per cent a year. Since 1971, when Nixon unilaterally broke the system of managed exchange rates, Western currencies have fluctuated more widely. This has made central bank cooperation more difficult and forced governments to rely more heavily on interest rates to control inflation. The resulting instability in currency and interest rates has contributed to slower Western economic growth since 1973 by making borrowing more expensive and long-term planning more difficult. Yet, despite the ending of fixed exchange rates, the debt crisis, persistent trade imbalances, great tides of currency speculation, excess liquidity, uncontrolled credit and the speculative dance of derivatives, central bankers maintained relative stability in the Western financial system. The cost of financial stability has been rising unemployment world-wide, penal debt repayments for the Majority World and grossly uneven economic development. Central banks have also secured the financial frontier between the West and the Majority World.

FINANCIAL GROUP AREAS

National currencies are the first line of defence of national economic sovereignty. By controlling convertibility between currencies, countries influence internal patterns of consumption and distribution independently of prices in other countries, provided the flow of goods can also be controlled. For example, if food produced by domestic farmers costs more than food from abroad, imports are likely to rise and farmers will be forced to cut costs or go bust. National currencies create a financial frontier, so that lowering the exchange rate makes foreign food more expensive, protecting domestic farmers and making export easier. On the other hand, prices for people who depend on imports will go up, so that the net benefit of high or low exchange rates varies for different groups. Import controls and subsidies are alternative mechanisms for protecting particular industries.

A strong currency enables a country to buy goods and borrow money more cheaply from other countries. Currencies stay strong so long as there are no other sources for their goods and people from other countries continue to buy. Western countries have a vested interest in maintaining strong or 'hard' currencies in relation to the Majority World to suppress the cost of raw materials while commanding higher prices for their own goods. Countries with hard currencies can also borrow money more cheaply, since it is more likely to keep its value. The effect is to draw a red line round countries with low credit ratings.

Countries like India, Brazil or Kenya may get short-term loans for trade deals, at a higher rate of interest than Western countries, or advice for a fee, but they find it more difficult to get long-term loans. Bankers' risk ratings in the *Institutional Investor* or *Euromoney*[3] read like the hierarchical classification of different groups for separate development. The top twenty-four countries are all OECD members apart from Singapore, Taiwan and Hong Kong. Asian-Pacific countries like South Korea have been able to defy the West's economic policy prescriptions by maintaining relatively high rates of domestic savings and subsidizing interest rates for selected export industries.

Because most Majority World countries compete against each other in crowded markets, it is almost impossible for them to protect commodity prices, which are therefore forced down, causing balance of payments difficulties. The combination of hard currencies and selective protectionism in the West means that many Majority World currencies are forced to devalue to stay competitive. Devaluation is equivalent to cutting wages and profits across the board, making their goods even cheaper for the West. Differences between 'hard' and 'soft' currencies reflect systematic inequality in the global economy. So long as they exist, there will always be currency flight and balance of payments crisis in the Majority World.

Hard currencies are almost equivalent to the gold standard which pushed the global economy into depression between world wars, except that now it applies mainly to the Majority World. In the nineteenth century, Western governments sent gunboats to small countries who defaulted on their debts as a result of balance of payments difficulties. Since 1945 the IMF has performed this task, as the fiscal police of the Western Economic System.

THE INTERNATIONAL MINISTRY OF FINANCE

The IMF performs certain functions of a global central bank and ministry of finance over the Majority World, under Western direction. The original aims of the International Monetary Fund were 'to facilitate the expansion and balanced growth of international trade, and to contribute thereby to the promotion and maintenance of high levels of employment and real income and the development of the productive resources of all members as primary objectives of economic policy'. This meant securing exchange stability between currencies, providing sufficient liquidity for world trade to expand without creating inflation, and making financial assistance available to countries with balance of payments difficulties to avoid protectionism. These aims reflected Western determination to prevent an economic depression like that of the 1930s. Although British India and Latin America were represented in planning its role, the IMF's fundamental principles were drawn up by the US Treasury, with some British influence. Majority World needs for stable commodity prices and investment finance were secondary to Western desires for stable currencies and low commodity prices. In practice, the IMF's main function is to enable member states to deal with balance of payments difficulties through short-term loans. Since 1976 it has only had a minor role within the West, although it played a major part in protecting the Western banking system from collapse at the start of the debt crisis.

The IMF is tiny compared with the colossal sums surging daily through the international currency markets, and much smaller than the combined weight of Western central banks. With less than $32 billion-worth of outstanding loans, it is much smaller than the World Bank, which has a portfolio worth $140 billion. Net IMF lending peaked at $11 billion in 1983 to meet the debt crisis. Since then the Majority World has repaid more every year than it has borrowed.

For Majority World countries with relatively low currency reserves and fluctuating income from exports, balance of payments difficulties are endemic and the IMF offers a financial lifeline. Since 1973, the Majority World as a whole, excluding oil producers, has had a persistent current account deficit.[4] The poorest countries had the worst position, many relying on international aid to bridge the gap, while the four 'Asian tigers' ran a surplus until 1991, then dipped slightly into deficit. For a great many countries, as we have seen, the international trading regime simply made it impossible to maintain a balance between imports and exports. Lending to these countries is like giving a blood transfusion to someone bleeding to death. In many cases, this means real deaths, as poverty forces families to go hungry and governments to cut spending on public services for the poorest. Although most trade is conducted privately through international markets, these harsh 'disciplines of the market' are enforced by the IMF as a public sector institution through political measures called structural adjustment programmes (SAPs). During the 1980s the IMF provided standby credits to over forty Majority World countries and structural adjustment programmes in eighteen.

The aim of structural adjustment is to make societies competitive in the global economy. The West's exclusive advantages mean that most Majority World countries are forced into fierce competition against each other for investment and markets. As argued in chapter 3, they are inhibited from turning raw materials into higher-value goods, so their only option is to cut costs. South-East Asian economies broke this pattern by defying policy prescriptions of the IMF/World Bank and pursing distinctive economic policies. Most other Majority World countries did not have the internal resources, opportunities, strong state intervention nor, frankly, the policies capable of overcoming the structural trade discrimination which causes balance of payments difficulties. Structural adjustment involves the IMF directly in countries' internal affairs. Its prescriptions 'to bolster economic growth and price stability in the developing countries' include 'reducing budget deficits by curbing public sector wages and employment, reducing subsidies' and reforms 'to help encourage private investment'. 'These countries had to create an environment conducive to capital formation and foreign direct investment.'[5] The IMF emphasizes 'growth orientated adjustment strategies' for developing countries. It is open about overriding sovereignty in the Majority World: 'To help us face the challenges of an ever more integrated global economy, the Fund's effective *surveillance* over members' exchange rate and macroeconomic policies becomes even more important' (emphasis in the original).[6]

The effect of structural adjustment is often devastating. Traditional producers are forced to compete against the industrialized mass production and agro-industries of the West, some of which are subsidized and protected by state aid (see pp. 80–1). The UN Commission on Africa reported that spending on health in IMF countries fell by half and spending on education fell by a quarter during the 1980s. Real wages in Africa and Latin America fell by over 25 per cent in the same period. Yet an internal study by the IMF in 1988 showed that most of its programmes failed to achieve their aims of increasing economic growth, cutting balance of payments deficits, lowering inflation or decreasing external debt. Assessment of the IMF's impact varies widely according to initial assumptions and criteria, but most recognize that the poorest have suffered significantly as a consequence of its intervention.[7] The appointment of Michel Camdessus as managing director in 1987 led to a shift of emphasis and greater recognition of the need to protect the poorest and increase the resources available to the Majority World, but this has been resisted by the IMF's Western shareholders.

The causes of trade imbalances which lead to IMF involvement in the Majority World and the impoverishment produced by its policies lie in the Western Economic System rather than the IMF. In dealing with international debt and structural trade imbalances, the IMF took on a role for which it was not designed. It filled an institutional vacuum, tackling problems for which its major shareholders, the West's political leaders, were largely responsible and utterly unwilling to confront.

The West imposed one-sided structural adjustment to force the Majority World countries to adjust their economies to meet the needs of Western markets. The IMF made no attempt to make Western countries address these issues and restructure their economies to make international trade fairer. Instead, it effectively bailed out the Western banking system at the expense of the

Table 11 Relative voting-power of G5 countries at the IMF/World Bank compared to percentage of world population

	IMF 1993 (% of vote)	IDA 1992 (% of vote)	IBRD (% of vote)	World population (%)
USA	17.86	17.59	16.71	4.7
Japan	5.56	8.01	9.82	2.34
Germany	5.56	6.19	6.91	1.47
UK	5.00	5.93	5.54	1.08
France	5.00	5.93	3.95	1.06
G5 total	38.98	43.65	42.93	10.65

Majority World and, to a lesser extent, Western taxpayers. For structural adjustment to work it must include stabilization of commodity prices and reduction of trade barriers by the West so that the Majority World countries can increase earnings from exports, as well as increasing aid and social protection on an equitable basis. This is unlikely so long as the Majority World has so little influence over IMF decision-making.

Decision-making

In 1993 the IMF had a membership of 175 countries, each with a seat on the Board of Governors, which meets twice a year. Executive power is vested in a committee of twenty-four Directors who meet at least three times a week. The Executive includes seven permanent members, the five Western powers plus Saudi Arabia and, since 1980, the People's Republic of China, plus fifteen members elected by region. Voting is proportional to the number of shares held by member states. The joint votes of the US and two other permanent members are enough to block financial assistance. Although the proportion of votes held by the G7 countries has fallen from 51 to 43 per cent, regional representation gives the West 66 per cent of the votes. When the West's share of the vote fell it changed the IMF's Articles to raise the majority required for crucial votes to 85 per cent. Yet decisions by the IMF have a much greater impact on people in the Majority World than on those in the West. Table 11 shows countries' percentage of votes in the IMF and in two branches of the World Bank, the IDA and the IBRD, compared with the percentage of the world population living in those countries. In theory, the Majority World could veto any issue if its representatives voted together. In practice, voting is rare and most decisions are taken by consensus. Western powers work together, meeting frequently to coordinate strategy and tactics. Western officials meet monthly at the Bank of International Settlements and regularly at the Paris Club (a gathering of creditor nations to discuss debt rescheduling), the Group of Ten most powerful countries, the Group of Five permanent members of the IMF board, and annual G7 summits. Majority World countries meet as the Group of 24 and Group of 77, but their diverse interests make a coordinated strategy difficult. Divisions between Western powers since 1994 have increased opportunities for Majority World representatives to influence decisions. As Western unity unravels, the balance of power shifts.

It is not surprising that the entire framework and context of the IMF's economic analysis is based on a Western viewpoint. Its 1993 *World Economic Outlook* starts: 'The recovery of global economic activity ... remains hesitant and uneven', despite the fact that in cash terms the Majority World countries grew by 6 per cent and China burgeoned by over 10 per cent. What mattered to the IMF was that the West only grew by 1.5 per cent. In cash terms, of course, 6 per cent growth in the Majority World was just 0.3 per cent of world growth. The cash value of 1.5 per cent growth in the West was five times greater than the 6 per cent growth enjoyed by the rest of the world. Average GNP per head in the West grew four times more than in the rest of the world – by about $200 compared with $50 – and so inequality continued to increase. The following year, average GNP per head in the West grew by about $900, compared with $350 among upper-middle-income countries and a *fall* of $10 a head for the world's 3 billion poorest people. The average increase across the Majority World was $50 per person.

Publications such as the IMF's *Annual Report* and *World Economic Outlook* reflect the hierarchy of global apartheid. They always begin with the concerns of 'industrial countries', then 'developing countries' and finally 'formerly centrally planned economies'. 'Industrial' and 'developing' countries are given roughly equal space, although the population of the latter is more than five times greater than that of the former. 'Industrial' and 'developing' are euphemisms, since some 'developing countries' are industrially bigger than several 'industrial countries'.

This subtle institutional racism is more explicit inside the IMF.

The managing director is traditionally a West European and the deputy a US citizen, but its 2,000 staff are recruited from 100 countries. According to one insider, the respected economist Davison Budhoo who worked for the World Bank and IMF for twenty-two years, 'racism makes itself felt in a wide range of organizational practices ... Among these is the classification of South Africa [in 1990] as a "European country" administered by our highly segregated, virtually "white staff only can work here" European Department.'[8] Moreover, 'certain Departments of the Fund are virtually segregated along racial lines, and "internal" race relations are deteriorating further.'[9] Since this attack the IMF has attempted to improve internal relations.

Budhoo also points out that officials who determine the fate of the world's poorest people earn 'more than the basic pay of every head of state in the world ... and about one thousand times more than the per capita income enjoyed by two thirds of mankind'.[10] His own salary and benefits package in 1988 was $143,000, tax free, augmented by generous subsistence allowances, medical insurance, a handsome pension, first-class travel, VIP treatment and diplomatic immunity. Budhoo accuses IMF officials of being the high priests and new nobility 'of Greed and Personal Ambition and Maintenance of the Status Quo'.[11]

Political conditionality

The IMF's monetary discipline is largely impervious to political or social consequences for the poor of the Majority World. In country after country, its officials have imposed financial conditions which forced down wages, cut public spending and increased unemployment in order to stimulate export-led growth. Arthur Schlesinger, historian and special assistant to President Kennedy, has observed that:

> If the criteria of the International Monetary Fund had governed the United States in the nineteenth century, our own economic development would have taken a good deal longer. In preaching fiscal orthodoxy to developing nations, we were somewhat in the position of the prostitute who, having retired on her earnings, believes that public virtue requires the closing down of the red light district.[12]

Its decisions have a powerful impact on the politics of every country in which it intervenes. In 1964 it imposed policies on the

Dominican Republic which rapidly reduced workers' living standards and put thousands out of work, leading to riots in which fifty people died, and to US military intervention the following year. When the fall of cocoa prices plunged Ghana into crisis in 1972, IMF borrowing conditions were so harsh that they prompted a military coup, ending Africa's first post-colonial democracy. In Jamaica, IMF policies after 1977 contributed to rising poverty, strikes and violent crime. After seven years of IMF-imposed free markets, unemployment was still 23 per cent, economic output was the same as in 1978, income per head had fallen by more than 10 per cent, foreign debt had grown, and over 40 per cent of exports were going on debt servicing. Transnational corporations benefited from lower costs and banks benefited from more reliable debt repayments, but most people became poorer.

When Brazil was forced to seek help in 1983, IMF officials demanded wage cuts of 20 per cent in real terms, price rises of 45–100 per cent for staple goods such as wheat and energy, and public spending cuts, as well as legislation to remove export duties, import controls and restrictions on profit transfers by transnational corporations. Strikes, riots and lootings of supermarkets were violently suppressed by the government. The governor of Brazil's central bank resigned and the Catholic church joined the crescendo of criticism against the IMF's austerity policies. But most of the IMF's measures were carried out and Brazil received a loan of $1.2 billion which enabled it to borrow another $11 billion from other sources, covering its balance of payments deficit and debt repayments. The IMF's deflationary policies cut imports by almost 30 per cent and industrial production slumped by 10 per cent, as bankruptcies and unemployment soared. Wages fell by half in real terms. But exports swung from deficit to a surplus of $13 billion. Big industrialists, merchants, contractors and big landlords gained. The poor and the environment were the main losers.

Political allegiance is a factor in IMF decisions, although it claims that loans are granted solely on technical criteria. In Chile, the elected Marxist President Allende was refused standby credit after the country had been thrown into turmoil by an economic destabilization strategy supported by the US. After Allende was overthrown and killed by a military coup in 1973, the IMF speedily assisted the dictator General Pinochet. The IMF's adviser, Carlos Sansom, welcomed the 'change from the chaotic conditions prevailing during the last part of the Allende government'[13] as the dictatorship slashed wages, cut public spending, removed import duties and devalued to win the IMF's coveted approval. Western banks and transnationals rushed in and the economy boomed, for some. While the richest 20 per cent increased their share of consumption from 34 per cent in 1972 to 51 per cent in 1978, the share of the poorest tumbled from 42 to 28 per cent. In spring 1979 almost the reverse scenario took place in Nicaragua. As the country was shaken by civil war and the Somoza dictatorship teetered, the IMF granted a loan of $60 million. Nine weeks later Somoza was overthrown in a genuinely popular uprising. The victorious Sandinistas undertook to repay the loan, but were unable to draw on IMF standby facilities.[14]

When South Africa suffered an economic crisis as a result of excessive military spending in 1976, it was granted a loan of $93 million to give the authorities 'some feeling of international support, which they deserve', in the words of British representative Peter Bull.[15] Five months after the Soweto uprisings, in which 1,000 young people were killed by the authorities, the IMF approved another loan of $186 million to compensate for falling gold prices. In two years, the apartheid regime received more from the IMF than any other country except Britain and Mexico, and more than the rest of Africa put together. The loans corresponded exactly to South Africa's increase in arms spending during the same period.[16] In November 1982 the IMF granted another loan of $1.1 billion, despite a UN vote of 121 to 3, with three abstentions, against IMF aid for apartheid.

Criticisms of the IMF have had some effect. It has acknowledged that its measures have sometimes been mistaken and have hurt the poor. In 1988 the managing director, Michel Camdessus, vowed that adjustment needs to 'give proper weight to social realities – especially the implications for the poorest'.[17] But still it draws up austerity measures and policy prescriptions in secret, running plans for the world's poor through computer models in Washington and delivering them first-class for Majority World governments to enforce.

Not all the IMF's prescriptions are wrong. Global financial stability is desirable and requires international cooperation. IMF criticism of excessive arms spending, subsidies for energy and grandiose plans are sometimes pertinent. Occasionally tough financial conditions may even be necessary. It may often be desirable to attach specific social, human rights or environmental conditions to loans. But these should follow the due processes of law within a democratic framework, not backroom pressure by the United States. Minority rule and the secretive, unaccountable and one-sided political nature of the IMF make it a pillar of global apartheid.

THE WORLD BANK: GLOBAL MINISTRY OF DEVELOPMENT

Where people are desperate, you have revolutions. It's in our own evident self interest to see that they are not forced into that.

Tom Clausen, 1980
President, World Bank, 1981–91[18]

While the IMF acts as a central bank over much of the Majority World, the World Bank is more like its Ministry of Development. It was set up to expand the global economy and 'promote the long-range balance growth of international trade' by encouraging investment and 'raising productivity, the standard of living and conditions of labor' (Article I). It grew and diversified in response to Western political needs as well as to the perceived needs of the Majority World. Like the IMF, it filled a void in global governance and took on many necessary tasks. The central questions concern its political direction, effectiveness and accountability.

The World Bank is the world's largest international state agency, with the possible exception of NATO. It costs almost $1 billion a year to run, dwarfing most Majority World governments in size, resources and expertise. It is the main multilateral public body for redistributing resources between countries, mainly in the form of subsidized loans. It lends $16 to $19 billion a year to over 100 countries, and receives similar amounts back in loan repayments. Net disbursements were $6.3 billion in 1992. This compares with about $45 billion total official aid and private direct investment of $53 billion (rising to $72 billion in 1993 and $80 billion in 1994). In 1992 the World Bank's total portfolio was $140 billion, compared with outstanding IMF loans of less than $32 billion and private foreign investment stock in the Majority World of over $338 billion. But World Bank approval often provides decisive 'leverage' for private funding, so that its loans attract almost three times more from other sources in matching funds. It is often more influential than elected politicians or officials of client states who are in a weak position to argue against its recommendations and money. This gives rise to 'pork barrel politics' in which the ability to wheedle World Bank loans creates political leverage that may not be in the best interest of local people.

The largest of its seven divisions is the International Bank for Reconstruction and Development (IBRD), set up to fund European reconstruction after the war. When Marshall Aid took over this task, the World Bank switched to financing roads, dams, power stations and ports in countries like Chile, India and Peru. Until the 1980s all loans were for specific projects which had to show a financial rate of return. The World Bank itself raises funds in world markets and mainly lends at commercial rates. As a state agency backed by Western governments, the bank is able to get lower interest rates than poor countries themselves. Over $235 billion has been loaned or committed to more than 3,500 projects by the IBRD since it began. The largest borrowers are, in descending order, Mexico, India, Brazil, Indonesia, Turkey, China, the Philippines, Argentina, Korea, Colombia, Morocco and Nigeria.

Since 1960 the bank has also allocated almost $78 billion in Western aid to the world's poorest countries in the form of 'soft' loans through the International Development Association (IDA). Repayments are spread over twenty-five to fifty years, with a service charge of less than 1 per cent a year. Currently countries with an average annual income (GNP) of less than $850 per head a year qualify, representing almost a third of the world's population.

Over a third of the bank's annual lending since the 1980s has been for structural adjustment loans aimed at integrating countries into the global economy. These loans were not tied to specific projects but linked to IMF prescriptions to remove government controls on agricultural prices, exchange rates and imports. They were regarded as 'absolutely fundamental to the Bank's assistance strategy' by President Conable.[19]

Like the IMF, the World Bank has come under sustained criticism for the damaging effect of its policies in the Majority World. Charities like Christian Aid and Oxfam have mounted major campaigns to make the bank more accountable and responsive to the poor. The bank has changed in response to pressures, but as a Western-run institution it cannot escape the dilemma of serving fundamentally conflicting interests. This is explicit in the bank's description of its twofold strategy for the 1990s. The first part encourages broadly based economic growth through productive use of the poor's most abundant asset – their labour. The second part requires investment in social services – especially basic education and health, family planning, and nutrition – to improve living conditions and increase the capacity of the poor to respond to income-earning opportunities arising from economic growth. The Bank recognizes that this strategy is 'more likely to be adopted in countries where the poor have a say in political and economic decision-making'.[20] If the poor majority had the final say over World Bank decisions it is questionable whether they would accept the assumption that poverty is best overcome by treating them as an abundant source of labour, since its abundance makes it cheap. The Japanese rejected similar advice after the Second World War and chose to invest in education, research and advanced technology rather than become cheap labour for Western companies.

The World Bank's place in global decision-making inevitably makes democracy difficult. Its primary clients are national governments, who often do not represent the poorest, even in the Majority World, while its structure and culture are biased towards large capital intensive projects like roads and dams, which show a financial return. Its economic assumptions emphasize export-led growth, which mainly means serving Western consumers.

More recently, the bank has developed a major role in directing, funding and advising on environmental policy in the Majority World, strengthening its role as the pre-eminent international public sector agency. Mainstream lending for environmental projects increased thirtyfold between 1989 and 1993, when a record $2 billion was allocated to twenty-three projects. In 1992 the bank was given joint responsibility with UNEP for the Global Environmental Facility (GEF) to support projects under Agenda 21 and other environmental agreements.

In many ways the World Bank is very similar to the South African Development Bank and associated agencies through which the apartheid state tried to relieve black discontent by improving economic and social conditions. The language, structure and processes of both sets of institutions are virtually interchangeable. South Africa launched a development strategy in 1981 to 'promote a more even spatial distribution of economic activity ... as well as a more equitable distribution of income by providing jobs where they are needed most.'[21] In the 1980s it embarked on 'new strategies to accelerate economic development in the Black territories to complement their consolidation and ensure their population a share in the prosperity of South Africa as a whole'. South Africa also stressed the importance of 'close consultation with the peoples concerned' and put the emphasis on 'projects that will provide jobs and raise income, increase production, expand markets, and provide basic essential services such as drinking water, schools and health services.'[22] In post-apartheid South Africa these same institutions continue under the auspices of the World Bank.

Emergence of the money mandarins

Following the Second World War the United States provided aid for European reconstruction and the 'developing world' as part of its cold war policy of containment – preventing Communism by stimulating private enterprise, improving economic conditions and strengthening democratic institutions. US Secretary of Defence Robert McNamara stated in 1964 that 'the foreign aid programme is the best weapon we have to insure that our own men in uniform need not go into combat.'[23] McNamara had been chief executive of the Ford Motor Company and directed the Vietnam war for President Kennedy before being appointed president of the World Bank in 1968. He told the world's finance ministers in 1973 'that the rich and the powerful have a moral obligation to assist the poor and the weak. That is what the sense of community is all about – any community: the community of the family, the community of the village, the community of the nation, the community of nations itself.'[24]

But it was – and still is – a community without a parliament serviced by self-appointing officials answerable only to leaders of the world's richest states. Like the more progressive officials of apartheid who aimed to 'uplift the blacks' under European leadership, McNamara saw the bank's role in terms of moral obligation and enlightened self-interest rather than democracy or justice. Under its Articles of Agreement, all staff 'owe their duty entirely to the Bank and to no other authority'. Loans were to be made on the basis of impartial 'economic considerations' and, in Keynes's words at the inaugural conference, 'absolutely objective and ecumenical, without prejudice or favour'.[25] This Olympian concept of an institution above politics, guided solely by its own internal policies, means that the World Bank is virtually a law unto itself. Public accountability is inhibited by a strict confidentiality code that withholds most project documents and background studies, although it is becoming more open.

The bank's presence in Washington, a short distance from the White House, the West's majority shareholding and the prevalence of Western staff, particularly at senior levels, means that it is deeply rooted in a particular kind of Western institutional culture.

More than half (58%) of higher-level staff were from the West in 1991 and 42 per cent from the Majority World,[26] although its work is almost entirely in the Majority World. Half the executive directors received all or part of their higher education in the United States. Most are economists and financial specialists, although the bank is actively involved in almost every area of policy from agriculture to social services.

The bank's expertise on the economic conditions, politics, people and environment of the Majority World is perhaps even more important than its money. It employs anthropologists, agronomists, ecologists, educationalists and other specialists, under the direction of financial experts. Its analysis is highly influential among government departments and development agencies throughout the world. It has a reputation for arrogance, knowing better than local people what is good for them, so that arguments which go against World Bank orthodoxy have a great deal of difficulty in getting accepted.

Like the IMF, the World Bank has been criticized for excessive running costs and incompetence. Michael Irwin, director of health services and an acting vice-president, resigned in 1990 out of frustration with 'the Bank's bloated, over-paid bureaucracy, its wasteful practices and its generally poor management'. Despite spending $150 million on reorganization in 1987, William Cosgrove, vice-president for personnel, admitted in 1989 that it 'only needs half the staff for the present workload'. Poor management means low morale, compensated for by tax-free salaries of $80,000 to $150,000, extensive perks, first-class travel and generous pensions for several hundred top staff.[27]

Rich rewards at the top contrast with the minimum wages of $6,000 a year paid to 250 cleaners employed by private contractors.[28]

Independent evaluations show that the record of World Bank lending is often poor. The bank itself has admitted mistakes. A vice-president confessed in 1988 that projects designed to reach the poorest 'were too poorly designed, and bound to be, because we are too remote, we cannot hope to understand the detail. Where we failed, it was often because we ignored the local frameworks.'[29] The bank's own Operations Evaluation Department has found that half its rural development programmes in sub-Saharan Africa had failed. Almost 40 per cent of all projects completed in 1991 were unsatisfactory and a similar proportion of current projects had 'major problems'. In 1987 its then president, Barber Conable, admitted that the bank was 'part of the problem'

of world development.[30] In December 1992 the bank published
the Wapenhans Report, a highly critical internal assessment of
project appraisal and implementation which identified deeply
rooted deficiencies and recommended many improvements.

One major failure acknowledged by President Conable in 1992
was a $300 million highway project in the Brazilian Amazon that
'had gone horribly wrong'. An invasion of loggers, gold hunters,
cattle ranchers and land speculators decimated indigenous peoples,
robbed timber from Indian reserves and wrought widespread
environmental destruction. A $167 million project aimed at repair-
ing the damage only perpetuated the problem.[31] Bank officials
were warned that the project would be a disaster for local people
and the environment as early as 1980. Its own appraisal acknowledged that 'this program will entail a higher-than-normal degree
of risks', including '(i) continued conflicts over land-related issues,
including some invasion of Indian lands; (ii) some indiscriminate
deforestation and unsound farming practices; and (iii) instances of
general lawlessness'.[32] A detailed first-hand report from an independent consultant predicted that corruption, racism and incompetence meant that the project was 'likely to prove counter-
productive',[33] and recommended smaller, more appropriate measures. The report was suppressed and its conclusions ignored. The
World Bank was determined to fund the project in order to enable
Brazil to increase exports and improve its balance of payments
position. But at 11.6 per cent interest, the loans added to Brazil's
debt burden.

The bank's policies can also cause massive relocations of people
in the Majority World. Internal reports estimated that 2 million
people would be displaced by projects in 1993 and another 600,000
would be moved in 1994. Most of these were poor landless
labourers or cultivators with customary tenure and little legal
protection or compensation.[34] In South Africa, the government
cleared black people out of white-designated areas to support
separate development. In the Majority World, the World Bank
relocates people in the interests of development driven by Western
economic priorities.

Politics of the World Bank

Like the IMF, ultimate authority in the World Bank is vested in a
governing board of the 176 finance ministers of its member states.

Real power is delegated to the president, traditionally a US citizen, and twenty-four executive directors who have similar unequal voting rights to those in the IMF. The West has five permanent seats on the board and the remaining nineteen board members are elected by groups of states on the basis of shareholding. Thirteen of the twenty-four directors are from the West, wielding almost 70 per cent of the total vote. The US share alone is enough for it to block decisions it does not like. The two African executive directors, representing forty countries and over 12 per cent of the world's population, have under 4 per cent of the vote.

This unequal voting power is based on the West's share of the bank's capital, although only 6 per cent is actually paid up. The rest is 'callable capital' which underwrites borrowing on the open market. More than three-quarters of World Bank loans to the Majority World are charged at commercial rates and earn a profit. There is therefore no justification for unequal decision-making over how these loans are allocated. Only a relatively small proportion of total loans is given as aid, namely the low interest rate charged on loans to the world's poorest countries.

Western governments have used their power in the World Bank to veto projects in countries they do not like. When Egypt tilted towards Moscow in 1955, the World Bank was forced to withdraw a $200 million loan for the Aswan Dam, an action which contributed to Egypt's nationalization of the Suez Canal and to the subsequent conflict with Britain, France and Israel.[35] The bank refused loans to Brazil's elected government in the early 1960s, then provided loans of almost half a billion dollars to the military regime after a coup in 1964. McNamara was more adept at resisting political pressure, refusing to withdraw from India when Kissinger favoured Pakistan,[36] but followed Western priorities in almost every other area. Indonesia under the socialist-inclined Sukarno was never granted any loans. After General Suharto seized power in a murderous coup of 1965, during which opponents claim that more than half a million people were massacred, Indonesia became a priority for the World Bank and loans amounted to over $600 million a year by the end of the 1970s. A report to the US Congress noted that 'fifteen of the world's most repressive governments will receive $2.9 billion in World Bank loans' in 1979.[37] Ronald Reagan also blocked loans to Nicaragua in order to undermine the Sandinista government.

The World Bank itself has also been more overtly political than the IMF. In 1968 its then new president, George Woods, commissioned Lester Pearson, former premier of Canada, and seven other men to reflect on the previous twenty years of aid and 'propose policies which will work better in future'. Their report, *Partners in Development*, drew attention to the widening gap between the Majority World and the West and called for an increase in Western aid to 0.7 per cent of GNP by 1975. The report was welcomed by many Majority World governments, but disregarded by most Western governments. In 1977, Robert McNamara again tried to influence the global agenda, persuading former West German Chancellor Willy Brandt and a broader-based commission to 'study the grave global issues arising from the economic and social disparities of the world community'. The Brandt Report, *North-South: A Programme for Survival*, proposed far-reaching broadly Keynsian reforms for increasing aid to the poorest, eradicating malnutrition, stabilizing population, international management of the global commons, disarmament, controlling transnational corporations, and reforming international trade, finance and governance. These proposals were dismissed by Ronald Reagan and Margaret Thatcher in 1981.

Another political intervention by the bank was its report on sub-Saharan Africa in 1989, which severely criticized authoritarian rule for corruption, incompetence and abuse of aid for military spending, luxury consumption and capital flight. It called for 'political renewal', respect for the 'rule of law, and vigorous protection of the freedom of the press and human rights'. It said that political reforms should be accompanied by an increase in aid and a grassroots revolution to enable 'ordinary people to take charge of their lives'. The report was based on extensive consultation with Africans and conveyed many home truths.[38]

The World Bank's policies for development, governance, public sector management and 'structural adjustment' of the Majority World are as extensive as those of any government. Its numerous guidelines and directives cover almost everything from energy, forests and water to culture, education, health and public services. Its environmental policies aim to assist 'member countries in setting priorities, building institutions, and implementing programs for sound environmental stewardship'; to address 'potential adverse environmental impacts from bank-financed projects'; and link 'poverty reduction, economic efficiency, and environmental protections.[39] It insists that all IDA borrower governments draw up National Environmental Action Plans (NEAPs) to improve environmental management.[40] It also develops regional strategies for areas such as Asia, Latin America and the Caribbean, Southern Africa and the Sahel. Its energy policies emphasize energy efficiency, conservation, independent regulation and the commercialization of state-owned power utilities to encourage private investment. Many of these policies are eminently sensible, but the bank does little to address environmental issues in the West, the world's main source of pollution.

A great deal of credit for the World Bank's involvement in environmental issues is due to campaigning by pressure groups during the 1980s. The bank has since formalized dialogue with Non-Governmental Organizations (NGOs),[41] much as the South African government coopted 'community leaders' into its development agencies. This is still far short of democratic accountability and transparency.

Dialogue almost certainty improved the bank's performance, to the extent that it was entrusted with the Global Environmental Fund following the Rio Earth Summit in 1992. This dialogue was reflected in a revised strategy called *Learning from the Past, Embracing the Future*, published in 1994.[42] This gave higher priority to environmental protection, women and 'investment in people' through universal primary education, access to health care and the elimination of malnutrition. Its other aims were to encourage the private sector and economic and political reform.

These are explicit political goals, established through a political process in which the majority of the world's people has only token representation. Whatever their merits, they lack the accountability advocated by the bank itself. Moreover, they have no influence over Western decisions which ultimately determine economic opportunities for most of the Majority World. Changes in interest rates, trading conditions or the flow of investment and pressure on the environment owe more to the internal policies of the West than to the World Bank, IMF or the entire Majority World. In order to address the root causes of global poverty and inequality, the IMF/World Bank must be reformed as part of a wider realignment of the global economic and political system, as outlined at the end of this chapter.

In this context it is worth recalling the immense transformation undertaken by the West itself during this century to mitigate and manage market forces. The relatively small amount of aid and investment allocated through the World Bank to the Majority World contrasts sharply with the massive redistribution within the West itself, summarized in chapter 3. This is one of the clearest demonstrations of different standards of humanity applied by the West to its 'own' people and to the rest of the world. Overcoming these differences is the central challenge facing the world.

MECHANISMS FOR GLOBAL ECONOMIC JUSTICE

Chapters 3–5 have argued that the West has used control of immigration and imports, privileged status for private enterprise and finance, and public spending to protect its people from unfettered competition with the Majority World and secure exclusive advantages in the global economy. These measures have produced unprecedented affluence for many in the West while suppressing wages and commodity prices in the Majority World, forcing it to supply low-cost goods and labour to Western markets. This systematic, structural inequality has many similar effects to apartheid in South Africa. Unlike South Africa, Western leaders did not consciously create an exclusive, discriminatory economic system, but simply sought to protect their national interests.

The global balance of power is changing as some Majority World countries increase their share of world trade, investment and income while a groundswell in the West increasingly demands greater protection from competition. Whatever happens, the status quo is not an option. The relentless growth of China and the Pacific economies, the vast productive potential of the former Soviet Union, Asia and Latin America, combined with US profligacy, will continue to tip the balance of economic power away from the West. It is as much in the West's interests to create a fair and democratic economic system as it is essential for sustainable development.

Most proposals for a fairer global economy, from the New International Economic Order, Brandt Report, Brundtland Report, South Commission, Human Development Report and Agenda 21 to the Commission on Global Governance, have been dismissed or ignored by Western leaders in their single-minded pursuit of economic advantage. The stark challenge of competition may yet make them listen.

The following points summarize some of the key elements needed for global economic justice:

1 *Economic policy*, which recognizes the primacy of non-traded wealth of families, communities and environment by:

- protecting rights of local communities to control their own lives and work, including women's rights over reproduction;

- enabling local production to meet local needs as far as

practicable, by strengthening local and regional economic management;

- developing the capacity of people to participate in political and economic development as creative agents rather than victims or servants of market forces;

- raising standards of environmental and social protection to match the world best, rather than forcing them down to the market minimum;

- enabling everyone to satisfy essential needs for food, shelter, health, education and a worthwhile livelihood through minimum wages and social protection.

2 *A fair trading framework*, which:

- preserves multilateralism in world trade and prevents economic bullying by global corporations and other Western powers.

- facilitates balanced, equitable trade;

- progressively removes one-sided protectionism against Majority World products, such as the Multi-fibre Agreement, quotas and escalating tariffs;

- pays tariff income into an international development fund or returns it to exporting countries as a tax on production and earnings (no taxation without representation);

- recognizes the right of all countries to promote self-sufficiency and self-reliance in food and essential needs, within an equitable multilateral framework;

- ends dumping of subsidized agricultural produce on world markets by the West;

- stabilizes commodity prices by managing supply;

- enables Majority World countries to manufacture raw materials and diversify their economies to free themselves from dependence on a few commodities.

3 *A framework for fair finances*, which includes:

- a UN-supervised programme of debt cancellation that increases funds for investment and consumption by the poorest;

- monetary reform to protect countries against excessive fluctuations in interest rates, exchange rates and terms of trade;

- a universal reserve currency denominated in purchasing power based on a basket of essential goods, convertible into any local currency at purchasing power parity;

- capped interest rates and fee-based financing, particularly for non-profit investment in social and environmental improvements;

- low-cost credit for the poor;

- a global monetary authority, publicly accountable to democratic governments, to manage this process and curb abuses of the international financial system;

- global taxation to redistribute resources equitably according to need rather than nationality.

Majority World countries could take the initiative to bypass a depreciating and unreliable US dollar by creating an international currency based on purchasing power parities for trade within the Majority World.

These measures are not impossible utopian fantasies. The West has managed its own internal affairs according to many of these principles for the past fifty years. Reform of global economic institutions can learn a great deal from the successes as well as shortcomings of the Western Economic System. Unfortunately the established mechanism for global negotiation through which a just economic framework might be agreed, the United Nations, is as undemocratic and exclusive as the economic system itself.

Further Reading

Global economic management

Adams, Patricia, *Odious Debts: Loose Lending, Corruption and the Third World's Environmental Legacy*, Earthscan Canada, Toronto, 1991.

Bird, Graham, *IMF Lending to Developing Countries: Issues and Evidence*, Routledge, 1995.

Cavanagh, John, Wysham, Daphne and Arruda, Marcos, *Beyond Bretton Woods: Alternatives to the Global Economic Order*, Pluto Press, 1994.

Corbridge, Stuart, *Debt and Development*, Blackwell, 1993.

Danaher, Kevin, ed., *Fifty Years is Enough: The Case Against the World Bank and the International Monetary Fund*, South End Press, Boston, Mass., 1994.

George, Susan, *The Debt Boomerang*, TNI/Zed, 1992.

Hancock, Graham, *Lords of Poverty*, Macmillan, 1989, Mandarin, 1991.

Hirsch, Fred, *Money International*, Allen Lane, 1967, Pelican, 1969.

Koerner, Peter, Maass, Gero, Siebold, Thomas and Tetzlaff, Reiner, *The IMF and the Debt Crisis*, Zed, 1992.

Rich, Bruce, *Mortgaging the Earth: The World Bank, Environmental Impoverishment and the Crisis of Development*, Beacon Press/Earthscan, 1994.

Sampson, Anthony, *The Money Lenders: Bankers in a Dangerous World*, Hodder & Stoughton, 1981, Coronet, 1982.

World Bank, *World Development Reports*, Oxford University Press, Oxford and NY, annual.

Institutions of Global Apartheid:
The United Nations System

The government of the world must be entrusted to satisfied nations, who wished nothing more for themselves than what they had. If the world-government were in the hand of hungry nations, there would always be danger. But none of us had any reason to seek for anything more. The peace would be kept by peoples who lived in their own way and were not ambitious. Our powers placed us above the rest. We were like rich men dwelling at peace within their habitations.

Winston Churchill[1]
British prime minister

We in South Africa prefer the danger connected with freedom under a democratic system to the safety connected with loss of freedom under a dictatorship.

P. W. Botha
South African minister of defence, 29 July 1969

The United Nations is promoted as 'the planet's town hall'[2] and, like many town halls, it is a hothouse of petty intrigue, patronage, some corruption and occasional dedication. It is also utterly dependent on central government – the West – for cash and power. Decisions which matter in global governance are made by the West, through G7 summits, OECD, NATO, and other internal structures, which are described in chapter 8. The elaborate structures of the UN are more like the labyrinth of departments for 'own affairs' in apartheid South Africa than an equitable and effective mechanism for global governance.

The UN was born in a marriage of idealism and high politics, the opposite of the parochial populism and political manipulation that crafted apartheid. It was a landmark of optimistic humanism and faith in the ability of international cooperation to secure universal peace and prosperity. Its commitment to 'human rights and fundamental freedoms for all without distinction as to race, sex, language, or religion'[3] was utterly unlike the sentiments that inspired apartheid. Yet the authors of both institutions had much in common and shared some crucial assumptions. Chief of these were the aim of retaining control within the West and among whites respectively, and the entrenchment of 'group rights' in national or ethnic sovereignty. In both cases this meant subordinating the majority to minority interests. Security and finance were concentrated in a few hands, while responsibility for social and economic development was dispersed among a hotchpotch of uncoordinated agencies. The parallels are not exact, and the West has shown greater tolerance of diversity and autonomy of the Majority World. Yet the points of comparison are illuminating and disturbing.

SOUTH AFRICAN PARALLELS

Apartheid was created within the Western democratic legal tradition, as white South Africans have been keen to remind us: 'The institutions of responsible government introduced in 1872 were modelled on Westminster.'[4] The Union of South Africa was established by a British Act of Parliament in 1909. The two parliamentary chambers in Cape Town, used until 1993, were almost identical to the British Houses of Commons and Lords, right down to the green and red upholstery. Under the preamble of the apartheid constitution, the white legislators

> solemnly declare[d] their conviction that it is necessary to stand united to:
> - uphold Christian values and civilised norms of the country and recognize and protect freedom of worship;
> - safeguard the integrity of the country and the freedom of its people;
> - uphold the independence of the judiciary and the equality of all before the law;
> - maintain law and order;
> - promote the happiness and spiritual and material welfare of all;
> - respect and protect the human dignity, life, liberty and property of all;
> - respect and promote the right to self-determination of all population groups; and
> - promote private enterprise and effective competition.[5]

White South Africa adopted a new constitution from 1984 which created three separate chambers – the House of Delegates, with forty-five members, representing 1 million Indians, and the House of Representatives, with eighty-five members representing

3 million Coloured (mixed heritage) people, alongside the House
of Assembly, with 178 members, representing 5 million whites.
This gave the white minority an inbuilt majority in the political
system and excluded the black majority entirely. The state president was elected by all three chambers and appointed a Cabinet
from all three. The government was elected from an electorate of
3 million whites, 8 per cent of the population. In 1986, the ruling
National Party took 52 per cent of the white vote – less than 1
million people, a mere 3.7 per cent of the population. Most
Western governments nevertheless recognized the minority regime
as if it were legitimate.

Below the national parliament was a maze of 'ministries of own
affairs', regional service councils and local authorities, made infinitely complex by the arbitrary rule of skin colour. For the black
majority, the government created ten 'self-governing' homelands,
four of which were granted 'sovereign independence'. Most were
a patchwork of poor black settlements surrounded by rich white
farms and factories, so that they were not even geographical units.
None of these fragmented 'statelets' were recognized internationally and all were highly dependent on the South African
state.

This constitutional warren offered thousands of black people
trappings of office and often considerable autonomy. Mangosuthu
Buthelezi, chief minister of KwaZulu, had more power than many
Majority World governments dependent on international aid and
answerable to the IMF, World Bank and Western markets. The
population of KwaZulu was larger than those of 40 per cent of
UN members, including Iceland, Ireland, New Zealand, Luxemburg and about seventy other independent states represented in
the UN.

The principles underlying the complex and ultimately unworkable constitution of apartheid South Africa were strikingly similar
to the cardinal principles of the United Nations – national
sovereignty and Western suzerainty. While the UN's creation
must be understood in the context of its time, it still remains an
agency of global apartheid.

ORIGINS OF THE UNITED NATIONS SYSTEM

We shall not make Britain's mistake. Too wise to try to govern the world,
we shall merely own it. Nothing can stop us.
              Ludwell Denny, *America Conquers Britain*, 1930

The West ruled most of the world when today's international institutions were created. They were first formed to contain growing competition between Europe's imperial powers. Diplomacy failed to prevent war in 1914 and four years of senseless slaughter brought the United States to the centre of the world stage. At the Peace Conference in 1918, President Woodrow Wilson called for national self-determination, a new world order and a 'general association of nations' to keep the peace. General Smuts, a member of the British Imperial Cabinet and prime minister of South Africa, added further ideas in his *League of Nations: A Practical Suggestion*. National self-determination was seen primarily in Western terms and did not imply independence for Europe's colonial possessions.

The League of Nations was established in January 1920 with forty-five member states: sixteen in Europe, four British Dominions, most of Latin America and India. Germany and the Soviet Union were excluded. The United States withdrew in 1920 after Woodrow Wilson lost an election to the Republicans and Congress passed neutrality laws which restricted US military commitments abroad. The League's subsequent inability to prevent the Second World War was a horrendous lesson in the need for decisive global governance, while its achievements, structure and experience provided a model for the United Nations.

American planning for the postwar world started less than two weeks after the Second World War broke out. Public and political opinion in the United States was against involvement in any overseas war. Even after Hitler's armies overran Czechoslovakia, President Roosevelt did not allow American industries to sell arms to Britain and France. But a relatively small number of influential academics, bankers, industrialists, journalists and lawyers energetically promoted a world role for the United States. Many of them were associated with the Council for Foreign Relations (CFR), a private think-tank linked to the Royal Institute for International Relations in Britain (see p. 206). The CFR was funded by the Rockefeller Foundation and Carnegie Corporation, whose fortunes had been made from oil and steel respectively. It had been formed during the First World War to draw up plans for the eventual peace settlement, but these had been ignored by President Wilson. This time they started planning before America entered the war.

In September 1939, CFR members met senior advisers to President Roosevelt, arguing that the war was a 'grand opportunity' to become 'the premier power in the world'.[6] They set up a secret War and Peace Studies Project, at arm's length from the State Department, 'to set forth the political, military, territorial and economic requirements of the United States in its potential leadership of the non-German world area including the United Kingdom itself as well as the Western hemisphere and Far East'.[7] Dubbed the 'Grand Area' in 1941, this was seen as 'the minimum "elbow room" the American economy needed in order to survive without major readjustments'. The memo continued: 'In the event of an American–British victory ... the Grand Area might be an important stabilizing factor in the world's economy ... perhaps it would be possible simply to interweave the economies of European countries into that of the Grand Area.'[8]

Already in April 1941 the group was clear about the need to distinguish between the United States' real war aims and public statements for propaganda purposes. They wrote:

> If war aims are stated which seem to be concerned solely with Anglo-American imperialism, they will offer little to people in the rest of the world, and will be vulnerable to Nazi counter-promises. ... The interests of other people should be stressed, not only those of Europe, but also of Asia, Africa and Latin America. This would have a better propaganda effect.[9]

The result was the Atlantic Charter, signed in August 1941 by US President Roosevelt and British Prime Minister Winston Churchill. This set out the war aims in terms of peace, freedom, equality and prosperity.

A week after Japan bombed the US fleet in Pearl Harbour in December 1941 and America entered the war, the Council's director Isaiah Bowman said: 'The measure of our success will be the measure of our domination after victory.'[10] Another member, General George V Strong, wrote that the United States 'must cultivate a mental view toward world settlement after this war which will enable us to impose our own terms, amounting perhaps to a pax-Americana'.[11]

In January 1942 representatives of twenty-six states, including South Africa, signed the United Nations Declaration. Organizational details were hammered out among a very small group. The Allies were determined to avoid the League of Nations' paralysis in the face of aggression by creating a tightly structured disciplinary system under their control in the Security Council. At the same time they wanted to avoid centralizing social and economic matters in case the General Assembly gained control over them.

Isaiah Bowman and other members of the Council for Foreign Relations formed the secret Agenda Group which drafted US proposals for a United Nations Organization during 1943. CFR members were also closely involved in drawing up proposals for the IMF and World Bank, based on plans by the British Treasury adviser John Maynard Keynes and his US counterpart Harry Dexter White.

The UN Charter and Bretton Woods institutions were modified in negotiations with other nations, but the substance reflected conclusions reached much earlier by the United States government.[12] When the war was won, the European-based League of Nations was replaced by United Nations institutions based largely in the US. They included the World Bank and IMF, set up by forty-four countries in 1944; the United Nations, formally established by fifty-one states on 26 June 1945; and the General Agreement on Tariffs and Trade (GATT), formed by twenty-three countries in Geneva in 1947. The Majority World was scarcely represented and the overwhelming emphasis was on the postwar problems of the Anglo-Saxon world.

Western preoccupations

When the postwar settlement was signed, Germany and large parts of central Europe were in ruins under allied occupation. The battered British empire embraced a quarter of the world's population and a fifth of its area. Much of Africa, Indo-China and Indonesia were under Belgian, Dutch, French and Portuguese control. The United States was the world's most powerful state. It dominated Latin America, occupied the Philippines, Japan and South Korea, and exerted immense influence in Europe.

Western decision-makers were preoccupied by three traumatic experiences: the Russian Revolution of 1917; the economic boom and slump of the 1920s and 1930s; and the savagery of two world wars. The US was also keen to weaken Europe's empires and gain access to their markets for its prolific industries. The new international institutions were therefore intended to:

● contain and counteract the influence of the Soviet Union and Communism;

● prevent the recurrence of war in Europe;

- maintain stable exchange rates and promote free trade within the West;

- reconstruct Western Europe.

Rebuilding war-ravaged Europe was a massive task. Under the Marshall Plan, the United States provided Europe with $13.6 billion over five years, 2 per cent of US GNP. This is equivalent to about $70 billion at 1991 prices. Two per cent of US GNP in 1991 was over $110 billion. Compared with official US overseas aid of $11 billion in 1990, just 0.21 per cent of GNP,[13] this was very generous for an economy half its present size. The US and Canada also lent Britain $5 billion at 2 per cent interest, with repayments spread over fifty years. The World Bank lent Europe a further $500 million on favourable terms, worth $250 billion at 1991 prices. In the early years, Europe accounted for two-thirds of all withdrawals from the IMF, which was primarily designed to serve the West. Marshall Aid was an excellent investment for the US. Most of it was provided in the form of foodstuffs, fertilizers, fodder and fuel produced in the US, stimulating its economy. It spread American culture and consumer values. And it played a major part in binding Europe into a Western alliance.

Grand principles and sharp practices

The Charter of the United Nations echoes the US Constitution, beginning with the words 'We the peoples of the United Nations determine'; it goes on:

- to save succeeding generations from the scourge of war

- to reaffirm faith in fundamental human rights, in the dignity and worth of the human person, in the equal rights of men and women and of the nations large and small, and

- to establish conditions under which justice and respect for the obligations arising from treaties and other sources of international law can be maintained, and

- to promote social progress and better standards of life in larger freedom.'

South Africa's prime minister, General Smuts was involved in drafting these words. When they were signed, racial segregation was still enforced in the southern United States and most black people did not have the vote. Britain, France and the Netherlands were imperial powers, with no intention of granting independence nor equal rights to their colonies. Like the US Constitution, human rights and freedoms were conceived in terms of 'civilized peoples', who had a duty to protect 'backward peoples'. Yet for many people living under colonial rule, the Charter and accompanying Universal Declaration of Human Rights were an inspiration for emancipation. It influenced the ANC Freedom Charter and the constitution of post-apartheid South Africa.

In practice, the UN has done little to achieve its lofty ideals. This was partly due to the cold war, but the main cause has been the West's single-minded pursuit of its own interests. The West's lack of commitment to these objectives was repeatedly illustrated by Europe's postwar resistance to independence and democracy among its colonies, by countless US interventions in Latin America and South-East Asia and by the West's support for white South Africa. While Western policies within the UN were neither consistent nor united during its first fifty years, the UN had much lower priority than Western solidarity through NATO, the OECD, European Union and other international groups and agencies from which the Majority World was excluded.

The United States began undermining UN independence within four years of its creation. The FBI put UN staff under surveillance and the Senate concocted a witch-hunt of suspected Communists. President Truman required US citizens working for the UN to sign a loyalty oath, in violation of the UN Charter and US Constitution. The UN's first secretary-general, Trygve Lie, colluded with the United States to sack dozens of US citizens from its staff.[14] This set a devastating precedent for government interference in the appointment and allegiance of staff, spawning a culture of caution and conformity across all UN agencies.

When the countries of the Majority World began to gain independence, the US actively prevented them from having any effective say in the world's affairs. President Nixon's ambassador to the UN, Daniel Patrick Moynihan, described his 'basic foreign policy goal' as 'breaking up the massive blocks of nations, mostly new nations, which for so long have been arrayed against us in international forums'. He went on: 'The Department of State desired that the United Nations prove utterly ineffective in whatever measures it undertook. This task was given to me, and I carried it out with no inconsiderable success.'[15]

The deliberate weakening of the United Nations by the world's most powerful state caused far-reaching damage. The less the West listened, the louder the rest of the world shouted. Impotence gave licence to incompetence. Under President Carter the US took a more conciliatory, largely paternalistic approach. In language reminiscent of many South African statements on 'native affairs', assistant secretary of state Charles Maynes declared that the US should be 'a sympathetic but tough parent, or brother, towards the UN. You don't give this dependent child everything it wants, because it will abuse the affection and attention. It needs to be both disciplined and supported.'[16] Later, President Reagan enforced sterner discipline by conducting extensive reviews of UN agencies, withholding funds and threatening to withdraw from membership. In many cases mismanagement in UN agencies deserved (and still demands) investigation. Greater scrutiny by elected governments is essential for accountability and equity as well as efficiency in global governance. But Reagan's aim was to curb criticism of US conduct by Majority World representatives, not to improve global accountability. Towards the end of the 1980s the United States changed its tune, insisting that its rights as a minority should be protected – in much the same way as officials of apartheid demanded minority rights before the transition to majority rule. Thus a senior US official argued in 1988 'that there have to be constitutional constraints to see that nobody abuses their power, compensatory structures to enforce a certain respect for the minority'.[17]

Group rights

Although the UN Charter begins 'We the peoples', the UN is an organization of *states*, not peoples, nor even nations. None of the national delegates to the UN is directly elected or answerable to national assemblies. Dictators have equal status with elected governments. Tiny statelets like Tuvalu, with 7,000 people, have equal status to India, with almost 900 million. Current membership criteria encourage big states (and UN agencies) to buy the support of small states with aid and other favours, positively inhibiting democratic development.

Article 2 of the Charter entrenches state sovereignty, asserting that 'Nothing contained in the present Charter shall authorize the United Nations to intervene in matters which are essentially within the domestic jurisdiction of any state.' These words were particularly important to South Africa, which argued that criticism of its policies on race and South-West Africa (Namibia) constituted interference in its internal affairs. The concept of 'group rights' was also central to apartheid as a system.

Although much of the UN's rhetoric is in terms of rights, national sovereignty effectively overrides the principles of human rights. The UN can only authorize intervention in another state, through economic sanctions or military means, 'with respect to threats to the peace ... and acts of aggression' (Articles 39–50). This protects the status quo of nation-states in world politics. This is central to Western power, because Western states are sufficiently powerful to sustain a semblance of sovereignty among themselves, while the rest of the world is subject to Western decisions for the global economy and environment.

UN separate development agencies

There are over 100 agencies in the UN system, scores of intergovernmental committees and coordinating bodies, as well as countless regional and functional commissions. Figure 2 indicates the formal relationships of the main agencies, but most have a high degree of autonomy, depending on chief officials and donor nations for direction, rather than on the UN as a whole. The UN system includes small technical bodies, strategic coordinating agencies such as the Universal Postal Union and International Telecommunications Union, as well as large agencies such as the Food and Agricultural Organization (FAO) and World Health Organization (WHO). Most agencies are ultimately governed by resolutions of periodic conferences representing all member states, creating cumbersome and unwieldy decision-making processes. The Economic and Social Council aims to create 'conditions of stability and wellbeing' but has very limited powers. The World Bank, IMF and World Trade Organization are not accountable to it and have no duty to carry out its wider aims.

The Commission on Sustainable Development was set up following the 1992 Earth Summit to monitor the implementation of Agenda 21. Governments agreed to submit an annual report on progress, which is a token of global accountability. By 1995 only

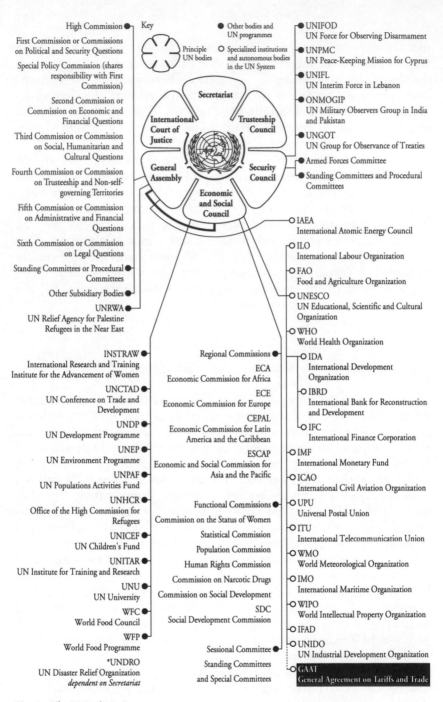

Fig. 2 The United Nations system
Source: UN.

about fifty reports had been received and many were public relations exercises rather than a serious step towards genuine accountability. The CSD is currently drawing up indicators and targets to make national reports more consistent and comparable, which could provide a meaningful way of monitoring progress towards environmental security. The Commission is a hopeful strand in the UN system, but, like the tattered banner of human rights, the early days of UNCTAD and previous promising initiatives, hope is pitted against the heavy hand of narrow self-interest.

Most UN agencies are relatively weak, struggling at the margins of world politics over Majority World concerns with minuscule means. Like the apartheid state, they create elaborate political climbing-frames far from the real centres of power. Unlike the majority under apartheid, many governments of the Majority World were seduced into this elaborate charade. Some participated with commitment and sincerity. Others succumbed to cynicism and sumptuous international salaries, enjoying the trappings of office without responsibility, like black officials of South Africa's discredited parallel structures. The complexity, inefficiency and sheer incompetence of many UN agencies suited the West very well. Like the homelands, here was visible proof that the Majority World was unfit for democracy. In truth, they were not given the chance to make it work.

UN Secretariat: an international civil service

The UN and its agencies employ about 55,000 international civil servants in over 600 offices throughout the world, not including the IMF, World Bank and GATT, which have over 10,000 staff and combined annual budgets over $20 billion, overshadowing the entire UN system. The UN itself has a budget of about $6 billion a year, of which the fastest-growing element is military peace-keeping, which cost over $3.2 billion in 1993.

The secretary-general has the immensely difficult task of dealing with the world's most powerful governments about the most extreme military and humanitarian crises while keeping the trust of diverse regimes. In practice, he has less status than a senior official in the US State Department or a middle-ranking Majority World head of state. Unlike the European Commissioner, for example, the UN secretary-general is not invited to G7 summit meetings, NATO or the OECD, where the West conducts its business, nor even the IMF, World Bank and GATT, which are nominally part of the UN system.

Appointment to top UN jobs is a remarkably haphazard affair, driven largely by jockeying among potential candidates within the UN itself. Posts are filled through an 'old boys' network which gives the five permanent members of the Security Council a veto over most appointments. The process does not include open advertisement, publication of job descriptions, scrutiny of candidates nor open election. Since 1946, 70 per cent of top jobs have been held by the West. Citizens from just a quarter (41) of UN member states have occupied all 136 posts: the US has held thirty-three; Switzerland, France and the UK ten each. Less than 30 per cent of post-holders have come from the rest of the world – and none from the Soviet Union or Eastern Europe. The first woman, Dr Nafis Sadak, director of UNFPA, was appointed in 1987, and by 1995 only four chief officers were women.[18]

The international civil service itself is mainly appointed by patronage within a quota system to achieve representation from member states, with many appointments made as a reward for loyal service and acceptability rather than ability.

THE WESTERN SECURITY COUNCIL

The Security Council is the supreme authority in the UN system and acts as legislature, judiciary and executive on global security issues. In signing the Charter, 'Members of the United Nations agree to accept and carry out [its] decisions' (Article 25), ceding some sovereignty to the Security Council. These powers are very much less than those of any national cabinet or even the European Council of Ministers and are usually exercised by appointed ambassadors rather than elected representatives.

The Security Council's five permanent members are the 'nuclear quins' of Russia (succeeding the Soviet Union), the USA, the UK, France and China, who each can veto decisions. The rest of the world is represented by just ten countries elected on a regional basis by the General Assembly to serve for two years. Since the permanent members are also the world's biggest arms-dealers, it is like putting foxes in charge of a chicken farm.

Permanent membership was barely justifiable in the context of the cold war, but is utterly out of date today. Proposals to make

Japan and Germany permanent members would strengthen Western dominance, while the suggestion that India or Brazil should join the veto powers is like the modernization of apartheid in South Africa during the 1980s when Coloureds and Indians were given the vote and token seats in the President's Council. A more equitable solution would be for each region of the world to nominate one or two representatives and to limit or phase out the veto.

The Security Council is intended to work by consensus, which gives enormous power to the permanent members, since no decisions can be made without their consent. Opposing Western interests in the Security Council can be costly for poor countries. The US cut aid to the Yemen after it voted against Western intervention in the Gulf.

Since the end of the Second World War, there has been almost continuous armed conflict somewhere in the Majority World, in which over 25 million people have been killed. Military capacity and insecurity have increased in tandem as the superpowers fought proxy wars in the Majority World. Until 1989 the Security Council was paralysed by the cold war, with the Soviet Union casting 114 vetoes, the West 117 and China three. Since then its role has increased dramatically. By the mid-1990s it was meeting almost daily, particularly over Bosnia. The Security Council is highly selective in the conflicts it chooses to deal with, ignoring many major disputes, particularly where permanent members are involved. It was largely silent over Vietnam, Laos, East Pakistan during 1971, Angola in 1974/5, the Iraq–Iran war and on many other occasions. Civil wars in Nigeria, Cambodia, Chad and Sudan were largely ignored, although they were no less international than those in Greece, Lebanon, Congo and the Yemen, which were discussed. Its powers of enforcement have been used more than twenty-six times. They are now being used in Angola, the Balkans, Cambodia, Cyprus, El Salvador, Kampuchea, Lebanon, Iraq, the Indo-Pakistan border, the Middle East, Mozambique, Somalia, Western Sahara and former Yugoslavia.

The increasing need for UN peace-keeping, and the failure of the UN to act effectively, amounts to gross dereliction of responsibility by the five permanent members. As founding members and the most powerful participants in the Security Council, Western countries bear considerable responsibility for this failure. Like South Africa's many interventions in neighbouring states and nominally independent homelands, the West is swift to intervene when its perceived interests are threatened. The United States

mobilized over half a million men and $50 billion to liberate
Kuwait in 1990/1. Britain dispatched a vast armada to eject
Argentina from the Falkland Islands in 1982, and the US invaded
Panama to arrest General Noriega on drugs charges. US intervention in Somalia was undertaken to satisfy domestic political
opinion, and when the US bungled it blamed the UN. It would
certainly seem that the West cares only for its own people and
interests.

During the 1930s, the inability of the League of Nations to cope
with conflicts in Spain and the Balkans and with great power
aggression plunged the world into war. Today the world is even
more unstable, better armed and less capable of maintaining peace
than ever. Global peace and security make it essential to strengthen
the capacity of the Security Council to mediate between warring
factions, regardless of state boundaries, and to intervene on the
basis of international law if necessary. In 1992, the secretary-
general put forward *An Agenda for Peace*, an integrated programme for early-warning, preventive diplomacy and deployment
of UN forces to deter hostilities. It recommended a wide range of
peace-building activities to repatriate refugees, restore essential
infrastructure, monitor elections, rebuild institutions and advance
human rights. But the West did little. It dithered over the escalating
crisis in Yugoslavia. It pulled troops out of Rwanda as genocide
was executed before their eyes and silent guns. It allowed UNITA
to defy UN-supervised elections in Angola. It permitted the
Khmer Rouge to regroup in Cambodia, and stood aside from
continuing conflicts in Afghanistan, Sudan, the crumbling Soviet
empire and elsewhere.

Peace, like policing, is too important to leave to factions in
global politics. Responsibility for global security must be shared,
with the Majority World taking a more proactive role within the
framework of international law. The task of the UN has never
been more urgent nor daunting and will grow sharply in the
coming century. But peace-keeping and humanitarian relief can
only be effective if the world community tackles the causes of
conflict, where the UN is even weaker.

THE PAPER PARLIAMENT

All 183 member states of the UN have an equal vote in the General
Assembly, but it is a powerless parliament. It can initiate or

endorse international legislation, like the Law of the Sea, and it has a limited role in relation to UN agencies. A majority vote can have moral authority as well as practical effect, which Western governments actively thwart except on rare occasions when they want to be seen as acting in the interests of the world. The General Assembly can make recommendations to member states or the Security Council (Article 11), although it cannot make recommendations on any matters considered by the Security Council unless asked. Under the 'Uniting for Peace' resolution of 1950, it may act if the permanent members of the Security Council do not, but it lacks forces and resources to act independently.

The West frequently ignores or plays down majority votes in the General Assembly. In 1971, the US Congress voted to import chrome from the illegal white minority regime in Rhodesia, in violation of UN sanctions. In 1967 the General Assembly passed Resolution 242, calling on Israel to withdraw from the occupied territories of Egypt, Jordan and Syria, yet the illegal occupation continued for decades with US assistance – in striking contrast to the swift expulsion of Iraq from Kuwait in 1991.

On the economic front, the World Bank asserted its independence from the UN as early as 1947 when it granted a substantial loan to the Netherlands as it launched a full-scale colonial war against Indonesian nationalists. After 1965 the World Bank again defied the UN by granting loans to Portugal and South Africa. While the West pursued its economic agenda through the IMF, GATT and the central banking system, the General Assembly adopted a Declaration and Programme of Action on the Establishment of a New International Economic Order (NIEO) in 1974 to establish a fairer economic system. The Declaration was followed by two decades of fruitless 'North–South Dialogue', volumes of resolutions, international conferences and reports. The West simply refused to engage with the grave social and economic disadvantages experienced by the Majority World.

Alongside the General Assembly, UN agencies hold international conferences which have increased in status and public profile through the involvement of non-governmental organizations and the press. Although their powers are largely symbolic, they can have a significant moral authority and develop a debate or consensus on issues such as population, women's rights or the environment. More specialized agencies have important regulatory and even legislative functions, while several run development programmes.

In many respects, however, the West pays less attention to majority views expressed in the General Assembly and UN agencies than the South African government did to its structures for 'own affairs' under apartheid. The West's unwillingness to accept majority verdicts even extends to the World Court, a body dedicated to the rule of law and imbued with Western legal traditions.

THE WORLD COURT

The International Court of Justice is 'the principal judicial organ of the United Nations' (Article 92). It was set up in 1946 as an integral part of the UN, replacing the League of Nations Court founded in 1919.

The Court has fifteen judges elected to nine-year terms by a simple majority in the General Assembly and the Security Council sitting independently. Permanent members do not have a veto on appointments. Judges may serve more than one term. Members of the court should be independent and impartial, rather than government representatives. The court may only include one judge of any nationality and should include 'representation of the main forms of civilization and of the principal legal systems of the world' (Article 9).

In 1993, six of the fifteen judges were from the West (France, Italy, Japan, Norway, UK, US), two from Eastern Europe (CIS, Poland), and seven from the Majority World (Algeria, China, Guyana, Madagascar, Nigeria, Sri Lanka, Venezuela). All were men until a British woman judge was appointed in 1994. Although the court's composition is less exclusive than that of the Security Council, the West is over-represented, with 40 per cent of the judges, while under half are from the Majority World.

The court's role is to settle legal disputes between states and to give advisory opinions on legal questions referred to it. Only states or UN agencies may apply to the court and be parties to actions before it. The court can only consider disputes if both parties –

1   agree to appear before it, or
2   are parties to a treaty which refers disputes to the court, or
3   have agreed to accept the jurisdiction of the Court.

Thus going to court is virtually voluntary, unlike national law. Unless states agree to be bound by its rulings, the court has no reliable means of resolving disputes. In the thirty-five years before 1992, the court dealt with eighty-eight cases, of which twenty were advisory on behalf of UN agencies and sixty-eight were contentious. The Soviet Union also rejected mandatory jurisdiction by the court until Gorbachev came to power.

Contempt of court

The court's limited jurisdiction means that powerful states can prevent most cases from even being heard. If this fails, they ignore rulings which go against them, without fear of censure from other big powers. When the court ruled (13–2) in 1971 that South Africa's occupation of Namibia was illegal, it had no effect. Two decades of fighting and thousands of deaths passed before Namibia became independent in 1990. New Zealand took France to court over nuclear tests in the Pacific in 1973. France refused to recognize the court's jurisdiction and continued testing. In 1986 the court found in favour of Nicaragua against US military intervention and ordered the US to desist and make reparations. America simply ignored the decision and continued arming the Nicaraguan contras. The US is also ignoring the court over the case brought by Iran over the shooting down of an Iranian airline in April 1988, which is still pending.

This catalogue of contempt mocks Article 1 of the UN Charter which states that the UN aims to bring about peace 'in conformity with the principles of justice and international law'. As in South Africa, the West has used the law as an extension of its power, rather than as an impartial instrument of justice, as will be considered in the next chapter. The United Kingdom is the only veto-wielding member of the Security Council to stick by a 1969 decision to accept the court's ruling on contentious cases.[19]

These weaknesses in international adjudication enable powerful states to act with impunity or arbitrarily impose sanctions against other countries, such as the US sanctions against Cuba and Vietnam. The lack of a reliable international court also gives countries like Libya grounds to fear that its citizens cannot get a fair trial abroad, as in the case of the two Libyans accused of the Lockerbie bombing. This case also highlights the need for an international criminal court to deal with terrorism, hijacking, drug-trafficking, genocide, war crimes and other offences which cross state frontiers or are of global significance but cannot be tried in one country.

REFASHIONING THE UN

Never before has the United Nations been so well poised to achieve the great objectives of its Charter – maintaining international peace and security, securing justice and human rights and promoting social progress and better standards of life in larger freedom.

Boutros Boutros-Ghali,
UN secretary-general, April 1992[20]

The United Nations was founded on aspirations for peace and security, but this meant Western peace, not world peace – much as the reconciliation between Afrikaner and English in the Union of South Africa created white peace at the expense of the majority. Western leaders are now seeking to reform the UN. As in South Africa in 1984, it could be restructured to incorporate the more affluent sections of the Majority World to modernize global separate development, not end it.

UN reform needs the vision and political will which inspired such defining documents as the Constitution of the United States, the UN Charter, or the ANC Freedom Charter. The following points set out some of the thorny issues which need to be addressed in any reform or replacement of the UN. These issues are dealt with more fully by the *Commission on Global Governance* and *Renewing the United Nations System*, but some more contentious proposals appear here for the first time.

Purposes need to spelt out very specifically and affirmed by member states. It is neither feasible nor desirable for the UN to become a world government, global state, or even a federal institution like the European Union, Brazil, India or the USA. Yet a multilateral forum in which the majority of the world's people are represented must be recognized as *the* central channel for global governance. So long as the UN does not fulfil this role, it will continue to be performed piecemeal by others, such as the G7, Western governments, the IMF/World Bank and transnational corporations.

Powers need to be very clear and focused on specific purposes in relation to human rights, environmental protection, economic cooperation, global peace and justice. The West must be willing to cede sovereignty on these issues, as it does within the EU and NATO, while the Majority World needs to recognize that it will be politically dangerous and difficult for Western leaders to convince their electorates that their security depends on deepening global cooperation.

Membership should belong to 'we the peoples' rather than national governments. It is absurd that states as big as California, with 24 million people, Szechwan with over 120 million, or the 80 million of Maharashtra are not directly represented, while 24,000 citizens of San Marino enjoy full diplomatic status and one vote – equal power to over 1.2 billion people of China. Over half of UN member states have populations of under 5 million. In theory representatives of just 100 million people could out-vote the other 5 billion. While small states need recognition and protection, citizens within larger states deserve an independent voice, and stateless peoples like Kurds or Timorese need a distinctive place in the world community. Several hundred million indigenous people are also excluded from nation-states and need direct representation. Possible measures to deal with these issues include:

- States and large regions could be represented separately, either through two chambers or a separate list within the General Assembly. Provision for a two-thirds majority of states on important questions could provide protection against domination by big powers.

- Member states must have a popular mandate in order to vote, the terms of which would be agreed by two-thirds of the General Assembly.

- The creation of a UN Parliamentary Assembly, consisting either of parliamentarians from member states or directly elected by universal adult franchise.

- The development of appropriate forums for under-represented groups and non-governmental organizations to participate more fully in UN deliberations.[21]

Accountability should be strengthened by requiring all UN representatives and agencies to report formally to elected assemblies in their own countries.

Security Council membership should move towards regional representation and the veto of the five nuclear powers phased out. Regional military alliances such as NATO, ANZUS and the CIS (the former Soviet Union) and all national armies should have additional accountability to the world community through the Security Council. The Security Council should relinquish judicial functions to an independent authority such as the World Court. It should develop policies on issues such as civil war, the use of mines, or rights of intervention to protect nationals, which should then be debated and agreed by the General Assembly.

Global security needs to be strengthened along the lines of *Agenda for Peace* and *The Commission on Global Governance*. The Security Council should consider every dispute as a matter of course. Government ministers should participate more regularly in order to give the council greater weight and increase press interest.

The General Assembly needs to become more purposeful and powerful, scrutinizing the work of the Security Council and specialist agencies; taking a greater role in the appointment and supervision of chief officers of the World Bank, IMF and WTO as well as UN agencies and the secretary-general, and exercising a stronger role in supervising international agreements such as Agenda 21, the Law of the Sea and the Biodiversity Convention.

Leadership of UN institutions must be strengthened and improved in order to mobilize the world community to deal more effectively with the growing number of international crises. It is vital that appointment or election to the top posts becomes more credible, open and accountable to attract both the most capable candidates and the widest support.

Strategic coordination must be strengthened, by bringing the Bank of International Settlements, IMF, World Bank and GATT/WTO as well as other agencies within the UN system and establishing a common site for UN agencies, as originally envisaged. Other necessary reforms are to:

- bring heads of appropriate agencies together through an Inter-agency Executive lead by the General Secretary or Deputy, with a more proactive, corporate role than the current Administrative Committee on Coordination (ACC);

- create an intergovernmental consultative board through which member governments can oversee and support the UN system;

- produce a common medium-term rolling programme and statement of priorities for the UN system as a whole. Each UN agency should be required to publish an annual work programme;

- give high priority to interagency teams so that issues of peace-keeping, humanitarian relief, human rights, basic needs and long-term development are linked;

- rationalize regional offices to end fragmentation, duplication and lack of coordination, as called for by General Assembly resolution 32/197 in 1977;

- require member governments to coordinate participation by delegates in the UN and its agencies, to debate an annual report and programme of the UN in national parliaments, and to ensure implementation of UN resolutions.

Regional coordination must be strengthened through reformed regional commissions and closer relationships with the Organization of African Unity, Organization of American States, ASEAN, the Commonwealth of Independent States and the European Union. At a national level UN agencies should work through a single office, headed by a UN coordinator appointed by the secretary-general in consultation with host governments.

Funding of peace-keeping, humanitarian relief and economic stability is too important to be left to the political preoccupations of member governments. Increased revenue should be sought through *global taxation* of currency transactions, trade, energy, use of non-renewable resources and pollution.

The International Court of Justice must be strengthened to replace arbitrary power politics with the rule of law. Recognition of the International Court as a Universal Supreme Court would give human rights and international law an independent arbiter. An international criminal court, permanent war crimes tribunal and court of the environment should be set up as distinctive branches of the World Court.[22]

For this vision to be effective we need a just basis for international law. The next chapter outlines how international law today serves the exclusive interests of the West.

Further Reading

The United Nations system

Childers, Erskine, ed., *Challenges to the United Nations: Building a Safer World*, CIIR/St Martin's Press, 1994.

Hazzard, Shirley, *Defeat of an Ideal*, Macmillan, 1973.

Luard, Evan, *The United Nations: How it Works and What it Does*, 2nd edn, rev. Derek Heater, Macmillan, 1994.

Righter, Rosemary, *Utopia Lost: The United Nations and World Order*, Twentieth Century Fund Press, NY, 1995.

Russell, Ruth B., *A History of the United Nations Charter*, Washington, DC, 1958.

Urquhart Brian, and Childers, Erskine, *Renewing the United Nations System*, Development Dialogue 1994: 1, Uppsala.

The Laws of Exclusion

Without Justice, what is the state but a robber band.

St Augustine, *c.* 411

We must acknowledge people's rights and ... make ourselves free by giving to others in a spirit of justice what we demand for ourselves.

President P. W. Botha, 1979

Laws express societies' decisions about what is right. Law is not just statute, but all customs, rules and principles accepted or enforced at any level. Every time a rule or law is enacted, interpreted or enforced, the prevailing consensus and balance of power within a society is resolved. Each decision becomes a precedent against which future decisions are tested. Law is never static, because circumstances and the balance of power change constantly, but change in law proceeds with greater deliberation than most other changes. Laws current in society at any time describe the 'settlement' between members of society. The word 'law' itself derives from the Old Norse or Saxon word *lagu*, meaning 'laid down' or 'settled'.

Every settlement includes decisions about who has a say in laying down the law, who interprets it and who enforces it. There is no universal rule for deciding what is a legitimate settlement, but general acceptance of the legal process is a precondition of its effectiveness. There will always be disagreements about particular laws, judicial decisions and enforcement, but so long as most people accept the process, then the settlement may be regarded as legitimate. Where acceptance is achieved through intimidation, coercion, deception or manipulation, it is clearly not a just settlement, although it may be legitimate in a narrow sense. A just settlement not only requires consent, but also equity. Where the majority opposes a particular settlement, as in South Africa, it is clearly illegitimate as well as unjust.

At a global level there is an apparent settlement, in which the United Nations, sovereign states and companies exercise power within an accepted framework. This chapter aims to show that the basis of Western international law is force, not justice, that Western international law denies the world's majority equal rights, and that when Western powers fail to get their way under this exclusive legal system, they break their own laws, using force or fraud. The parallels with the South African legal system are profound.

LAWS OF APARTHEID

Legislation to protect the minority and exclude the majority in South Africa began the moment Europeans settled the Cape in 1652. Roman–Dutch law spread with the invaders and continued when Britain took control in 1806, although British common law, statutes and legal practice gained influence. European courts applied to everyone, but the white authorities permitted black chiefs to try and punish black people offending against common laws as again well as indigenous law and custom.

The European minority used the law to justify and extend minority rule every time it was threatened. Apartheid legislation was the product of bitter struggles between groups within the white minority, each seeking its own interests but all united in the conviction of white superiority. Black resistance was dismissed or savagely repressed, while black collusion, division and servitude were actively fomented.

Over the centuries Europeans created a vast edifice of discriminatory laws, customs and regulations which was enforced with the utmost severity. The most important principle underlying the web of apartheid legislation was Afrikaner sovereignty and self-determination. This was the battle-cry of Dutch settler-farmers defending their collective self-interests against imperial Britain, indigenous Africans and entrepreneurial Indians. The 'settlement' of 1910 reconciled Afrikaner and British interests under the South Africa Act, passed in Westminster. It excluded Africans from the legislative process, stating that 'a member of the House of Assembly shall be ... a British subject of European descent.' Until 1936, black men who owned property could vote in Cape Province, although only white men could be elected. White women did not get the vote until 1930. Parliamentary sovereignty gave apartheid its claim to legitimacy and justified the suppression of extra-parliamentary action by the black majority.

The legal system of apartheid enacted after 1948 consolidated and entrenched existing segregation in a 'settlement' that aimed to protect European civilization. It was in many respects the ultimate expression of a process that began with the creation of modern Europe. Racial classification was neither the first nor most important piece of legislation in the apartheid arsenal. The Population Registration Act of 1950 was introduced thirty-seven years after the Native Land Act confined black land-ownership to 7 per cent of the territory. Legal measures to restrict economic participation included the Asiatic Land and Trading Act of 1919, the 'civilized' labour policy of 1924, and countless other regulations.

Many apartheid laws were expressed in such a way that they appeared to give equal rights or protection to the black majority. King Ngqika told a British official in the Cape: 'When I look at the large piece of country which has been taken from me, I must say that, though protected (supposedly) by Britain I am rather oppressed by my protectors.'[1] Writer and an ANC founder-member Sol Plaatje wrote of the Native Land Act that 'by adroitly manipulating its legal phrases, it seems that it was recast in such a manner as to give it a semblance of a paper restriction on European encroachment on native rights'.[2] Black people were removed from the common voters' role under the Representation of Blacks Act of 1936, excluded from existing universities under the Extension of University Education Act of 1959 and denied South African citizenship under the Promotion of Bantu Self-Government Act, 1959.

At its height, the legal structure of apartheid was a thicket of laws which secured white superiority in every sphere of life, from the Immorality Act prohibiting sexual relations between people of different racial classification, to controls on the media, suppression of opposition and many more. These laws may be grouped into ten sets of acts:

1 conquest and denial of the pre-existing customs, laws and right of indigenous peoples;
2 imposition of Western legal concepts and norms;
3 assertion of superior rights of white people as a group;
4 classification of people into racial population groups;
5 restriction of citizenship, political participation and voting rights to white people;
6 pass laws and influx controls curbing freedom of movement by non-whites;
7 unequal rights in employment, enterprise and economic participation;

8   restriction of ownership and use of land by black people to 13 per cent of the area, thus designating most of the country for white use;
9   separation of amenities and services, including education, housing, medical care, hotels, parks, beaches, etc.;
10 disregard for the law in order to protect minority interests.

The West did not need race classification to deny the majority equal rights in international affairs, institutions, opportunities or amenities. The laws of sovereignty, nationality and property were sufficient to protect minority rule within the postwar settlement.

LAWS OF CONQUEST

Conquest gives a title which the Courts of the conqueror cannot deny.
                                            US Chief Justice Marshall, 1823[3]

I gave Whites permission of living on my country ... They have never obtained any right to property to the soil from me. Had I granted that, such a right should have been contrary to the law of the nation which allows no such alienation of land.
                                            King Mosheshwe I of Lesotho, 1859[4]

The rule of law is upheld as fundamental to Western civilization. Yet the primary fact of Western law is conquest. The Romans conquered most of Europe, which was then conquered and re-conquered by Germanic tribes, who in turn forged nation-states that conquered the world. The legacy of conquest is profound, as generations of conquerors, rulers and ruled accommodated their demands and customs to each other.

Conquest itself is rarely, if ever, legitimate. But once established every regime seeks a legal basis – by extending its own laws to the new territories, by seeking justification in existing laws and customs, by creating a new constitution on its own terms, or by a mixture of all three methods. However established, dominant regimes invariably find legal justifications for subordinating the conquered while rewarding collaborators and repressing resistance. Such pretexts take many forms:

● the land was uninhabited;

● the land was inhabited but not owned by anyone;

- the land was not being used productively;
- by treaty;
- by purchase;
- by invitation of a section of the population;
- by conquest, if all else fails.

International law upholds the Roman legal principle that no one but the owner can give a good title – *Nemo dat quod non habet*. Once occupied, possession itself can grant legal title under English law. Common law has long provided that action to recover ownership must be made within a certain period, twelve years under English law.[5] The principle of limitation also means that events cannot be brought to court after a certain period. Exceptions to this include crimes against humanity, such as the Nazi genocide against Jews.

International law also upholds the Roman legal principle that natural reason concedes ownership to the first occupier – *quod nullius est, id ratione naturali occupanti conceditor*. Europeans justified their settlements on the grounds of *terra nullius* (land belonging to nobody), which meant that the country was *res nullius* (property belonging to no one). This entitled the settlers to treat the indigenous inhabitants as *filius nullius* (bastards, or rightless people).

A great deal of colonial history propagated in the West aims to demonstrate that territories were neither occupied nor owned. The 'founding myths' of Australia, Canada, New Zealand, Russian Siberia, South Africa and the United States evoked the idea that the land was empty or inhabited by a few nomadic savages. In almost every case this was untrue and a deliberate lie.

European settlement of North America was a triumph of law-breaking, subsequently legitimated by the same legal principles which underpin the present global settlement. The American rebellion against Britain was, among other things, a challenge to King George III's attempt to curb westward expansion and appropriation of Indian territories. In 1773 the king complained of 'great frauds and abuses ... committed in purchasing lands of the Indians, to the great prejudice of our interests, and to the great dissatisfaction of the said Indians'. The king declared in vain 'that the several nations or tribes of Indians with whom we are connected, and who live under our protection, should not be molested or disturbed ...'.[6] American self-determination was exacted from the indigenous people, not from the king of England, just as Afrikaner independence was won at African expense, not from Britain. While British conquest usurped native sovereignty, the Declaration of Independence in 1776 finished the freedom of native Americans and made them foreigners in their own lands.

Descendants of the original inhabitants of America, Australia and New Zealand are challenging European conquest through the courts, with potentially far-reaching implications. In 1993 the Australian High Court overturned the legal basis of Captain Cook's claim on the continent in 1770, in what is known as the Mabo Ruling. Prime Minister Paul Keating welcomed this as 'an historic judgement ... recognising in law the fiction of *terra nullius* and the fact of native title. With that alone, the foundation of reconciliation is laid, because after 200 years we will at last be building on the truth.' In Canada the Inuit negotiated self-governing status for nearly 356,000 km², C$1.73 billion compensation, mineral rights and a share of royalties from resource development of federal lands. These issues are far from resolved anywhere in the world. Demands for restoration of indigenous rights and for reparations are bringing the spectre of Europe's colonial holocaust into international negotiations and domestic politics.

The truth is that the pre-existing legal systems and status of Africa, America, Asia and Australia were suppressed and supplanted by Western law. This became the basis of international law, just as Dutch–Roman–English law and a British Act of Parliament provided the legal basis of apartheid in South Africa.

WESTERN INTERNATIONAL LAW

The rule of law requires a recognized source of law, a system of law enforcement, and a means of resolving disputes by reference to agreed rules. These conditions do not depend on a legislature, nor courts, nor the authority of a centralized state. All three conditions clearly exist in practice in international law. Although there is no world parliament, there is a well-established body of international law. This consists of:

● customary rules and principles which are generally accepted (referred to as *opinio juris*), mainly covering state practices such as diplomatic relations;

- treaties and agreements voluntarily adopted by states;

- rules for the international public interest (referred to as *jus cogens*).

While the West has avoided giving the United Nations legal powers, near-unanimous resolutions (over 90%) of the General Assembly amount to international law-making.[7] The International Law Commission of the UN, established in 1947, has codified a substantial body of relatively uncontentious law concerning the sea, statelessness, diplomatic relations, international treaties, and the succession of state property, archives and debts.[8] Despite this, the West consistently ignores decisions by the General Assembly with which it disagrees, as, for example, over the Israeli occupation of the West Bank, the New International Economic Order, the Law of the Sea and, until 1989, South Africa's illegal occupation of Namibia.

The West is more willing to treat the Security Council as a reliable source of legitimacy, for the simple reason that it can veto proposals it does not like. Even then the West is highly selective when deciding to obey Security Council resolutions. When it voted 13–0 to condemn the South African Constitution Act 1983 and declared it null and void (Resolution 554), the United States and Great Britain abstained and continued to treat the minority regime as the legal authority. This contrasts sharply with the thirty-year blockade against Cuba or economic sanctions against Libya.

The West's selective use of the United Nations and its self-appointed powers to make and enforce Security Council resolutions gives global apartheid legislative capacity with less accountability or legitimacy than the white parliament in Cape Town. That was at least directly accountable to an electorate and passed laws in public, whereas the Security Council is only indirectly accountable to Western voters.

The most explicit form of international law is the treaties and conventions mutually agreed between states. These laws are not binding on a state until signed and ratified by it. Thus France did not sign the 1963 Nuclear Test Ban Treaty and continued to detonate nuclear weapons in the Pacific Ocean, against the wishes of neighbouring states. States may even add reservations or disapply particular clauses. Agreements such as the Law of the Sea must be ratified by a minimum number of states before they can come into force.

International law gains its legitimacy and strength through consent, so a great deal of effort is made to reach agreement. Consensus-building is a very positive aspect of international law-making, but consent between unequal partners often involves coercion. The mask of consensus gives the United States and its allies immense power to impose its laws or frustrate treaties it opposes. The West's minority veto power in international law is a further legal pillar of global apartheid.

Public interest, or *jus cogens*, refers to rules which the international community regards as 'necessary to protect the public interests of the society of states or to maintain the public morality in them'.[9] There is no definitive list of laws covered by *jus cogens*, but aggression by one state against another, piracy, war crimes, slavery and genocide are generally accepted as illegal. Aeroplane hijacking, terrorism and drug-smuggling are increasingly recognized under this heading. Apartheid was declared illegal and a 'crime against humanity' by the UN General Assembly in 1973,[10] with ninety-one votes in favour and twenty abstentions. Britain, the United States, South Africa and Portugal voted against. Destruction of the common environment or possession of nuclear weapons may one day be prosecuted under this category, but the international community is still too divided for this to be accepted.

Any country or the international community as a whole can enforce international laws covered by the principle of *jus cogens*, whether or not the offending state has agreed to be bound by it. This principle of 'no hiding-place' means that any state can prosecute a person for piracy or war crimes, no matter what their nationality or where the alleged crime took place. In practice the definition and status of *jus cogens* depends on the power of enforcement, which is highly unequal between the West and the Majority World. Western powers are effectively exempt from prosecution or from implementing 'public interest' laws which they oppose.

Jus cogens is akin to the concept of natural law, an important source of inspiration for justice and equality in Western history. It was used by the church to outlaw enslavement of Christians – a process that took over 1,000 years to achieve. It was a source of the Universal Declaration of Human Rights. But the fundamental principles of Western international law are not derived from natural law, based on human equality, but from national sovereignty.

NATIONAL SOVEREIGNTY

Obedience to the law is the greater part of patriotism.

Thomas Jefferson

Western international law is based on the principle that sovereign states rule their own affairs unless bound by treaty, custom or the recognized public interest of the international community. This derives from the Roman legal concept of *jus gentium*, or 'law of the peoples'. In origin, this was a form of common law based on prevailing ideas of equity, fair dealing, common sense and public utility at a time when the civic laws of Rome could not be applied to the tribes of Italy. This principle eventually extended to the empire and became the basis of European international law.[11] In Roman legal philosophy, *jus gentium* was also distinguished from natural law, or *jus naturae*. One significant difference was that *jus gentium*, like Roman civic law, permitted slavery, whereas natural law saw all men as free and equal. Women were not mentioned.

The principle of national sovereignty developed over a long period out of the ancient imperial practice of indirect rule. It was established in central Europe by local rulers resisting external authority exercised by Spain in the name of the Holy Roman Empire. In 1648, the Peace of Westphalia ended both the Eighty Years War between Spain and Holland and the Thirty Years War in Germany, thus setting limits on imperial power. The treaty recognized the sovereign right of states to make and enforce their own laws. Paradoxically, this facilitated the growth of absolutist states and autonomous state power as well as democracy within states.

'National sovereignty' was used by white South Africa to justify separate development and resist external criticism of its 'internal affairs', including the illegal annexation of Namibia. When the Universal Declaration of Human Rights was adopted, both South Africa and the Soviet Union objected that it did not specifically mention the sovereign rights of states. South Africa also said that it 'would not be in the interests of the less advanced indigenous population' if everyone had the right to reside in a particular area, since this 'would destroy the whole basis of the multi-racial structure of the Union of South Africa'.[12] Similar arguments had been used against the Constitution of the United States, when slave-owners demanded 'Who authorized them to speak the language of We, *the people*, instead of We, *the states*?'[13] National sovereignty gives little protection to small nations like Estonia, Guatemala or East Timor unless they have great power connections, as Kuwait had in 1991. Nor is national sovereignty any consolation to stateless peoples, like the Palestinians, or those who feel themselves to be subordinated within a state they reject, like the Basques or Tamils.

National sovereignty also determines who has access to the law on what terms, much as skin pigment and racial classification did in South Africa. Western citizens can appeal to an extensive legal apparatus, but an Algerian, Mexican or Colombian citizen in the West without appropriate papers has few rights and may be detained or deported without legal redress. This unequal status of individuals according to nationality makes the principle of *jus gentium* and state sovereignty a fundamental legal pillar of global apartheid.

National sovereignty among unequal states also creates a hierarchy of citizenship in world affairs, with similar effects to those of racial classification, creating separate bodies of law for the Western minority and the non-Western majority, as explained in the next three sections.

EXCLUSIVE CITIZENSHIP AND SUBORDINATE RIGHTS

The principle of one man, one vote has long been accepted in South Africa. It all depends in which structures you want to apply it.
President P. W. Botha, 5 Sept. 1986

Citizenship is a complex concept best expressed in terms of civil liberties or human rights, including the right to participate in government and to vote. Citizenship requires both legal rights and the ability to exercise those rights in practice. In international law there is no 'world citizenship', only citizens of sovereign states. In this respect, individuals are recognized only in terms of their group identity. As in South Africa, there is a hierarchy of group rights:

1 the USA, UK and France, whose citizens can elect governments that control the Security Council, NATO, IMF/World Bank and global economic regime;
2 OECD countries and the Western Alliance, whose citizens have the vote, recourse to effective courts and Western solidarity;

3   other independent states represented on a regional basis in the Security Council and IMF/World Bank, which are party to human rights conventions;
4   independent states which are not party to human rights conventions or do not adhere to them;
5   occupied territories and peoples without states;
6   refugees, asylum-seekers and stateless persons. The last are covered by a separate convention which had been ratified by only twenty-nine states by February 1993.

Although not explicitly classified by race, this hierarchy is banded by colour. Groups 1 and 2 are 'part one' countries within the World Bank, usually called the 'developed' or 'industrialized' countries. They are mainly white. Groups 3 to 6 are mainly non-white. Within the West, it is much easier for citizens of groups 1 and 2 to get visas, travel, seek protection under the law and obtain social benefits. Black citizens of the West are much more likely to be stopped at borders, asked for proof of identity, arrested 'on suspicion' and challenged when seeking social security benefits than are white people. Non-white citizens of groups 3 to 6 are likely to have much greater difficulty getting into group 1 and 2 countries and are subject to much greater constraints than non-nationals from within the West.

Nationality laws of most countries and the European Union explicitly enshrine this 'classification'. Most citizens of group 3 countries with rights of residence and work in group 1 countries cannot travel freely in other group 1 countries. Thus Jamaicans who grew up in Britain or Algerians brought up in France face physical restrictions in Europe more discriminatory than those of South Africa during the 1980s. People of Turkish descent born in Germany do not automatically acquire German citizenship, although they know no other homeland.

This 'classification' has the force of common international law in so far as it is embodied in international institutions and treaties. The precise terms vary, but the division into 'developed' and 'developing' countries is so deeply ingrained that even the humane UN Human Development Report publishes separate tables for 'developing' and 'industrial' countries. The IMF similarly compiles separate tables for the twenty-three 'industrialized countries', 130 'developing countries' and twenty-four 'countries in transition', meaning the former centrally planned economies. 'Developing' countries are further classified by the IMF by predominant export – fuel (19 countries) and non-fuel (111), including exporters of manufactures (11), primary products (54), services and private transfers (33) or those with a diversified export base (13). Alternatively, the Majority World is sometimes divided according to financial criteria, such as creditor, debtor and nations which are heavily in debt.[14] These systems of classification describe people in terms of their usefulness to the West. Their religion, culture, or other attributes do not count. Despite its massive debts, the US is not listed as a debtor country, nor has the West been reclassified as 'overdeveloped' or 'mal-developed' since its damaging impact on the environment became recognized. Ranked by rates of murder, rape or crime, the US would appear among the 'least developed' countries of the world. But the West sets standards against which all other countries are measured.

International classification has a powerful influence on how people are treated. It is as arbitrary, intricate and exclusive as South Africa's racial classification, and serves the same function without the stigma of racism. This pillar of global apartheid is reinforced by limitations on civil liberties and immigration controls, considered next.

EXCLUSIVE CITIZENSHIP AND QUALIFIED RIGHTS

Civil liberties describe the formal rights of all citizens. In practice, most rights are qualified by a large number of conditions. The former Soviet Union had the most impressive bill of rights of any country, all circumscribed by state security and national interests. In the US, UK, South Africa and most European countries, the franchise was long restricted by gender, property ownership and sometimes education. Today the most widespread qualification of effective citizenship is wealth. In many respects money is the chief qualification for international citizenship.

Most people in the Majority World have much less effective citizenship than people in the West. French and Japanese farmers had greater influence on the GATT negotiations than the more numerous Indian farmers. Western officials, lobbyists and pressure groups far outnumber the Majority World in global chambers of power. For the people of Zaire, East Timor, Chile under Pinochet, or of other Western-backed dictatorships, the 'free world' could be more oppressive than Soweto or the Transkei.

In many Western countries the non-white minority do not even have the vote, even though they may have lived and worked there for decades or even since birth, such as Turkish people in Germany. Where they have the vote, many do not go to the polls, because no party which represents their interests stands any chance of winning. Even where they could win, they lack the most important power of all in affluent Western democracies – money to sponsor candidates and lobby between elections. Thus white right-wing candidates were elected as mayors in Los Angeles and New York in 1993, although most voters were poor and non-white. The dispersion of black communities within Western countries also makes it more difficult for their concerns to be represented within existing political structures. The fact that Wales is a distinct geographical entity within Britain, for example, gives Welsh people a substantial political presence, including members in Parliament, a Welsh government department and a secretary of state in cabinet. This had made it possible for Welsh to be recognized as an official language, have its own television channel and get state support. There are more black people in Britain than there are people in Wales, and perhaps as many speakers of Urdu as of Welsh, yet these communities have no distinctive recognition within existing structures. This is not to argue for ethnic represen-tation along South African lines, but to acknowledge that political systems need to be more flexible and inclusive to represent multi-ethnic diversity in decision-making.

Although non-white people in the West have much greater political freedom than in South Africa, and are represented in Western assemblies, under-representation of different communi-ties within Western political structures leads to social tensions and injustice.

LABOUR LAWS AND INFLUX CONTROLS

One of the clearest measures of global apartheid is the way in which the movement of non-white people is increasingly restricted, as it was in the development of apartheid in South Africa. State control of the movement of people is incompatible with free markets, which inevitably increase pressures on people to migrate in search of work. Yet deliberate intensification of global market forces has been accompanied by greater restrictions on the movement of people. These restrictions have not been explicitly based on race, although colour has been a significant factor.

All European states have steadily been closing their borders since the late 1950s, particularly after the 1974 recession. Britain has enacted over ten pieces of legislation restricting the entry of non-white people since 1962. The effect of this can be seen in refusal rates for visitors. In 1993, one in sixty-three Jamaicans was refused entry, as was one in eighty-two from Bangladesh and one in 100 from Nigeria, compared with one in 3,011 from the USA and one in 4,319 from Sweden. Belgium and Holland stopped immigration for work and began deporting 'irregular' workers. France tightened controls on African migrants from 1970 onwards, introduced voluntary repatriation in 1977 and in 1980 began deporting French-born West Africans by force. In 1986 it removed the basic rights of due process for migrants facing deportation and 17,000 people were deported the following year. The interior minister, Charles Pasqua, instituted a policy of 'zero immigration', although checked by the country's constitutional court. In 1995 the government increased its target to 20,000 compulsory repatriations a year. As in South Africa, deportations are justified on grounds of 'racial harmony'. Similar sentiments are evident across the United States. In November 1994 60 per cent of Californians voted to deny health and education benefits to illegal immigrants and to prevent their children, born in the USA, from becoming citizens, under Proposition 187. It still faced constitutional hurdles and opposition from public service workers, but similar demands are gaining momentum across the US states. Meanwhile the border with Mexico has been fenced off.

At the same time as Britain reduced rights for its non-white Commonwealth citizens, other Western Europeans were given rights to live, work and claim social security without any historic links to the country concerned. Increasing restrictions on non-white people while extending citizenship rights to white people of different nationalities echoes a similar process in South African history, when the vote was gradually removed from black people in the Cape at the same time as the Union of South Africa was strengthened. Although the two processes are different, the parallels are uncanny. Fortress Europe entrenches separate development by stealth.

The West is not alone in discriminating against migrant workers, inviting them when their labour is needed and expelling them when the economy turns down or political conditions change. Ethnic, religious and other forms of discrimination are widespread throughout the world. The key issues are the underlying economic causes, the legal responses by the world's most powerful states and the diminution of human rights as a consequence.

As the global economy becomes more integrated, growing numbers of people will have little choice except to migrate in search of work. Much of the migration follows investment and demand from Western markets, such as oil-workers in Nigeria and the Middle East or assembly-workers in China and Indonesia. Increased employment for Filipina maids across South-East Asia is largely due to income from trade with the West, just as lack of employment in the Philippines is caused by the falling prices of agricultural exports. Western political–economic policies have a powerful impact within the Majority World. Immigration to the West is only the outermost ripple of powerful forces shaking the Majority World.

Discriminatory immigration controls are an essential pillar of global apartheid. They are likely to increase as Western societies continue to close their borders in response to competitive pressures.

EMPLOYMENT AND ECONOMIC DISCRIMINATION

Legal discrimination against the Majority World in economic affairs was described in chapters 3 to 6, and includes extensive privileges of company law and finance, import controls and unequal trade restrictions. Although these exclusive economic advantages are not based on race, they arise from a similar economic logic to that of apartheid: the protection of particular groups from competition. The most fundamental and pervasive legal instruments of Western economic discimination have been property rights.

THE RULE OF PROPERTY RIGHTS

> The rich people buy their apartheid with large residences and properties. The poor man must live wherever he can afford. I am on the side of the white worker.
>
> P. W. Botha, 28 Feb. 1987

Property rights are fundamental to the Western world order. Property is private sovereignty. People's ability to exchange property is the basis of the market, trade and commodity production. Property gives people security, the means of production and the motivation to produce. Ownership brings wealth and power. People without access to property from which to produce a livelihood are forced into servitude or even destitution unless protected by other rights.

Property rights and private ownership have become so well established that they appear to be common sense, beyond question, like laws of nature. But they are relatively recent legal concepts which have enabled the Western Economic System to expand through its internal momentum. The enclosure of common lands, the creation of joint stock companies and stock exchanges, the development of credit and debt, the growth and abolition of the slave trade, the appropriation of colonies, the protection of intellectual property and privatization of public assets are all stages in the evolution of private property. This complex bargaining process between different interests continues as property rights acquire entirely new meanings and powers in the fields of telematics, genetics, or pollution.

Property rights provide a clear basis for making a claim on what has been produced. Private property is a legal invention which gives the owner the right to use, dispose, or earn a rent from something. It is a social mechanism for sharing what people produce. In economic terms, ownership has no value unless the thing owned is used for production. Ownership gives the right of a share in production even if the owner did nothing to produce it, or the right to sell property even if other people depend on it for their homes and livelihood.

As a legal invention, property ownership has many benefits. It disperses decision-making, enabling people to make transactions without reference to authority. It provides a reliable framework for action and for resolving disputes. The market value of property provides a reference for calculating opportunity costs of using monetized resources in different ways. There are powerful arguments to say that strong property rights give individuals, communities and the environment better protection than state regulation, since the state often overrides property rights to appropriate land or build roads, dams and nuclear power stations against the wishes of local residents. Many of the most devastating violations of nature and civil liberties have been through state action, sometimes in concert with private corporations.[15] The benefits of personal property rights often conflict with other interests. During America's helter-skelter economic expansion in the nineteenth century, many entrepreneurs declared that property was merely a 'social institution', 'subject to those limitations and instructions, which increase its tendency to the ... general welfare', 'a creature of civil government' and no more than that 'which the law declares to be property'.[16] They wanted to build railways, dams or oil pipelines across the land of recalcitrant farmers, and most Western states took the power of compulsory purchase to help them. When a business failed, they wanted to abrogate property rights through bankruptcy and begin again. Where absolute property rights conflicted with private enterprise and the interests of the state, they were often suspended.

At the other end of the scale, property rights entitle landlords to clear unprofitable people and plants to make way for cash crops, regardless of wider social or environmental consequences. Thus Scottish trees and crofters were swept away in favour of more lucrative sheep or El Salvadorian peasants were cleared out to plant coffee groves. The very word 'private' derives from the Latin *privare*, to deprive.

As property rights are extended by GATT, the World Trade Organization and international treaties to cover plant varieties, genes, the air and the seabed, it is essential to recognize that 'property', like 'sovereignty', is fundamentally an exclusive concept. The extension of private property rights can become a process of appropriation unless it also carries explicit responsibilities. Most of the world's resources do not and could not have a 'market value'. Not everything can be bought and sold. The concept of property rights has absolute limitations.

Property is a privilege, not a right

The concept of private property *rights* violates a fundamental principle of rights – universality. Unless property rights mean that everyone owns some property by right, then protection of private property cannot apply to everyone equally, since it would exclude those without property. If private ownership of property were a right, it is logically possible for people without property to be excluded from everywhere. They would become slaves to those with property, since they have nothing to sell except themselves. Most wage-earners in the West are protected from virtual slavery by employment laws and social security. These social rights override absolute property rights. Social rights, like property rights, are established in law through political decisions. In the

Western Economic System, as in apartheid South Africa, the dividing-line between who is or is not protected by particular 'rights' can have life-or-death consequences.

Where social rights are absent, as for illegal immigrants, some non-waged married women, and factory workers in some export-processing zones, conditions are little better than slavery. Vast numbers of landless people in the Majority World are effectively slaves of land owners, employers or pimps. International debt holds whole countries in virtual debt bondage. Property rights can be a contributory cause of famine, since those with purchasing power (which is an expression of property) have a prior claim on resources, driving up prices in times of shortage and causing those without property to starve, as happened in the Irish famine from 1846. Amartya Sen's study of famines in Bengal (1943), Ethiopia (1973 and 1974), Bangladesh (1974) and the Sahel (1973) show that 'Starvation deaths can reflect legality with a vengeance.'[17] Property is usually protected against the hungry, homeless, or disenfranchised, so that protection of property rights entails slavery for the propertyless. People can only be protected from virtual slavery if they have rights that override property rights. In which case, 'property rights' cannot be universal rights, but would more accurately be described as privileges.

The term 'privilege' means private law, an exclusive licence to something. Intellectual property rights, such as patent and copyright law, are explicitly based on the concept of privileged protection. The very word 'royalty', the payment for permission to use a patent, publish copyright material or extract minerals from sovereign territory is based on royal privilege. There are many circumstances where granting privileges serves a useful function and should be protected, but these are political decisions which should be based on principles of justice.

In the new South Africa, the ANC's draft Bill of Rights seeks to reconcile two totally different concepts of property rights – 'the birthright of all human beings to a little piece of space called home, and the rights conferred by the state on holders of title not to be disturbed in their possession'.[18] The first of these principles is the basis of land reform and protection for smallholders in many parts of the Majority World, although it is often condemned as a restraint on free trade by the West, while the second has been used by the West to justify intervention in the Majority World. Neither concept is adequate to understand the privileges and reciprocal obligations inherent in just ownership.

The effects of one-sided property rights damage everyone.

Western property rights increase inequality, because they enable those who have most property to acquire more with less effort than those who have no property but work for a living. Large property-owners have greater power over purchasing and investment, therefore more say over what is produced. They are less likely to be frugal with resources and more likely to cause waste. The widening wealth gap weakens social cohesion and sense of community as those with everything defend themselves against those with little or nothing.

Property ownership is a powerful and important privilege. Ownership places a trust on someone for which they are accountable. People do not cease to be part of society through private ownership. Property is still part of the commonwealth, whatever its formal legal status. Personal property contributes to or damages the welfare of all, depending on how it is used. The case for private enterprise, from Adam Smith to Milton Friedman, is ultimately based on the argument that it is the best means of bringing prosperity to all. Where it clearly fails to do so, then society has a right to define duties of property ownership in law.

Constant pressure from global corporations to enforce and extend property rights, entrench equal rights for investment, or deny traditional communal rights and reject concepts of the common heritage of humanity, emphasize the importance of property rights for the Western Economic System. The simple, seemingly innocent concept of alienable and transferable property rights has put most of the world's resources at the disposal of the wealthy through the market mechanism.

The power of property rights to provide privileged protection to a minority and exclude the majority makes them an essential legal pillar of global apartheid.

Grabbing the global commons

At one time the whole world was a 'global commons' in which people lived as part of nature. John Locke, apostle of property rights, revealingly wrote 'in the beginning all the world was America.'[19] Over time, as human populations grew, groups of people divided the land between families, tribes, churches, nations, empires and companies. Western society was created by transforming landholding at home and grabbing land abroad. In Britain, the enclosure acts turned common land into private property and created landless labourers, while the East India companies laid the foundations for British rule and the dispossession of India and South Africa. At the height of European imperialism, between 1880 and 1914, over 70 per cent of the earth's surface was ruled by white men. This had hardly changed when the UN was created, although independence in Africa and Asia rapidly reduced Western rule to 40 per cent of the land surface (excluding Antarctica). The West continues to control the largest share of the world's air, sea, mineral, biological and other environmental resources through markets and one-sided treaties, as outlined below.

The law of the sea

The development of marine law, like that of all law, reflects struggles between conflicting interests. Spain and Portugal divided the oceans between them under the Papal Bulls of 1493 and 1506, extending their national sovereignty across the globe. This conflicted with the commercial interests of North European states, who asserted freedom of the high seas under the concept of *res communis*, communal territory,[20] the basis of current law. Over the past forty years, the West has increasingly abused its greater economic power to exploit this common territory as a resource and a dumping-ground for waste. President Johnson foresaw the dangers of 'a race to grab and hold the land under the high seas' and in 1966 proposed an international agreement to ensure that 'the deep seas and ocean bottoms are and remain the legacy of all human beings.'[21] The eventual outcome was the Law of the Sea Convention, which regulates all aspects of the sea by defining rights and obligations over navigation, economic activities and pollution, with legal procedures for settling disputes. It introduced the concept of international taxation, obligatory technology transfer and a supranational Seabed Authority for deep-sea mining. Agreement took fourteen years of hard bargaining. When it was signed by representatives of 119 nations in December 1982 it was celebrated as 'the victory of the rule of law and of the principle of the peaceful settlement of disputes', symbolizing 'human solidarity and the reality of interdependence'.[22] For most signatories it was an attempt to establish a 'just and equitable international economic order' governing the ocean. No sooner was it agreed than the West blocked its implementation.

This unique international treaty gives legal status to the concept of the 'Common Heritage of Mankind'. It is a rare example of a resolution by the UN General Assembly becoming international law, enacting the 1970 declaration that 'the area of the sea-bed and ocean floor and the subsoil thereof, beyond the limits of national jurisdiction, as well as its resources, are the common heritage of mankind, the exploration and exploitation of which shall be carried out for the benefit of mankind as a whole'.[23] The Convention is a complex package of delicately balanced compromises between widely divergent interests. The West won very substantial concessions during the negotiations. For example, the Convention granted a 200-mile 'exclusive economic zone' giving coastal states access to resources in 40 per cent of the oceans. A third of this total is claimed by just six countries – Australia, Japan, New Zealand, the Soviet Union, the United Kingdom and the United States. Britain did well, with micro-colonies like the Malvinas/Falkland Islands dotted around the globe. In exchange, the West agreed that an international Seabed Authority would be set up, with powers to regulate all commercial mining of the seabed beyond national economic zones. Industrial countries agreed to transfer mining technology to enable 'developing' countries to participate. Developing countries would also receive a share of the revenue from seabed mining in recognition of their stake in global resources.

The Convention required ratification by sixty states in order to become law. After twelve years, Iceland was the only Western state which had ratified. The US and its allies blocked ratification because they want to keep the right to mine the deep seabed. They objected that 'By denying the play of basic economic forces in the market place, the Convention would create yet another barrier to rational economic development.'[24] Conservative critics denounced it as 'global socialism' and a prelude to world government with a source of revenue independent of nation-states. President Reagan wanted a 'frontier mining code' under which 'you can do what you want' on the high seas.[25] Anger at the US stand shows through the restrained words of Tommy Koh of Singapore, the president of the conference:

> The doctrine of freedom of the high seas can provide no legal basis for ... exclusive title to a specific mining site in the international Area.... Any attempt by any State to mine the resources of the deep sea-bed will earn the universal condemnation of the international community ... All speakers have addressed an earnest appeal to the United States to reconsider its position.[26]

Despite lack of ratification, most countries sought to observe the spirit of the Convention and no significant deep-sea mining took place. In 1994 the Clinton administration obtained agreement from the G77 to radical modifications of the seabed mining regime, enabling the US to ratify the Convention without conceding its principal objections. The International Seabed Authority was inaugurated in November 1994 and seabed mining is not intended to start until 2008. It is just possible that international law may prevail in this modest but potentially significant unravelling strand in global apartheid.

Laws of the Air

The global atmosphere is our most precious common resource. Awareness of the dangers of atmospheric pollution has grown over the past century and is enacted through laws to protect clean air in most Western countries. More recently, international agreements have been made to protect the atmosphere in three vital areas – acid rain, erosion of the ozone layer and global warming. The first two have been moderately successful, mainly because solutions were technically feasible without major change, although problems remain.

Global warming is of an entirely different order of magnitude. Scientists estimate that increased global warming, largely due to emissions of carbon dioxide (CO_2) from burning fossil fuels, is likely to cause a significant rise in sea levels, turbulent climate change and potentially catastrophic damage to agriculture and the environment during the coming century.[27] The issue is complex, since global temperatures fluctuate naturally and many factors affect climate change, including emissions of other gases and 'sinks' which absorb CO_2, such as plant life, particularly trees and ocean plankton. The central fact remains that CO_2 emissions from fossil fuels are the major cause of global warming and must be cut to preserve our shared environment. On the precautionary principle, the scientific consensus recommends that total CO_2 emissions must be cut by about 60 per cent. This means that the atmosphere, like the land and the sea, can no longer be used as a limitless domain, but must be treated as a finite resource. Its limits are bound by the capacity of the environment to absorb CO_2 without raising average global temperatures above the level at which human life can be sustained.

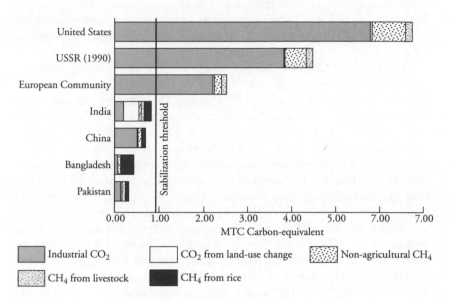

Fig. 3 Per capita emissions of greenhouse gases
Source: Global Commons Institute.

About 80 per cent of all CO_2 emissions are produced by the West and the former Soviet bloc, which in effect are therefore occupying 80 per cent of the global atmosphere. The West as a whole produces over half of all emissions and the United States a quarter. This means that less than 5 per cent of the world's population uses more of the earth's atmosphere than the 75 per cent living in the Majority World.

Where resources are finite they can be shared through rationing, trading, or by force. The issue at the heart of global negotiations over climate change is which of these three options is embodied in international law. In principle, it has been agreed that this should be dealt with equitably, but what this means in practice is almost entirely open. A majority of the Western Alliance is determined to hold on to its unequal use of the global atmosphere by using financial power to disenfranchise the Majority World.

The stakes are high. Cutting CO_2 would mean a massive transformation of industry, transport and consumption in the West. Rapid industrialization by the Majority World is increasing CO_2 emissions, although most countries are still below per capita sustainable levels (see figure 3). The Majority World cannot significantly increase its use of fossil fuels without causing irreversible damage to the atmosphere. Economic development by the Majority World on present patterns is almost as constrained by environmental limits as black economic development was limited by land ownership in South Africa.

The Global Climate Convention, aimed at curbing human-induced global warming, was agreed at the Earth Summit in Rio in 1992 and signed by over 158 states. The Convention acknowledged that climate change is a 'common concern of humankind' and resolved to stabilize greenhouse gas concentrations in the atmosphere 'on the basis of equity and in accordance with their common but differentiated responsibilities and respective capabilities. Accordingly, the developed country Parties should take the lead in combating climate change' (Article 3). Actual commitments under the Convention (Article 4) are limited, requiring industrial countries of the West and Eastern Europe to stabilize CO_2 emissions to 1990 levels. Under President Bush, the US tried to block the Convention on the grounds that it infringed national sovereignty. The Clinton administration has since signed, but is failing to cut CO_2 emissions, which continue to rise in most Western countries. On 21 March 1994 the Convention became law, having been ratified by at least fifty states. Negotiations continue in annual meetings of all signatories.

The rapid process of agreement and ratification is impressive, reflecting recognition of the gravity of global warming. The high level of participation by non-governmental organizations, such as the Climate Action Network and Global Commons Institute, is also a small step towards a more open international system. But the difficult task of cutting emissions has barely begun. The battle has now shifted to technical arguments, where Western negotiators are devising ingenious ways of defending the status quo. Although many in the West are seriously grappling with their legal obligation to cut CO_2 emissions, including governments like those of Holland and Denmark, most are pursuing economic policies that increase carbon emissions. Unlike the West's outright rejection of the New International Economic Order, negotiations over the Convention are taken seriously by most Western governments, thus enhancing the legitimacy of global law-making. Systematic efforts by the US administration to undermine the treaty are a disappointing repetition of its obdurate approach to the law of the sea. US efforts to create tradable pollution quotas and buy off groups within the Majority World through a process euphemistically called 'joint implementation' is reminiscent of the way in which its first settlers appropriated common lands from Native Americans. Joint implementation is a sophisticated diversionary tactic that is absorbing a huge amount of intellectual, institutional and political energy. It is being vigorously promoted by global corporations and the United States government because it offers them most benefits at least cost, but it will do little to avert global warming and may well accelerate it.[28]

Negotiations over global climate change provide two other powerful illustrations of global apartheid in action. The first is that cost-benefit analysis by Western economists estimates potential damage from global warming by valuing a 'statistical life' at $1.5 million in the West and $100,000 in low income countries.'[29] While economists innocently reflect global inequality as scientific fact, these calculations have a significant effect on the bottom-line figures which politicians use to make life-and-death decisions about global warming.

Second, describing carbon emissions in terms of property rights leads to the obvious conclusion that the West owes the Majority World a substantial 'debt' for past emissions.[30] The value of the debt depends on the assumptions made. One estimate based on a sustainable level of output per ton of carbon produces a figure of $3.4 trillion dollars.[31] India's minister of environment, Kamal Nath, claimed that 'at a conservative estimate, the privileges enjoyed by the North for excess emissions are worth 100 billion dollars annually [in] "environmental rent" that ought to be trans-ferred to developing countries every year...'[32] This dimension of property rights has been totally rejected by Western economists and politicians eager to promote joint implementation and unequal life valuations.

These examples illustrate how technical economic assumptions inserted into the footnotes of global negotiations can have a powerful influence on the development of international law. Neither of these issues is settled.

Law of space

Space is the fulcrum for future control of the planet. Western satellites constantly survey the earth's surface, relaying streams of valuable commercial and military data. Remote sensing scours for minerals, oil, and growth or disease among crops, giving Western firms powerful advantages over local producers and governments. Space also has lethal potential as a celestial citadel from which

Western weapons could wage war on a rebellious earth. Perhaps the most potent use of space is cultural and ideological. While most people in the Majority World cannot even communicate with their fellow-citizens by telephone, television, press or post, television satellites beam Western soaps, films, news and advertising into almost every cranny of the globe. The ideological implications of this are considered in chapter 9.

The law on outer space agreed in 1967 was virtually a bilateral agreement between the US and the Soviet Union, the two main space powers. The treaty provides for freedom in space limited by considerations of public interest. It states that

> space exploration shall be for the benefit of all countries, irrespective of their degree of economic or scientific development; that outer space shall be the province of all mankind ... on a basis of equality and ... not subject to national appropriation; and that celestial bodies shall be used exclusively for peaceful purposes.[33]

These brave words did not prevent the US spending billions of dollars on Star Wars or commercial developments that only benefit private companies and their home states.

Principles governing the use of satellites for international television broadcasting were adopted by the General Assembly in 1982. But the technology of commercial satellite communications has overtaken international and national law, leaving the skies virtually free to companies like News International. Even Western countries have difficulty regulating the invasion by satellite television. For the Majority World, 70–90 per cent of television already originates in the West. Satellite technology is breaking down barriers of even the most restrictive regimes such as China and Myanmar (Burma). In future, broadcasting rules are more likely to be dealt with under GATT than the UN. This will make domestic media even harder to protect against the Americanization of global television and the total commercialization of culture and politics.

Rules for remote sensing were dealt with in 1986, when the UN agreed that all activities should benefit all countries, respect state sovereignty over natural resources, and protect the earth's environment. There is no legal constraint on observing territories or broadcasting from space. In practice, this gives the West unlimited power to do what it wants, because few other countries can afford the freedom of space. States observed can obtain the raw information gathered about them in space at a reasonable price, but this is almost useless without the capacity to analyse the data. Space powers argue that because analysis is done on the ground, it is not a space activity and can be kept secret or sold at commercial rates, which are prohibitive for all but the largest companies and countries. By law, information relating to environmental protection and natural disasters should be provided to territories observed in an analysed form, but this is interpreted very narrowly since it also has great commercial value.

Cyberspace and information inequality

During the past decades the West has created an entirely new virtual geography of global communications networks, known as the internet or cyberspace. Its foundations were laid by the state, and funded through public spending on the military, space exploration and the universities, which are still the main providers. It has since expanded rapidly through commercial enterprise and the spectacular development of information technologies. These new communications technologies open immense potential for human freedom and development. They also accelerate commercial forces shifting investment and production around the world, transforming every society in their wake.

The laws and codes of this new world are effectively being laid down by the commercial companies which control the technology, leaving national governments and the International Telecommunications Union scrambling in the rear. The clear pattern emerging is that access to the new world of instant communications and infinite information on demand will be as unequal as the world out of which it grew, although the low cost of the technology offers possibilities for unlimited equality of access. These issues are beyond the scope of this book, but access to advanced telecommunications is the global equivalent of the Land Act in South Africa. This unequal pattern of development will accelerate as technology and information amplify the ability of powerful users to transform the world. In a world governed by information, exclusion from information is as devastating as exclusion from land in an agricultural age.

The laws of life: diversity and survival

Diversity is essential for evolution, biological and cultural. The Majority World is richest in both. Tropical rain forests cover only 7 per cent of the earth's surface, but contain about half of all living species. Indigenous peoples use and understand many properties of these species, not only as particular products, but as organic, interrelated ecosystems upon which they depend.

The spread of Western industrial civilization has already wiped out hundreds of indigenous peoples and thousands of species, replacing diversity with single-minded monocultures driven only by self-interest. The quest for profit and private ownership has extended some forms of human ingenuity and productivity at the expense of other civilizations and of nature.

The Majority World was the source of bananas, beans, coffee, cotton, hardwoods, indigo, maize, marrows, peanuts, palms, potatoes, rubber, spices, sunflowers, tomatoes and many other species which the West now takes for granted. Countless medicines owe their genesis or mass production to discoveries in the Majority World. The commercial value of genetic resources taken from the Majority World is probably greater than all the gold and other minerals extracted over centuries of conquest. Vandana Shiva, science and environment adviser to the Third World Network, has estimated that wild germ plasm contributed $66 billion to the US economy. It is estimated that its annual value to the pharmaceutical industry will rise from about $4.7 billion now to $47 billion by the year 2000.[34] The contrast between the West's approach to biodiversity and the law of the sea is a powerful illustration of one-sided law-making. With the law of the sea, the West refused to recognize the ocean floor as part of the common heritage of mankind. Since only the West had the capacity to exploit mineral resources below the seabed, it saw no reason to share control with anyone else. But since the greatest variety of plant species is in the Majority World, the West has insisted that they belong to the 'common heritage of mankind'. This rich stock of raw material is therefore used free of charge by Western transnational corporations to develop high-priced, patented biological commodities which are then sold back to farmers in the Majority World. The selective testing, gathering and breeding of plant species by generations of farmers in the Majority World is almost totally disregarded.

The legal framework for plant crops was first set in the early

1960s by the Union for the Protection of New Varieties of Plants (UPOV) Convention, which agreed to free exchange of existing seeds but gave plant-breeders protection for new varieties. These 'plant-breeders' rights' were the first step in creating property rights over living organisms. They did not, however, prevent farmers from saving seeds for replanting or other breeders from developing new varieties. Restrictions now being introduced will enable commercial breeders to demand royalties for the sale of crops and new varieties developed by others. Under pressure from Western countries, the Food and Agriculture Organization agreed in 1989 to exclude new varieties from the 'common heritage of mankind'. This restricted the right of farmers to sow seeds from each harvest or to develop new varieties from them. As a concession to the Majority World, the FAO recognized farmers' rights with respect to traditional varieties, but these rights accrued to governments rather than to the farmers themselves. This reinforced the principle of 'group rights' and gave the West another lever over Majority World governments.

The second area of international legislation on biodiversity is the 1993 GATT agreement, which established uniform rules to protect intellectual property rights (TRIPS), including the patentability of new plant varieties. This will increase control by the small number of giant corporations which dominate the seed and pharmaceutical trade, including genetic resources taken from the Majority World for free.

The Convention on Biological Diversity signed at the Rio Earth Summit on 5 June 1992 was the latest attempt to manage ownership and the control of biological diversity on a global level. For the West and transnational corporations, the key issues were intellectual property rights and patent protection, as well as access to vast genetic resources in the Majority World. For the Majority World, the main issues were the rights over the commercial exploitation of genetic resources, including material already in crop gene banks; the rights of local communities to conserve local ecosystems; access to and control over biotechnology; protection against the potential dangers of genetic engineering; and the fact that the Western-controlled World Bank will be responsible for financial mechanisms under the Convention.[35] Intensive work by the G77 countries and the Third World Network ensured that issues of biotechnology, safety and some concerns of the Majority World were included in the Convention, causing US President Bush to declare it 'seriously flawed' and to refuse to sign. President Clinton has since signed. But the Convention still cedes extensive control over the world's life-forms to Western companies, who can gain exclusive monopoly rights over genes extracted from the Majority World with no redress. This process is not only unjust, but has a far-reaching and destructive effect on the biological and cultural inheritance of the world's people.

Environmental space

The concept of 'environmental space' gives a tangible measure of the amount of physical resources which support human life. Friends of the Earth and the Wuppertal Institute calculated the environmental space used by the European Union in 1990. This shows that consumption in the EU 12 used a net area of about 121,000 km² (0.037 hectares per capita) of land outside its borders, equivalent to an additional 10 per cent of its agricultural land, an area slightly greater than Bulgaria, Malawi, or Nicaragua, or about half the size of the United Kingdom. Calculations for non-renewable material and energy use show that Europeans use about 80 per cent more resources than are available on a sustainable basis, most of them imported.[36] Average material consumption in the Majority World is many times less than this. But as more and more people aspire to dreams of consumption projected by advertising, the cost of resources may rise, conflicts increase and environmental constraints loom ever larger. All of these issues demand greater global cooperation, which depends on a common agreement on fundamental principles of justice and equity.

Unfortunately the West's selective, narrow and self-interested interpretation of international treaties means that space, air, oceans and life itself are seen as effectively within its domain. They are still treated by most Western governments as '*terra nullius*', free for appropriation by the powerful. Western control over the global commons is almost as sweeping as the Native Land Act of 1913, by which whites entrenched their ownership of 93 per cent of South African land.

Despite its overwhelming control over global resources under international law, the West frequently violates the sovereignty of the Majority World by breaking its own laws through covert destabilization and military intervention.

UNDERMINING THE LAW

Never once did I hear anybody, including myself, raise the question: is this course of action which we have agreed on lawful ... We were just naturally pragmatic.

Walter Sullivan, FBI, 1976[37]

Western disregard for international law is most evident in its support for dictatorships and its opposition to democratic or popular regimes it does not like. Like white South Africa's support of UNITA in Angola, Renamo in Mozambique and of other covert action, the West preferred to use front organizations or indirect measures to protect its interests. Secretary of State Robert McNamara wrote in 1967:

> The United States cannot be everywhere simultaneously. The balance of forces and the variable alternatives which challenge us in the changing contemporary world can only be conquered with faithful friends, well-equipped and ready to carry on the duty assigned to them ... The Military Aid programme has been devised to conquer such forces and such alternatives, since it helps maintain military forces which complement our own armed forces.[38]

The American war in Vietnam, Cambodia and Laos, in which about 4 million people were killed, had no basis in international law. McNamara has since confessed that it was utterly wrong. US military aid for the Nicaraguan Contras violated its own laws as well as international law. Covert support for the mujahidin in Afghanistan, UNITA in Angola, the military government of Indonesia, and many other unsavoury regimes had no legal justification. John Stockwell, the highest-ranking CIA official to denounce US covert action, has estimated that the United States was involved in over 3,000 major covert operations in which at least 6 million people were killed.[39] Stockwell himself served in the Congo and Vietnam before directing the CIA's war in Angola, where the CIA and South African Defence Force both supported UNITA.

After the shame of Watergate in the 1970s, American political leaders were concerned that cavalier attitudes to international law would damage the United States' reputation. In March 1974 Congress published a report, *Human Rights in the World Community: A Call for US Leadership*, which claimed that this attitude had 'led the United States into embracing governments which practice torture and unabashedly violate almost every human rights guarantee'.[40] The Carter presidency showed more respect for the law, but this did not prevent his administration from *increasing* military supplies to Indonesia after its murderous and illegal invasion of East Timor in 1978, bypassing congressional restrictions by sending jets via Israel,[41] providing military and moral support for General Chun's suppression of South Korea's democracy movement, or approving a $600 million loan to that country's military government just a few days after it inflicted horrendous violence on demonstrators in May 1980.

Under Presidents Reagan and Bush, the latter a former CIA chief, the secret services resumed covert wars in defence of US interests. Illegal action against Nicaragua resumed in 1982. In 1989 US forces invaded Panama, killing between 2,000 and 4,000 Panamanians. The invasion was illegal and contrary to the UN Charter and the charter of the Organization of American States. It was condemned by the United Nations as a 'flagrant violation of international law', in a vote of 75 to 20, with forty abstentions. The stated aims were to protect 35,000 US citizens in Panama, restore democracy and arrest the Panamanian leader, General Noriega, on drugs charges. Its true aims were to abolish Panama's armed forces, renegotiate President Carter's agreement to restore Panamanian sovereignty over the Panama Canal in the year 2000, and secure the future of the United States' military bases in Panama. These aims were finally achieved when President Clinton signed a new agreement with Panama in 1995. The military bases in Panama take US forces 2,000 miles South of Miami, extending their control over the Caribbean basin, South America and the Pacific Ocean. It was the twenty-first military intervention in Panama by US forces since 1903, and the most violent.[42] The United States had long tolerated illegal occupations of West Papua (Jaya Irian) and East Timor by Indonesia, of its neighbouring territories by Israel, and of Tibet by China, but in 1991 it led an international force of over half a million men to eject Iraq from its illegal and brutal invasion of Kuwait. John Stockwell cites evidence that the US provoked the Iraqi president, Saddam Hussein, to invade, in order to distract domestic opinion from the dire condition of the US economy and to 'erase the Vietnam war syndrome'.[43] The US covertly supported Iraq's illegal war against Iran and ignored atrocities committed against its Kurdish population. US companies profitably armed Iraq over many years, along with other Western countries, China and the Soviet Union. Whatever the exact truth, war was very convenient for President

Bush. Former US attorney Ramsey Clark visited Iraq during the war and condemned the indiscriminate destruction of civilian areas in which thousands of people were killed, as 'lawless violence' and 'most grievous violations' of International Laws of Armed Conflict.[44] Since the war, the Iraqi people have continued to suffer the collective punishment imposed by the West.

The Geneva Convention (1949) defines war crimes as indiscriminate air-bombing and military attacks, preventing medical attention from being given, and the use of weaponry that causes unnecessary suffering. Tragically, there is extensive evidence that the West, particularly the United States, has repeatedly resorted to criminal military action rather than use the International Court of Justice to resolve disputes.

Global interdependence makes a reliable and just system of international law essential for peace and security. There can no longer be any place for a private law of the rich and privileged which gives every tyrant a right to rule so long as they do not challenge the status quo.

SUMMARY

Laws of national sovereignty, private property and one-sided treaties, coupled with a ruthless disregard of the law when expedient, give the West unparalleled control over the world's resources through international law, just as white South Africans legalized their unequal control over the land. The hierarchical classification of people and countries into 'developed', 'less developed' or 'stateless' is used in international administration as a kind of common law population registration act with as much power over people's lives as racial classification in South Africa. This is enforced through immigration controls and routine decisions of the IMF, World Bank and other agents of the West.

Chapter 8 will describe how the West organizes its own affairs, protects its interests and secures global governance under minority control.

Further Reading

The global legal system

Mothersson, Keith, *From Hiroshima to the Hague: A Guide to the World Court Project*, International Peace Bureau, Geneva, 1992.

Pheko, S. E. M., *SA: Betrayal of a Colonised People: Issues of International Human Rights Law*, ISAL Publications, 1990, Skotaville, Johannesburg, 1992.

Postiglione, Amedeo, *The Global Village Without Regulations*, Giunti, Florence, 1992.

Sachs, Albie, *Advancing Human Rights in South Africa*, Oxford University Press, Cape Town, 1992.

Shaw, M. N., *International Law*, Grotius Publications, Cambridge, 1986.

Williams, Robert A., Jr, *The American Indian in Western Legal Thought: The Discourses of Conquest*, Oxford University Press, Oxford and NY, 1990.

The Western Alliance Government

American voters are going to choose a president – not just of the United States, but really the leader of the entire world.
President Bush, Oct. 1992[1]

I am not prepared to sacrifice my rights so that the other man can dominate me with his greater numbers.
President P. W. Botha, 1987

International law, the United Nations and agencies such as the World Bank, IMF and World Trade Organization are relatively marginal in global governance. While they often wield immense influence in the Majority World, most important decisions are made within exclusive institutions of the Western Alliance, including:

● informal communication channels, international think-tanks and forums;

● internal power structures of the US, Japan and EU;

● the Organization for Economic Co-operation and Development (OECD)

● the G7;

● the central banking system;

● military alliances such as NATO, ANZUS and the Western European Union (WEU), assisted by the secret services and covert action.

The unity of purpose between Western powers after centuries of intense conflict is one of the most remarkable achievements of the postwar world. For centuries war and fierce competition between European states were recurrent, despite intimate links among European rulers and royal families. Every Western state was deeply divided by class and regional conflict. Over half a million people were killed in the American civil war, more than 100 million died in Europe's many battles, and Western states slaughtered each other's people in two horrendous world wars. The unique feature of the postwar period is the extent to which deep differences have been settled within a common strategy.

Western power is the product of ceaseless conflict resolution and negotiation to contain competition and protect common interests. Western nations pooled their sovereignty, resources and military strength to an extent unprecedented among independent states. Weaving the intensely competitive states of America, Europe and Japan into an alliance was never easy. It continues to convulse with divisions, bridged only by a profound understanding that unity is power which open conflict would destroy. This is a truth which the white minority of South Africa well understood.

SOUTH AFRICAN PARALLELS:
A STATE OF BROTHERHOOD

White South Africa was created out of an uneasy union between four hostile territories after Britain crushed the Dutch republics in the savage Boer War. Despite deep internal differences, the white minority forged a powerful state capable of dominating the black majority through a web of cultural, economic, political and military institutions. Afrikaner, English and other white groups never fully integrated, but most accepted implicitly that survival depended on white unity.

For over half a century, South Africa's political direction came from the Broederbond (Brotherhood), a secret society of Afrikaners at the top levels of government, the military, church, media, academia and commerce. Founded in 1918, the Broederbond provided the mission and means for the Afrikaner minority to wield hidden power across the country. Its members ran cultural organizations, a youth movement, student groups, charities, trade unions, think-tanks, two universities, a teacher training college, an investment company and even a burial society. From the 1930s its members developed the principles of apartheid which were carried out with single-minded ruthlessness by the National Party. For over forty years the main planks of government policy were first discussed in secret and canvassed through informal channels of the Broederbond, creating a high degree of internal consensus and support. At its peak in the 1970s, the Broederbond was reputed to have 12,000 carefully selected members, organized into about 800 cells.[2] White unity was also maintained through careful distribution of power between the four provinces, with parliament in Cape Town, government in Pretoria, supreme court in Bloemfontein and the commercial industrial centre in Johannesburg. While the institutions of state, finance, industry and civil society worked closely together within the relatively closed Afrikaner society, each maintained a degree of autonomy that ensured debate about and joint ownership of key decisions, rather than transmission of them from a central authority. White provincial and municipal government also enjoyed considerable autonomy, raising most of their revenue from local taxes (rates) and service charges rather than from central government. Scope for debate within Afrikanerdom narrowed during the late 1970s as the security apparatus tightened in response to rising black resistance. In order to contain conflict, central government bypassed the *verkramptes* (narrow-minded) provincial politicians and white electorate to set up parallel structures to which more reliable *verligtes* (enlightened) businessmen, military officers or technocrats were appointed to modernize apartheid. Blacks, Coloureds and Indians were coopted alongside whites, under the direction, protection and pay of central government. Creeping centralization increased the sense of powerlessness among sections of the white minority while efforts to appease the majority deepened their insecurity.

White unity flowed, above all, from rising prosperity due to buoyant international gold prices, industrialization and plentiful low-waged black labour as well as privileged access to education, jobs, housing and welfare. For many whites, all this seemed threatened by reforms of the 1980s. Paradoxically, the Broederbond's success in securing Afrikaner prosperity reduced its importance. The business elite wanted to improve the skills, conditions and aspirations of black workers to meet rising consumer demand, while white workers, farmers and small businesses feared the erosion of their privileges. Government attempts to accommodate the non-white majority split the movement. Apartheid finally came to an end when white unity was no longer sufficient to sustain it.

BEHIND CLOSED DOORS

The world is governed by very different personages from what is imagined by those who are not behind the scenes.

Benjamin Disraeli (1804–81)

The West does not have one tightly knit group working behind the scenes, like the Afrikaner Broederbond, but many informal and exclusive international networks among academic, business and political elites. Considerable credit for the consistency of policies across the West is due to think-tanks such as the Council on Foreign Relations, the Bilderberg Group and the Trilateral Commission. Members of these groups influenced critical moments in Western development, helping to create the League of Nations, British Commonwealth, United Nations, Treaty of Rome, NATO and the G7 summits. Funding for these groups was almost entirely from charitable bodies set up by corporations such as Carnegie (steel), Chase Manhattan Bank, Ford, and Rockefeller (oil). In 1976 more than half of the world's 115 largest corporations and banks were represented on the Trilateral Commission.[3] There is a remarkable historical link between these groups and South Africa. Cecil Rhodes, flush with money from South Africa's gold and diamond mines, founded a secret society in 1881, which became the original Round Table Group in 1909. Rhodes aimed to create a federation of English-speaking peoples and to bring all habitable portions of the world under its control. Under the trusteeship of Alfred (later Lord) Milner, governor general of South Africa from 1897 to 1905, this group became a major influence in British imperial and foreign affairs up to 1939. Its members founded the Council on Foreign Relations (CFR) in America and the Royal Institute for International Affairs (Chatham House) in Britain. During the US isolation of the 1920s and 1930s, the CFR kept alive the flame of internationalism, collective security and free trade in its debates, research and policy papers. High points of the CFR's influence were planning the United Nations institutions and its policy of containment towards Communism. Its study groups prepared the ground for US intervention in Vietnam and Guatemala in the 1950s.[4] Dialogue and cooperation across the Atlantic were strengthened by close relationships with Chatham House. This shaped a common agenda on European integration, Atlantic alliance and management of the postwar world.

Since the 1950s, annual Bilderberg conferences have offered leading businessmen, bankers and senior politicians a 'high-ranking and flexible international forum in which opposing viewpoints can be brought closer together and mutual understanding furthered'.[5] President Eisenhower (president 1953–61) 'always had one of my people' attend[6] and sent his domestic policy chief Gabriel Hauge, who became director of the CFR from 1964.

Other influential participants included Secretary of State Dean Rusk, Ralph Dahrendorf, Paul Nitze, Robert McNamara and the first secretary-general of the OECD, Thorkil Kristensen.[7] In 1970 Bilderberg participant Zbigniew Brzezinski called for the formation of 'a community of the developed nations' composed of the US, Western Europe and Japan. He proposed a 'high-level consultative council for global co-operation, regularly bringing together the heads of governments of the developed world to discuss their common political-security, educational-scientific, and economic-technological problems, as well as to deal from that perspective with their moral obligations toward the developing nations'. Such a council 'would be more effective in developing common programmes than in the United Nations, whose efficacy is unavoidably limited by the Cold War and by north–south divisions'.[8] This led to the creation of the Trilateral Commission in 1971, with Brzezinski as director, and the first G7 summit in 1975.

The Trilateral Commission was initiated by Bilderberg members under the leadership of David Rockefeller of Chase Manhattan Bank in order to bring the rising economic power of Japan within 'the councils of real world powers'.[9] Its purpose was 'to generate the will to respond in common' to 'opportunities, challenges and responsibilities', and 'to promote among Japanese, West Europeans and North Americans the habit of working together on problems of mutual concern, to seek to obtain a shared understanding of these complex problems, and to devise and disseminate proposals of general benefit'.[10] Jimmy Carter was an active member of the Commission, crediting it with being 'a splendid learning opportunity'.[11] He drew heavily on it for his election strategy, domestic programme and foreign policy as well as key staff in his administration (1977–81). But in his acceptance speech for the Democratic presidential nomination, Carter implicitly criticized its influence as 'a political and economic elite who have shaped decisions and never had to account for mistakes nor to suffer from injustice'.[12] The radical right saw the Trilateral Commission as a liberal establishment conspiracy. William Loeb, publisher of the *Union Leader* in New Hampshire and early champion of Reagan's presidency, warned that 'this group of extremely powerful men is out to control the world.'

When the radical right gained power during the 1980s, the Trilateral Commission was eclipsed by free-market pressure groups such as the American Enterprise Institute for Public Policy Research (AEI), the Council for Inter-American Security, and the

Heritage Foundation in the US, and the Institute of Economic Affairs, Centre for Policy Studies, Adam Smith Institute, and Aims of Industry in the UK. The Reagan–Thatcher–Bush administration rejected every concession to the Majority World in favour of narrow Western interests. Together they stood firm against the New International Economic Order, Brandt Reports, debt forgiveness, sanctions against apartheid, Law of the Sea, regulation of transnational corporations and thousands of proposals aimed at improving conditions for the Majority World, right up to President Bush's defiant isolation at the Earth Summit in 1992. They brought about what is often called the 'lost decade for development'. This powerful regime was based on unprecedented coordination between conservative leaderships, to the extent that the same people advised on election campaigns, economic policy and social legislation on both sides of the Atlantic, including the South African National Party in the 1994 election campaign.

Members of the Trilateral Commission continued to influence the global agenda by working more closely with like-minded elites from the Majority World through high-level international commissions, including:

- two Brandt Reports on North–South relations in 1980 and 1983;

- the Palme Report, *Our Common Security*, in 1982, which advocated disarmament to pay for development;

- the Brundtland Report, *Our Common Future*, in 1987, on the global environment;

- Agenda 21, agreed at the Earth Summit in 1992.

Maurice Strong, secretary-general of the Rio Earth Summit in 1992, was a member of the Trilateral Commission, a trustee of the Rockefeller Foundation, chairman of Petro-Canada, head of the first UN conference on the environment in 1972 and first executive director of the UN Environment Programme. *Changing Course*, the manifesto of the global Business Council for Sustainable Development, came about at his request.

Compared with that of the Reagan era, the influence of the Trilateral Commission was benign, much as the relaxation of apartheid under P. W. Botha improved on the hard-line Verwoerd and Vorster regimes. But the debate about global governance was confined to a narrow constituency at the apex of Western power.

Options for wider participation or global democracy were not even on the agenda.

THE GLOBAL POWER ELITE

America is run largely by and for about 5,000 people who are actively supported by 50,000 beavers eager to take their places. I arrive at this figure this way: maybe 2,500 megacorporation executives, 500 politicians, lobbyists and Congressional committee chairmen, 500 investment bankers, 500 partners in major accounting firms, 500 labor brokers.

Robert Townsend, 1972, head of Avis car rental[13]

Most important decisions in the world are made by relatively few people – the top echelons of a dozen ruling parties, a few hundred massive corporations and finance companies. They in turn are served – and influenced – by senior civil servants, policy analysts, editors, a few thousand lobbyists, pressure groups and think-tanks: perhaps a quarter of a million people, less than 0.03 per cent of people in the West.[14] Each country has different power structures and degrees of decentralization, openness and accountability, but their elites often have more in common with each other than with their fellow-citizens.

At the pinnacle are a few thousand super-rich. They inhabit a world which scarcely recognizes national boundaries, served by a worldwide network of private clubs, private planes, private estates and private health care. Alongside them are the chief executives of the largest corporations which control a quarter of the world's production and 70 per cent of world trade. Occasionally individuals like Rupert Murdoch, Ross Perot or James Goldsmith use their wealth to take an overt political role. But most of their influence is indirect, through patronage, trade associations, advertising, media ownership, lobbyists and the pervasive power of money, ideas and organization. These powerful circles overlap with the political elites and senior civil servants who run nation-states. Although the leaderships of private, public and political institutions are increasingly interchangeable, they are distinct and subject to different pressures. While most may share certain assumptions, forces of competition frequently prevail over aspirations for cohesion.

These elites pursue a global agenda, sometimes in the face of fierce opposition within their own countries and ruling parties. The main elements of this agenda are free movement of capital, open markets, deregulation, privatization, currency stability, Western unity, high defence spending and access to low-cost resources. Western governments have sometimes overruled national considerations to support this agenda, in a genuine belief that it is in the best interests of their country as well as Western unity. The single market and European Union, NAFTA and the GATT agreement were pushed through at considerable political and social cost in many Western countries. Successive Japanese governments have suffered intense internal strife as a result of US pressure to cut direct taxes, reduce trade surpluses and increase military spending. Western European governments have maintained a united front over nuclear weapons and US wars in Korea, Vietnam and the Gulf, despite domestic opposition or a lack of any clear national interest.

The American elite has been particularly successful in keeping certain issues off the agenda and acting decisively against allied states which pursue independent policies. Regulation of transnational corporations, the arms trade, disarmament, global inequality and reform of international institutions are some of the issues which have been kicked into the margins.

These elites do not form a conspiracy or unified power bloc. As in South Africa, rivalries and shifting alliances within these exclusive circles often determine where the main power struggles of the West are fought and won, or lost. Ross Perot and James Goldsmith are notable for openly opposing the elite agenda. Behind the scenes Western institutions for coordination and consensus-building, notably the OECD, G7 and NATO, seek to reconcile differences and translate the agenda into practical politics.

THE ORGANISATION FOR ECONOMIC CO-OPERATION AND DEVELOPMENT

The OECD is unashamedly a rich man's club. It began in 1947 as a coordinating committee for European recovery and the Marshall Plan. It became the OECD in 1960 and now includes twenty-four of the world's richest industrial nations, plus Turkey and Mexico, with South Korea in the wings. Mexico was admitted to develop the political cohesion needed to manage the North American Free Trade Area (NAFTA), although Mexican average income is a quarter that of South Korea, Hong Kong or Singapore.

The OECD's role was candidly described by its secretary-general, Jean-Claude Paye, for its thirtieth anniversary celebrations in 1990:

> The OECD differs from any other international organisation in a number of ways ... First, there is the homogeneity of its composition ... The real common denominator of the club – for that is what it is – is to be found in its shared values. In the economic sphere, this means the market economy. In the world of politics, it is pluralist democracy, which all members have now recognised as providing the fertile ground which is needed to nurture the market economy, itself founded on individual freedom and initiative.
>
> Second, the OECD is notable for the way it works. In more than 150 committees and working parties, government officials and ministers ... experts from the academic world, business and the unions, meet to consider how to implement the best possible policies in their own particular areas of interest ... The collective wisdom it generates influences policy formation and development in member countries.

The article concluded: 'A club it is and a club it must remain – but certainly not a closed one.'[15] Monsieur Paye lists the 'dynamic Asian economies, Eastern Europe and 'Last ... a number of Latin American countries' if they are 'able to implement the policies that are necessary in order for them to play their full part in world growth.' In other words, 'you can join us by becoming like us'. In December 1990 the OECD adopted a Partners in Transition programme for the dynamic Asian economies (DEA) to become part of the OECD.[16] Africa, India and China – respresenting half the world's population – are beyond the perimeter walls.

This subtle process of selective cooption and creeping incorporation into the West contrasts with the equivalent exercise in South Africa, where elections for Indian and Coloured representatives led to riots among the excluded majority. The West is careful not to put too much emphasis on democracy until the outcome can be guaranteed. Thus NAFTA is a first step to incorporating Mexico, without any talk of North American political union as in Europe.

OECD membership is fundamentally about Western political cohesion and control. Many Majority World countries have higher industrial production than the small European OECD states, but they are not even invited as observers. For political reasons, Turkey is a member of both NATO and the OECD, although its average income is lower than those of twenty Majority World countries, including Brazil, Chile, Algeria and South Korea. On the other hand, Turkey's application to join the EU is repeatedly rebuffed, although about 3 million Turks live within EU borders. Turkey's political ties with the West are closer than those of former Communist states, yet the latter are ahead in the queue for membership.

While the OECD acts as a secretariat and think-tank for the West, global decision-making is undertaken by ministers and officials of the G7 richest nations.

THE GLOBAL CABINET

The annual G7 summit is the 'cabinet' of the Global Apartheid System. It brings together the heads of state, foreign ministers and finance ministers of the West's seven major industrial powers plus the president and top officials of the European Union. The summits have a key coordinating role in world affairs. Meetings address a wide range of economic, political, security, social and environmental matters. G7 decision-making includes regular meetings of ministers and senior officials during the year as well as working groups on specific problems such as airline hijacking or drug-trafficking. G7 finance ministers caucus before meetings of the IMF/World Bank while trade ministers worked closely together during GATT negotiations.

Like most national cabinets, G7 discussions are secret and its decisions express a consensus after hard bargaining behind closed doors. Its final declarations give symbolic authority to the values and principles which shape Western decision-making. The meetings also document changing preoccupations, priorities and emerging problems in the global system as perceived by its paramount rulers. Only three topics have been discussed at every meeting between 1975 and 1994 – monetary issues, trade and North–South relations. International debt, energy, environment and structural reform have been discussed at most meetings.

The summits were particularly important for developing a coordinated response to OPEC's oil-price rises after 1974 and to the issue of Majority World debt after 1982. They reaffirmed faith in free trade and low inflation as global economic priorities during the 1980s. They have reinforced Western resolve to tighten monetary policy and raise interest rates despite high unemployment in the West and devastating debt burdens for the Majority World. They have attempted to manage exchange rate fluctuations between Western currencies and defused conflicts between G7 members, particularly over agricultural subsidies, the collapse of the Soviet empire, environmental protection and GATT. They have confirmed common approaches to issues such as Afghanistan, East–West trade and arms negotiations, Vietnamese refugees, the Lebanon and hijacking. Above all, they have maintained the illusion of the legitimacy of Western control over global economic affairs, a charade perpetuated by most Western media.

The G7 is under growing pressure to become more representative. Since 1994 the president of the Russian Federation has joined summit meetings, making the exclusion of Majority World states even more conspicuous. China has a larger economy than Russia or all G7 countries except the US and Japan, and a bigger population than all eight countries together.

Michel Camdessus, the IMF's managing director, has suggested that the IMF's Interim Committee should replace the G7. This brings together twenty-four finance ministers from both the West and the Majority World in roughly equal numbers. It currently meets twice a year. Members have unequal voting rights and their focus is narrower than the G7's, but it is more representative. The Commission on Global Governance recommends that the G7 should be replaced by an Economic Security Council within the UN system, with twenty-three members representing the world's largest economies according to purchasing power parities and regional representation.[17] Replacing the G7 with more representative decision-making structures is essential if global economic instability and inequality are to be addressed. This is for the sake of Western communities as much as the Majority World, because ultimately we all suffer from a divided world.

But the G7 is neither the only nor the most powerful decision-making body in the Western Alliance. Far more powerful are the central banks, working closely together behind the scenes as I have described in chapter 5, and NATO, which is much more than a military alliance.

THE WESTERN SECURITY MANAGEMENT SYSTEM

Defence strategy embraces much more than military strategy ... It involves economy, ideology, technology, and even social matters ... all countries must, more than ever, muster all their activities – political, economic, diplomatic and military – for their defence. This, in fact, is the meaning of 'Total Strategy'.

P. W. Botha, South African minister of defence, 1975[18]

> Our new strategic concept reaffirms NATO's core functions and allows us
> ... to realize in full our broad approach to stability and security encom-
> passing political, economic, social and environmental aspects, along with
> the indispensable defense dimension ...
>
> NATO's Strategic Concept 1991

Every war is a civil war in an interdependent world. The West,
like white South Africa, has developed a concept of total security
which reaches deep into the economic, political and institutional
fabric of society. The sheer size of the West and its geographical
separation from the Majority World means that security is less
pervasive, less intrusive and more tolerant of dissent than it was in
apartheid South Africa. But for peoples who dared defy Western
dominance in Algeria, Vietnam or Latin America, its military
power was often even more deadly.

The West is responsible for over half of the world's military
spending, a quarter of its soldiers, 60 per cent of arms sales and
the world's most advanced weaponry. It has direct military
involvement in three-quarters of all countries, with permanent
bases on every continent, in the ocean and in space, protecting less
than one-sixth of the world's population. As in apartheid South
Africa, Western security is widely deployed among the excluded
majority, in the townships of Panama, the Philippines, Korea and
Central America. As in South Africa, the brunt of frontline
fighting is borne by men and women from the non-white majority.
Conflict with the Majority World rarely spills over into the politics
of the West itself and therefore appears invisible, but even this is
changing. The Palestinian war against Israel forced the aircraft
industry to increase security. Algeria's civil war flares up in the
streets of France. Intensification of global competition and population growth will undoubtledly increase Majority World wars
and bring them into the West.

For almost fifty years the cold war obscured underlying conflicts between the West and the Majority World, but NATO's
terms of reference have quietly been redefined. Western political
leaders are divided over future strategy and public opinion is
increasingly reluctant to support foreign wars without clear domestic benefits. This uncertainty creates opportunities to build
political support for an equitable system of global security. Military parallels with South Africa are less immediate than parallels
in other areas, although there are some common points of doctrine.

SOUTH AFRICA'S TOTAL SECURITY STRATEGY

White minority rule in South Africa required ever-increasing military control and repression of the majority during the 1970s as black resistance grew. In response, the government developed a security strategy based on French, US and Israeli experience in Indo-china, Algeria and the Middle East. Considerable power was vested in a National Security Management System, set up in 1986, with five broad aims:

- regional supremacy;
- total mobilization of white society;
- cooption and incorporation of as many black people as possible;
- ruthless suppression of opposition; and
- material improvements to buy off black discontent.

The first was largely achieved through overwhelming military power, while the second was attempted through an intense ideological onslaught. Cooption of black people partially succeeded by creating almost total dependence on the white economy, but it was an unreliable rankling subordination. The last two failed because they did not address black political aspirations.

South Africa became a regional superpower, dominating southern Africa militarily and economically. Neighbouring countries either submitted to cooperation on Pretoria's terms or became targets for destabilization. A senior apartheid official said: 'We want to show that we want peace in the region, we want to contribute and we can help a lot. But we also want to show that if we are refused we can destroy the whole of southern Africa.'[19] At home, Botha developed his 'total strategy'. Education, politics, the media and the economy were infused by the ideology of security at all costs. Whites were not allowed to know the arguments of the 'enemy', as the ANC and other opposition groups were totally banned from the media. All white men were conscripted into the Citizens Force for two years and could be called up until the age of 55. White society became the most militarized in the West, with the largest body of trained soldiers in Africa. Defence spending assumed immense economic importance, with over 20 per cent of the state budget directly or indirectly allocated for police and security purposes, over $3 billion (R9 billion) in 1985/6, almost a tenth of GDP.[20] Differences between black organizations were actively manipulated, fomenting a cycle of intercommunal violence. Homeland police forces were trained in repression. Traditional leaders and township entrepreneurs were wooed with patronage and protection, while opposition was ruthlessly crushed. Its leaders were imprisoned or eliminated, its supporters hounded and its arguments suppressed. Emergency regulations gave security forces sweeping powers to ban organizations, meetings and protests, detain people without trial and constantly harass any resistance. During the 1980s, over 30,000 people were detained, including 8,000 children and 3,000 women.[21] By destabilizing black communities at home and undermining neighbouring states, the minority government made it appear that black people were incapable of governing themselves and always fighting each other, so that white rule seemed a beacon of order and stability in a continent of chaos.

WORLDWIDE WAR ZONE

This has become a very small planet. We have to be concerned with all of it – with all of its land, waters, atmosphere, and with surrounding space.
                                        Dean Rusk, 1965, US secretary of state[22]

Since 1945 the United States has extended its global military presence as Europe withdrew from empire. It had military treaties with fifty states and supplied military aid to forces in about 100 countries. It had a million soldiers, marines and airmen stationed in some 400 major and 3,000 minor military bases across the globe.[23] Earthly fortifications were reinforced by military satellites, surveillance centres and the billion-dollar Strategic Defense Initiative ('Star Wars') in space. The US Department of Defense spends over $300 billion a year, more than the entire GDP of India ($215 billion in 1992).

Western political leaders continuously justify high military spending by asserting that the world is a dangerous place. General Douglas MacArthur, commander-in-chief of Allied forces in the Pacific and head of the military government in Japan from 1945 to 1951, declared in 1957:

Our government has kept us in a perpetual state of fear – kept us in a continuous stampede of patriotic fervour – with the cry of grave national emergency. Always there has been some terrible evil at home or some monstrous foreign power that was going to gobble us up if we did not blindly rally behind it by furnishing the exorbitant funds demanded. Yet, in retrospect, these disasters seem never to have happened, seem never to have been quite real.[24]

US intervention was as ruthless and unprincipled as that of apartheid South Africa. Support for authoritarian 'National Security States' in Latin America and Asia was as much part of US global policy as support for black dictators in the homelands was for South Africa. Like South Africa, it preferred quick military strikes against offending states such as Panama, Libya or Grenada, rather than the slow process of international law.

Since the army offered a career with better pay and training than anything available in inner-city ghettos, a disproportionate share of US military duty was borne by African–Americans. During the Vietnam War, 18 per cent of those enlisted, and over a quarter of all casualties, were black, compared with 11 per cent of the population as a whole.

During the 1981–9 Republican presidency, the doctrine of 'peace through strength' became a total security strategy almost equivalent to that of South Africa. Secretary of State George Schultz described this in a speech to a Pentagon conference on low-intensity conflict in 1986:

> We have seen and we will continue to see a wide range of ambiguous threats in the shadow area between major war and millennial peace. Americans must understand ... that a number of small challenges, year after year, can add up to a more serious challenge to our interests. The time to act, is not when the threat is at our doorstep, when the stakes are highest, and the needed resources enormous. We must be prepared to commit our political, economic, and, if necessary, military power when the threat is still manageable and when its prudent use can prevent the threat from growing.[25]

Although fear of Communism justified military intervention in the Majority World, the US military knew that the underlying causes 'exist within developing nations themselves and will not necessarily diminish even if Soviet international behaviour continues to moderate'.[26] General Gray wrote in the *Marine Corps Gazette*:

> The underdeveloped world's growing dissatisfaction over the gap between rich and poor nations will create a fertile breeding ground

for insurgencies. These insurgencies have the potential to jeopardize regional stability and our access to vital economic and military resources. This situation will become more critical as our Nation and allies, as well as potential adversaries, become more and more dependent on strategic resources. If we are to have stability in these regions, maintain access to their resources, protect our citizens abroad, defend our vital installations, and deter conflict, we must maintain within our active force structure a credible military power projection capability with the flexibility to respond to conflict across the spectrum of violence throughout the globe.[27]

Election of a Democratic Party administration in 1993 made little difference to the US war machine. Spending on nuclear weapons systems and Star Wars was reduced but not axed. Intervention in Iraq and Somalia continued. Training for low-intensity warfare went on, with 50,000 troops going through the *Cortina* programme every year in Arkansas and Oklahoma.[28] More effort was put into making other countries pay for American armed forces through a policy of multilateralism. The UN was still used to create the appearance of legitimacy, not as a genuine means of joint decision-making. President Clinton told the *Washington Post*: 'I still believe we ought to be aggressively engaged in the world' but said that 'you're never going to have the American people looking outward again, except when they think their interests are affected.'[29] With US interests spanning the globe, this would justify intervention anywhere, restrained only by a wary public opinion.

The cost of constant war

Every gun that is made, every warship launched, every rocket fired represents, in the final analysis, a theft from those who hunger and are not fed, who are cold and are not clothed.
Dwight D. Eisenhower, US president, 1953–61

In the thirty years after 1945, the world spent over $17 trillion on arms (at 1986 prices). Most of this money was wasted on cold war confrontation, but much was used in Majority World conflicts. Up to 1990, NATO and the Warsaw Pact accounted for over 80 per cent of world military spending and more than 90 per cent of all arms exports. In the 1980s, they dissipated $8 trillion of the world's resources, in cash terms – the equivalent of three years' income for all 4 billion people of the Majority World. Since then Japan and the Majority World have substantially increased military spending. This drain of resources was as damaging as the devastating use to which it was put.

Over 25 million people have died in wars since 1945, over 60 per cent of them civilians, almost all in the Majority World. Over half were in the Far East, particularly Korea and Vietnam, where the West was directly involved. The end of the cold war did not bring peace. Almost half a million people were killed in violent conflict during 1992, the largest numbers in Somalia and the former Yugoslavia. This figure was overshadowed in 1993 when three years of intensifying conflict in Rwanda erupted into genocidal massacres as hapless Western forces stood aside. Ruth Leger Sivard, Director of World Priorities and a former senior official of the US Arms Control and Disarmament Agency, summarizes the devastation of war since 1945:

> Deaths in wars represent only a fraction of the human losses. Judging from records available for recent wars, the number seriously injured may be several times larger. Material losses – in national income and foreign trade, in wrecked schools, homes, crops – depress living conditions and demoralize lives.
>
> The legacies left by the big wars of recent decades will stay to haunt generations to come: hundreds of thousands of mines in Afghanistan's fields, the defoliated forests of Vietnam. The costs in terms of global progress are incalculable. In property losses alone, one estimate is that they could reach $500 billion ... Deliberate manmade famine and destruction, however, lay a burden on aggressors and arms suppliers, as well as victims, which can fester like a wound that never heals.[30]

The West bears enormous responsibility for this waste of lives, resources and opportunities in the Majority World, from the legacy of colonialism to its projection of the cold war into the Majority World. European imperialism denied and delayed the Majority World's aspirations for self-determination. Imperial strategies of divide and rule deepened hostility between population groups. Indirect rule undermined traditional relationships of accountability between local leaders and the majority, strengthening authoritarian and rapacious rulers. Colonial frontiers served imperial interests and cut across traditional boundaries, sowing generations of antagonism. Since the Second World War, support for oppressive authoritarian rulers has perpetuated conflict. Both East and West have supplied arms which enabled local disputes to

become major conflicts. By denying local aspirations for independence and supporting repressive regimes the West has often created
opportunities for Communist intervention, opening the door to
advice and arms from China or the Soviet Union. In Angola,
Cuba, Nicaragua, the Horn of Africa, Vietnam and many other
countries and regions, national liberation movements have often
experienced Communists as friends of freedom in the face of
oppression and economic exploitation. The Security Council, in
which the West as well as the Soviet Union (now Russia) and
China have a blocking veto, has utterly failed to fulfil its duty
under the UN Charter, preserving only peace between themselves
and dividing the world into markets for their own arms and
influence.

The war business

As in South Africa, military spending and the arms trade have
created extensive vested interests dependent on tax dollars and arms
exports. During the 1980s, the US sold $134 billion-worth of
weapons and military services to 160 states and political movements.[31] Under President Bush, US arms sales doubled after the end
of the cold war, from $7.8 billion in 1989 to $18.5 billion in 1990.[32]
Sales leapt to $31 billion in 1993 as President Clinton continued the
high-pressure sales drive in desperation for jobs and economic
growth. Britain is second in the international arms bazaar, with sales
of $7.8 billion (£5.2 billion) in 1993, rising to $9 billion in 1994, over
a fifth of world arms exports, sustaining over 100,000 jobs.

Millions of people are employed directly or indirectly by the
military, individual and institutional shareholders rely on guaranteed rates of return, and arms manufacturers donate millions of
dollars to political campaign funds. Military spending creates a
pernicious web of 'pork barrel' politics which severely inhibits
any US government from reducing arms spending. Similar influences pervade all major weapons producers, including the post-
apartheid government of South Africa. It regards the industry as a
'very important technological base without which numerous job
opportunities would be lost'.[33] The ANC defence minister curtly
defended continued arms sales at its biannual military trade fair:
'We spent billions developing this technology ... We are faced by
enormous debts and our people are suffering.'[34] The arms industry
is a lethal trap ensnaring all who enter.

Table 12 NATO countries: military spending and resources as percentage of the world total (1986)

	No./amount	% of world total
Population	652 m.	12.8
Soldiers	6 m.	23.4
Spending	$395 bn.	48.0

In defence of common values

The core of Western security is the North Atlantic Treaty Organization (NATO), formed in 1949. It brings together the West's major military powers under a unified command. Its sixteen member states include the United States, Canada and most countries of Western Europe. France is a semi-detached member. NATO is above all a political organization, with economic and social goals set out in the Preamble to the NATO Treaty:

> to safeguard the freedom, common heritage and civilisation of their peoples, founded on the principles of democracy, individual liberty and the rule of law. They seek to promote stability and wellbeing in the North Atlantic area.

In 1986 NATO commanded half of the world's military spending, almost a quarter of its armed forces and its most advanced weaponry (see table 12).[35]

The end of the cold war led to gradual reductions in both spending and personnel, so that by 1992 NATO defence spending had fallen to $358 billion (1985 prices) and the number of soldiers had been cut to just over five million. At the same time, spending and militarization by the rest of the world continued to increase.

Within the West, NATO is largely seen as 'above politics' and supported without question by all major political parties, with some exceptions in Greece and Spain. One of its prime movers was Ernest Bevin, British foreign secretary in the reforming Labour government of 1945–51. In contrast to discussions on the European Union, there has never been a public debate about the irreversible decision to pool sovereignty in NATO, although it gives the power to make life and death military decisions to foreign commanders and demands greater financial commitments than the EU, without the political oversight by an elected assembly.

The political purpose of NATO is probably more important than its military role. NATO provides for continuous cooperation and consultation in non-military fields through civilian committees on political affairs, challenges of modern society, science, economics, communications, budget, infrastructure, armaments, defence review, nuclear planning, air defence, logistics and crisis management.[36] The North Atlantic Council is the highest authority in NATO and acts as a 'standing committee of governments'[37] for continuous consultation and coordination. It consists of the foreign and defence ministers of member states, who meet twice a year, and permanent representatives at ambassador level who meet at least weekly, and usually more often. A large number of committees prepare the Council's work and carry out its directives. As in all powerful institutions of Western rule, decisions are 'not taken by majority vote, but by common consent. Consensus is the rule throughout the Organization'.[38] The North Atlantic Assembly consists of 188 parliamentarians from member states and is part of the process of building support for NATO rather than a mechanism for public accountability. It meets twice a year and has committees covering civilian, economic, military, political and scientific affairs.

NATO's wider political purpose was first set out in a document know as the Three Wise Men's Report on Non-Military Cooperation,[39] accepted in 1956. This recommended that NATO's deterrent role depended on strengthening 'internal solidarity, cohesion and unity' which 'can be discharged only if the political and economic relations between its members are cooperative and close' (§9). The report was a highly significant statement of key principles underlying Western cooperation:

> In a shrinking nuclear world it was wise and timely to bring about a closer association of kindred Atlantic and Western European nations for other than defense purposes alone; that a partial pooling of sovereignty for mutual protection should also promote progress and cooperation generally. (§12)

The report contained many detailed recommendations for cooperation in cultural, information and scientific fields, based on a recognition that the autonomous sovereign nation-state was virtually obsolete:

The fundamental historical fact underlying development is that the nation state, by itself and relying exclusively on national policy and national power, is inadequate for progress or even for survival in the nuclear age ... the growing interdependence of states, politically and economically as well as militarily, calls for an ever-increasing measure of international cohesion and cooperation. (§36)

The report noted that 'it will be very difficult for member governments to carry [these recommendations] into effect' and emphasized the importance of a vigorous, concerted political effort to 'carry this conviction into the realm of practical government policy' (§38). This commitment to political integration of the Atlantic Community contrasts sharply with the West's policy and behaviour within the UN. The report emphasized the importance of 'continued and increased collaboration' through organizations such as the OECD, GATT, IMF/World Bank and UN Economic Commission for Europe, but warned against NATO members forming 'a "bloc"' since this 'would only alienate other friendly governments' (§65).

In order to consolidate political solidarity, wealthier NATO members contributed substantial aid to poorer members, particularly Portugal, Greece and Turkey. NATO economic policy includes a commitment to 'economically underdeveloped areas for reasons of enlightened self-interest and to promote better relations among peoples' (§35). In 1980, NATO's ministers 'reiterated their determination to work vigorously for a more effective and equitable world economic system'.[40] During the following decade global inequality grew more rapidly than before.

Extending the Western security cordon

The end of the cold war made the roots of conflict in poverty and inequality more visible. Within NATO this was recognized at the North Atlantic Council meeting in May 1989, when heads of state and governments set out their aspirations for 'a new pattern of relations between the countries of East and West, in which ideological and military antagonism will be replaced with cooperation, trust and peaceful competition'. They declared a commitment to 'search for solutions to those issues of universal concern, including poverty, social injustice and the environment, on which our common fate depends'. And they acknowledged that 'we will increasingly need to address worldwide problems which have a bearing on our security, particularly environmental degradation, resource conflicts and grave economic disparities'.[41]

This was reflected in an explicit recognition that future wars would be in the Majority World. The first US National Security Strategy of the new era, presented in March 1990, foresaw 'that our military power will remain an essential underpinning of the global balance, but ... the more likely demands for the use of our military forces may not involve the Soviet Union and may be in the Third World'.[42] Since almost every use of Western military force since 1945 has been in the Majority World, NATO policy was effectively catching up with reality.

In 1990 and 1991, NATO's heads of state and government issued three declarations setting out its new 'strategic concept' and opening the door to a wider international role. These were not widely discussed in public, although their implications are as profound as those of the Maastricht Treaty on European Union. The declarations commit the alliance to greater use of 'multinational formations ... within the integrated military structure' and

> mutual co-operation among sovereign states in support of the indivisibility of all of its members. Solidarity within the Alliance, given substance and effect by NATO's daily work in both the political and military spheres, ensures ... equal security amongst the members of the Alliance, regardless of differences in their circumstances.

They state that 'The risks to Allied security that remain are multifaceted in nature and multidirectional' including economic difficulties and ethnic rivalries in Eastern Europe as well as 'disruption of the flow of vital resources, and actions of terrorism and sabotage'.[43] Central to the new strategy is enlargement through the 'Partnership for Peace' Programme involving twenty-two Central European states, particularly Poland, Hungary, the Czech Republic, Slovakia, Romania and Bulgaria. North Atlantic states such as Mexico, Morocco, Senegal, Venezuela, or the Caribbean islands have never been considered for NATO membership, while Central European states became serious contenders for membership immediately after the end of Soviet rule.

Integration of the European wing of NATO through the WEU and the European Union is also continuing, although Western leaders face a dilemma between strengthening democratic accountability through the political structures of the EU or developing the WEU as a more secretive supranational structure alongside it.

Beyond Europe, the West is protected through numerous pacts, including the ANZUS Treaty of 1951 between Australia, New Zealand and the United States, and SEATO, the South-East Asia Treaty of 1954, committing the United States, Britain, France, Australia, New Zealand, the Philippines, Pakistan and Thailand to mutual defence.

NATO and other alliances are part of the intense but routine high-level coordination within the Western club which enables member states to present a united front against any challenge to their global interests. But the interests of Western countries are not identical and often conflict. Without the unifying fear of the Soviet Union, these conflicts are coming into the open, as has been demonstrated by the war in Bosnia. The West's ability to maintain political and military unity is increasingly tested by military conflicts throughout the world as well as by intensifying economic competition between Western powers themselves.

Competition for resources, frustrated aspirations and sheer deprivation in the Majority World and former Soviet Union are erupting into ever more numerous conflicts. The number of refugees worldwide is growing and will almost certainly increase. Wars, natural disasters and crises such as the floods of Bangladesh, famines of Africa, the Kurdish conflict and Rwandan genocide will inevitably grow in number unless the root causes are addressed.

CONDITIONS FOR GLOBAL SECURITY

Global security will only be possible if the West creates a just settlement with the Majority World. Lasting resolution of economic, political and military conflicts requires an equitable framework trusted by all sides. Only then can we begin to use the human ingenuity, material resources and lives now wasted on military effort to create real security. The experience of postwar Europe is a positive example of deeply hostile states deliberately pooling sovereignty and resources to tackle the causes of conflict.

The extension of the Nuclear Non-Proliferation Treaty in 1995 was another positive step towards greater global security, despite the decisions by France and China to continue testing. Much more needs to be done to:

- reduce and destroy nuclear arsenals under UN supervision;

- cut arms production and convert military industries to peaceful purposes;

- ban or severely restrict Security Council members from trading in arms and impose tight controls on all trade in weapons;

- strengthen economic, environmental, political and social measures to reduce the causes of military conflict;

- increase capacity for conflict resolution, through trained mediators as well as high-level political support through the UN and regional organizations;

- bring NATO, ANZUS, SEATO, CIS, the Pentagon and other regional military alliances under UN supervision and make them internationally accountable;

- create a UN Volunteer Force under the direction of the Security Council, capable of stalling military aggression;

- give whole-hearted commitment to the UN *Agenda for Peace*.

The twenty-three recommendations of the Commission on Global Governance also merit support.

There will always be a need for effective military forces to intervene in conflicts like those of Angola, Bosnia, and Rwanda, or even the war between Iraq and Iran. But intervention must be authorized and supervised within an equitable political framework based on just laws. To achieve this the exclusive institutions of Western rule must be opened to include the world's majority.

Opening the West

Western leaders frequently talk about 'bringing developing countries into the world economy'. The Majority World has been part of the world economy since the conquistadors plundered Mexico and Peru for gold and silver, African slaves were taken to America, and South-East Asia supplied spices to Europe over 500 years ago. Four decades of pledges to increase aid, open Western markets, and improve 'dialogue and partnership' with the Majority World have not addressed the fundamental inequalities in the West's use of global resources nor its control over decision-making. Reform of the West's own decision-making processes are therefore essential alongside the changes proposed in other chapters. The first steps should be to:

- abolish the G7 and replace it by a global coordinating body answerable to a reformed UN General Assembly;

- merge the OECD into a global social-economic partnership with the Commonwealth, the non-aligned movement and equivalent bodies;

- build international networks to enable people from all sections of society and the world to share experiences, learn from each other and develop a common understanding about world issues and local needs;

- give regional assemblies, such as the European Parliament and US Congress, an explicit role within a reformed United Nations, alongside the development of regional assemblies worldwide;

- enact statutes to limit powers of regional governments to those matters best dealt with at a regional level, such as protection of the environment, liberty, justice and equitable trade, as well as security;

- limit the accumulation of powers by state and private organizations and entrench the rights of subsidiary powers by local governments;

- make all states answerable to a permanent commission of the UN General Assembly for the effect of their decisions on other peoples;

- tackle the causes and manifestations of xenophobia and racism;

- deepen and develop civil liberties and democracy.

Such measures would bring global as well as local considerations to bear on decision-making within the West itself. They will not, on their own, abate the fears fuelling xenophobia and one-sided protectionism. For this we need to address the ideological foundations of the Western world order.

Further Reading

The Western alliance

Ambrose, Stephen E., *The Rise to Globalism*, Penguin, 7th edn, 1993.
Chomsky, Noam, *Deterring Democracy* (Verso, 1991), Vintage, 1992.

Gross, Bertram, *Friendly Fascism: The New Face of Power in America*, Black Rose Books, Montreal, 1980.

NATO Information Service, *The North Atlantic Treaty Organisation, Facts and Figures*, Brussels, 1989.

Schulzinger, Robert D., *The Wise Men of Foreign Affairs: The History of the Council on Foreign Relations*, Columbia University Press, New York, 1984.

Sklar, Holly, ed., *Trilateralism*, South End Press, Boston, 1980.

Wolfe, Alan, *The Rise and Fall of the 'Soviet Threat'*, Policy Studies Institute, Washington, DC, 1979.

9

The West Knows Best: Values and Ideology of Global Apartheid

[Our] way of life is based upon the will of the majority, and is distinguished by free institutions, representative government, free elections, guarantees of individual liberty, freedom of speech and religion and freedom from political oppression.

President Truman, Mar. 1947

South Africa is a democratically-governed state and it is a civilized state.

President P. W. Botha, 5 Sept. 1986

People need to believe in a system to make it work. When a society or group is under threat, ideology provides a rallying-cry to mobilize people to its defence. When an ideology loses credibility, as happened with state Communism in the Soviet world, the system crumbles. Empires which lose faith in themselves lose power.

Apartheid in South Africa was created piecemeal by a minority electorate frightened for their jobs and sense of identity, convinced of their innate superiority, and determined to keep exclusive control of 'their' country. They fought, prayed, schemed and voted to protect their privileges out of deeply rooted convictions. They institutionalized their beliefs through church, state, schools, families, media, laws and the very geography of the land. Their beliefs withstood powerful challenges over many decades. Apartheid ended as the ruling elite realized that the country's problems could not be resolved without a just settlement with the excluded majority.

Western power is motivated by beliefs more deeply rooted, diverse and enlightened than apartheid. Yet identifying common elements between these European belief systems may help us address the complex relationships between belief, action and social organization which perpetuate global inequality.

IDEOLOGY AS IDEAS IN ACTION

Ideology may be defined as the beliefs and assumptions of a particular society or social group. Ideology is not just an abstract set of ideas, but basic principles embedded in rituals, institutions and patterns of existence. It is a collective – and selective – memory, retaining ideas and assumptions for interpreting experience, answering fundamental questions, formulating aspirations and informing decisions. It enables people to act without going back to first principles. It creates a shared sense of meaning and purpose within which people develop their own ideas, goals and measures of achievement. Above all, it unites people in times of crisis.

Ideologies are complex social processes, constituting an all-pervasive fabric of thought and feeling through which we pattern our actions. Constantly recreated in everyday life and institutions, ideologies are never static, but respond to and shape experience. Ideologies are rarely homogeneous, but are as differentiated as society itself. Diversity of religion, politics, culture, nationality and beliefs within the West offers many options and conceptual resources to deal with social problems. This ideological diversity is a great strength which enabled Europeans and their American descendants to adapt and keep power despite centuries of conflict. Ruling groups have changed or been replaced, societies transformed, alliances reconfigured. Yet continuity has been maintained.

The ideas which inform the ground-rules, institutions and actions of those in power constitute the dominant ideology. These are not necessarily the most widespread ideas, but those which have greatest power over people's lives. They are not necessarily expressed, nor is the expressed ideology necessarily dominant. The real test is what takes precedence when a group or society is forced to choose. For instance, was access to global markets and finance ultimately more important than self-determination and local supremacy for the Afrikaner *volk*? Is national sovereignty more important for member states of the European Union than larger markets? Is the brotherhood of Islam more important than the statehood of Algeria, Libya, Egypt or Sudan? At a personal level, fundamental beliefs are similarly tested by choices between family or firm, friendship or faith, profit or principles. The degree of conviction with which different beliefs are held is decisive in times of crisis, when people are forced to choose. Everyday assumptions are stripped to the core for which people are willing to fight and give up everything, even their lives.

Values are the essential core of ideology. They answer the question 'why?' and express ultimate meaning and purpose. These beliefs are often emotional rather than intellectual, rooted in feelings and fears. Emotions express social bonds that go beyond conscious understanding, reaching realities deeper than reason. These include reflexes for preservation and protection of the self as part of society, such as love, loyalty and identity. Recognizing emotion as the foundation of values and ideology is not to abandon reason, but to understand its motive power.

Much ideology is instrumental, defining *how* things should be done, treated or seen. When circumstances change, old ways of doing things cease to work and people are forced back to basic values. Sometimes these inspire new ways of achieving ancient aspirations. Sometimes values themselves change as experience defies deeply held beliefs. Change itself is often generational, as elders give way to younger people growing up with new realities.

Everyday decisions by governments, courts, companies, media workers, teachers and individuals constantly test and revise the prevailing ideology. But there are defining moments when societies or institutions make crucial ideological choices that determine the future. Such moments are often cumulative. Countless individual choices imperceptibly mount up until one particular path becomes compelling. Like points in a railway line, that choice virtually closes down other options.

The union of South Africa in 1910 and elections in 1948 were two such moments, but there were many others before and after when individuals, institutions or sections of society made fateful choices establishing apartheid. In the United States, the rebellion against England, the Constitution, civil war and New Deal were decisive moments which built a powerful central federal authority rather than a patchwork of autonomous states, as in Latin America. The Allied victory in 1945 and creation of the IMF, World Bank, NATO and other institutions were decisive moments in the postwar settlement.

At the time of writing most strands of a new global settlement remain unresolved and open to influence. Creation of the World Trading Organization is a decisive movement towards a new global settlement, but significant details are still open. Revision of the European Union Treaty and the US presidential elections in 1996 and 2000 will be crucial moments. The prospect of unprecedented global instability over the coming decade is likely to crystallize in several defining moments that could either entrench global divisions or begin to overcome them.

The underlying issue, as in so much of modern history, is the conflict between extending competitive markets and protecting people from the adverse consequences of competition. This is not a theoretical issue, to be decided once and for all on the basis of abstract principles, but a process of political judgements which must include people's aspirations as well as assessments of the prevailing technology, economic conditions and likely consequences of any decision.

For the past fifteen years most governments and international institutions have emphasized wider markets and increased competition. This brought benefits to many people, but also created losers. As competition continues to intensify it is almost certain that pressure for protection will grow. The most likely outcome is one-sided protection that perpetuates the West's exclusive advantages in the global economy. Or it could be a step towards wider democratic participation and the development of more equal standards of protection worldwide.

In order to influence these epoch-making moments, it is not enough to know what is at stake in any particular decision. We need to address the core convictions which motivate people and the underlying forces at work in that moment. The lessons of white South Africans' search for protection against unrestrained competition are particularly relevant in the creation of a single global market today.

THE IDEOLOGY OF APARTHEID

We want each of our population groups to control and govern itself as in the case with other nations. Then all can co-operate as in a Commonwealth ... South Africa will proceed in all honesty and fairness to secure peace, prosperity and justice for all by means of political independence coupled with economic inter-dependence.

Prime Minister Verwoerd, 1961[1]

Like all ideologies, apartheid was never static. Its main principles, institutions and laws were created under British rule. 'Apartheid' only became explicit as an election slogan in 1948, when the word united the Afrikaner people against economic domination by the English minority and competition for jobs with the black majority.

It was rich with references to Christianity, divine destiny, civilized values and democracy, but the core beliefs were simple:

- Afrikaner nationalism;
- white superiority;
- submission to authority, notably God, church, state and the father within the family;
- fear of losing one's identity, of black people and of Communism.

These convictions changed in response to circumstances. Under Verwoerd, Afrikaner identity conceded parity to its ancient English adversary in order to maintain a common European union against the non-white majority. In response to external criticism, the blunt term 'apartheid' became 'separate development' or even 'separate freedoms'. During the 1980s there was a belated attempt to incorporate Coloured and Indian populations into the circle of privilege. Afrikaner economic success gradually eroded support for a state-dominated economy and gave way to faith in market competition. Black resistance also confronted the white minority with a radical threat to its privileges. These two forces gave rise to the central convictions of late apartheid ideology:

- national security and the ruthless protection of white interests;
- market liberalization as the main source of prosperity.

During the 1970s and 1980s the state was increasingly driven by security concerns. Responsibility for economic affairs was ceded to the private sector, although ultimately bound by security considerations. Both these changes also eroded Afrikaner identity and culture, particularly in the cities. Finally, as ever-increasing security failed to bring peace and market forces increased black economic power, the dominant minority was forced to reassess its overriding ideological principle – white superiority.

The gradual ideological shift at the heart of Afrikanerdom was fundamental to the transfer of power from the white minority. Frederik van Zyl Slabbert, leader of the anti-apartheid Progressive Federal Party, observed in 1984 that 'it is quite clear that those who govern have lost the ideological solidarity which first united them as a party. Bluntly, they no longer believe apartheid or separate development is going to pull us through.'[2] Loss of confidence was reflected in a change of rhetoric, from confrontation to talk of consultation, consensus and compromise. 'At the same time', van Zyl Slabbert observed,

> the degree of repressive tolerance has increased as this new rhetoric has flourished. Coercion and repression of extra-parliamentary opposition has become far more subtle and sophisticated. It would be very foolish to interpret this loss of ideological cohesion and the new 'reasonable rhetoric' as symptoms of a loss of will to dominate.[3]

The persistent, unchanging purpose of separate development as an ideology was to justify the privileged protection of the white minority. Decades of academic, anthropological, constitutional and theological contortions were ultimately no more than a rationalization of double standards. The question is, to what extent do the central principles of the West also justify double standards?

NAMING WESTERN IDEOLOGY

Unlike white South Africa, the West scarcely needed to justify its global dominance. Previous chapters have documented Western double standards in trade, finance, aid, defence, law and international institutions. Separate development is an institutional reality that does not need an explicit ideology like apartheid because it is built so deeply into the way the world works.

The difficulty of naming Western dominance makes it elusive and hard to challenge effectively. Colonialism gave national liberation movements a clear target, yet the eventual removal of direct rule left many peoples subservient to Western economic power. Anti-capitalism and the Communist cause inspired many, but even victory often brought disappointment and sometimes dictatorship, leaving Western hegemony undiminished. The most successful challenges to Western power are in global markets, where authoritarian South-East Asian states and corporations cooperate to undercut and out-perform Western producers. While specific aspects of Western power have come under attack, there has never been widespread opposition to minority rule in global governance, as there was over apartheid in South Africa.

'Global apartheid' refers to all aspects of minority rule in global governance through which Western states separate their 'own' people from the world's majority. Previous chapters have aimed to show that this structural injustice is as deep and as injurious as apartheid in South Africa, even though there are many differences between them. Global separate development was not an overt strategy but a consequence of the deliberate pursuit of common interests. Many Western leaders who sincerely pursue their nation's interests may even be horrified to realize that under present conditions this amounts to global apartheid. It is therefore essential to identify the specific elements of Western ideology underlying global apartheid in practice.

ELEMENTS OF WESTERN IDEOLOGY

Two world wars and the Great Depression taught Western leaders that the nation-state and nineteenth-century free-market economy were at an end. While they created supranational institutions to manage trade, finance and defence, domestic politics continued as if they were independent of the new global realities. For most of the postwar period, international affairs were largely bipartisan and conducted above national politics, often in secret. This separation between national and international affairs embodies the ideology of global apartheid, just as the separation of white parliamentary democracy from the black majority embodied the ideology of apartheid in South Africa.

The core convictions of Western unity were spelt out in the Atlantic Charter of 1941, with the key words freedom, democracy, development, human rights, peace and prosperity. But the underpinning political principle of Western unity was not liberty for all, but defence of Western interests and containment of Soviet influence. Fear of Communism was used to convince US public opinion of the need to spend large amounts of money on defence, rebuild Europe and Japan, and to intervene forcefully in other countries across the globe. Western unity required vigorous ideological effort throughout the cold war period. Democracy, human rights and the rule of law were often little more than rhetoric in the propaganda war with the Soviet Union rather than fundamental principles. Although the West tolerated much greater freedom than the Soviet Union, many of its interventions in the Majority World and the hounding of internal opposition betrayed its own ideals.

The core convictions underpinning Western unity are bound up with a bedrock of assumptions about Western civilization, the exercise of power, economic growth and the nature of human existence. A detailed analysis of Western ideology is beyond the scope of this book, but four fundamental principles may be clearly identified:

- an assumption of certainty and superiority, that Western ways are best, or indeed the only ways;

- national sovereignty and the defence of Western security, so that reasons of state override the rule of law in international affairs;

- the imperatives of property and market forces as the main means of increasing prosperity;

- democracy as an exclusive and national process about winning and holding state power.

Fear of Communism was a major factor throughout the cold war, particularly in the United States, but was not fundamental throughout the West, since Communist parties continued to win significant electoral support in Western European countries. Issues of identity played a recurrent part in most countries, but were not central, as they were in South Africa or in Germany under the Nazis. Western traditions of civil liberties, tolerance and the rule of law were important, but not central in the conduct of international affairs. The following sections consider the contribution of these four dominant assumptions to global apartheid and the selective way in which the media shape public perception.

Western superiority and the assertion of certainty

[C]onsider what a difference there is between the life of men in the most civilized province of Europe, and in the wildest and most barbarous districts of the New India; he will find it great enough to justify the saying that 'man is god to man'.

Sir Francis Bacon[4]

Throughout the epoch of Western expansion, men – and it has generally been men – have acted with the utmost conviction that they were right. Despite personal doubt and fierce debate among themselves, they knew best and acted accordingly. This profound sense of certainty was stoked by ceaseless competition for grades at school, admission to university, jobs, promotion, election, market share or the Nobel prize. By definition, Western leaders are winners. They know they have succeeded in a tough contest. However weak or insecure they may feel, winning means putting on a powerful front, for the prize is great and the winner takes all.

Certainty and an inherent sense of superiority are central to European action, although not unique to it. Ruling elites frequently believe themselves to be superior to the majority and many ethnic or religious groups believe they are inherently better than others. In many societies rulers exercise almost arbitrary powers of life and death over ordinary people. In the West – as in South Africa under apartheid – such powers are largely regulated by law. Western superiority is similar to white superiority in South Africa in so far as Western power is entrenched in international institutions, Western citizens have unequal protection under international law and Western economic policies prevail across the world.

Assumptions of superiority reach far into Western thought and feelings about the world. Rationality and the scientific method explicitly aimed to make men 'masters and possessors of nature'.[5] Marxism, Leninism and Trotskyism were no less certain than their opponents. The escalation of US intervention in Vietnam was inspired by certainty of victory, deaf to its adversaries or the terrible fate of its victims. Today the World Bank and IMF assert they know better how to develop the Majority World than those who live there. Likewise Western economists confidently calculate the costs and benefits of dealing with global climate change, dismissing alternative views as unbalanced. The West's faith in market-led economic growth is pursued regardless of casualties.

This one-sided cast of mind is perhaps the deepest and most powerful aspect of Western ideology, because it permits actions that seem contrary to nature, emotion, intuition or justice, but which deliver the desired result. Western certainty is more subtle than white supremacy. It permits, even encourages, people from the Majority World to participate, provided they learn Western ways. Vandana Shiva illustrates how single-minded certainty reduces complex relationships between people and trees to a functional, one-dimensional transaction based on cash.[6] Simple certainty replaces diverse natural and social systems with monocultures and wipes out sophisticated ecological resilience.

Paradoxically, the West acquired the power to assert its convictions as a consequence of humility, individual conscience, critical enquiry, due process of law, and values developed in opposition to authority. The challenge for a global society is to create a commitment to equality and diversity that recognizes the intrinsic value of each human being wherever he or she is born. One of the greatest obstacles to equality is the arbitrary distinctions between people according to nationality.

The imperatives of power: Western security and national sovereignty

In *United We Stand America* there's one filter, everything must go through it: is it good for our country?

Ross Perot, 1992
US presidential candidate[7]

National sovereignty and security form the core of Western ideology, just as they were the core of apartheid and Afrikaner nationalism. Both share assumptions and experience of European expansion, nationalism and conquest of non-white peoples. Democracy, free enterprise, free speech, social justice, rule of law, even private property and specific national interests have all been sacrificed for security.

The conceptual and emotional foundations of Western sovereignty are rooted in a sense of order, hierarchy and absolute rule that was only partially reformed by democracy. Nationalism grew out of ancient tribal sentiments and was used to integrate the diverse communities of Europe and the United States into multinational states. It inspired liberation movements in the struggle against colonialism. But nationalism, particularly ethnic and religious nationalism, has often proved an unreliable basis for states and has frequently been used to justify immense cruelty.[8] For many countries of the Majority World national sovereignty is little more than a brave flag and battered ship tossed on stormy commodity markets, currency flows and great power conflicts. In the poorest countries international agencies have more influence than the countries' own citizens.

The nation-state is ultimately about power, concentrating decisions and resources in a few hands to win in the competition between states. Since the First World War, no Western state has exercised complete sovereignty over its own affairs. This was explicitly recognized after the Second World War, as Western states increasingly 'pooled' sovereignty in NATO, the European Union and other institutions. The process was often uncomfortable as national pride, sometimes even national economic interests, were subjugated in the interests of the Western Alliance.

National sovereignty remains vital to the rhetoric of Western ideology because of its power to mobilize people, even at the cost of great personal sacrifice. It creates a sense of common interests uniting poor and rich in defence of the realm. National unity is not just about identity. It is underpinned by the franchise, public education, national currency, the rule of law, the defence forces and income redistribution designed to maintain social cohesion. It appeals to people's sense of belonging to a wider community rather than just being 'individuals and families' or an aggregate of consumers. 'National security' acknowledges that people have collective interests needing protection.

As global economic forces dissolve even the most powerful states into a multitude of niche markets, seize control of national currencies and obliterate national borders with electronic highways, national sovereignty is being replaced by private sovereignty that owes allegiance only to self-interest. It is too late for individual states to assert their power over money markets and global corporations. People can only regain control over their own lives if states pool their sovereignty to regulate the global economy.

The imperatives of property: market forces, consumer sovereignty and economism

> There are people who for a century have made it their point of departure that simply everything – even the survival of white civilisation – must be made subordinate to their so-called economic laws ... It is fortunate that under a Nationalist government these worshippers of economic laws have never had their way but that a higher and nobler goal has been strived after – the maintenance of white civilisation.
>
> *Die Transvaler*, 11 Oct. 1958

The dramatic extension of markets as the fundamental principle of society was the ideological triumph of the 1980s, as it was in Britain in the nineteenth century. Markets are in many respects the antithesis of apartheid, since traders disregard colour, religion or community in pursuit of profit and competitive advantage. Yet free trade brought Europeans into southern Africa, provoked apartheid into being and sustained the apartheid regime. Getting to grips with the power of markets is the central ideological

challenge for the twenty-first century, as it was for the first half of
the twentieth.

The ability to choose in markets is a liberating and creative
force, improving productivity, increasing opportunities and reducing central authority. But without fair rules, competitive pressure
leads to ruthless exploitation of people and the environment. The
West, like white South Africa, laid down rules for trade and
finance that gave its citizens better protection from the worst
effects of market forces and exclusive advantages over the world's
majority. The West never fully risked the dangers of a real free
market and protected itself through tariff barriers, immigration
controls, social security and extensive state intervention in industry
and finance, with some countries managing markets better than
others. Free enterprise is a flag of convenience for global corporations and the financial sector, which enjoy extensive privileges
and protection, as argued in chapter 4. Free-market rhetoric gives
the West a powerful justification to control Majority World
economies through unequal purchasing power, while restricting
their ability to compete on their own terms.

For a long time many Majority World countries were unable to
challenge the West's economic hypocrisy because they believed
markets themselves were the source of their problems. And they
were right, to the extent that they were forced to compete in
markets over which they had no say. Western markets were rigged
against them and they had little chance of protecting themselves
against the negative consequences of competitive markets while
reaping none of the benefits. Outright hostility to market mechanisms has largely evaporated among leaders and policy-makers in
the Majority World, to the extent that even Communist China and
Vietnam have embraced market forces.

Economic growth and the pursuit of material wealth have
become the dominant belief system ruling the world. Market price
has become the ultimate value against which everything, including
people and the environment, is measured. Growth is the primary
preoccupation of almost every society, political party and international negotiation. The pursuit of growth is entrenched in the
aims of the world's most powerful institutions, from businesses to
state treasuries, banks and the World Trade Organization. As the
most powerful and widespread ideology in global politics, it is
both deceptive and dangerous.

Increased prosperity and better material standards of living are
highly desirable, and essential for over a billion people living in
absolute poverty. But market forces alone cannot meet their needs.

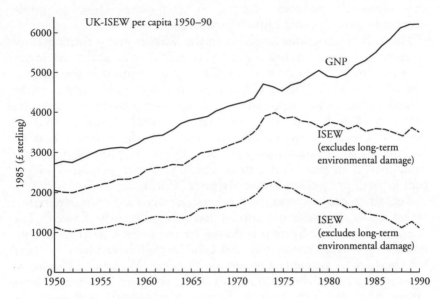

Fig. 4 Index of Sustainable Welfare
Source: New Economics Foundation.

The poor cannot buy what they need unless they work for the wealthy to earn money. If the wealthy do not buy, the poor remain idle. Often they cannot even buy basic implements to provide for themselves. The West used Keynesian arguments to manage markets, redistribute resources among themselves and secure social cohesion, while excluding the Majority World. Keynes still offers profound lessons for a new global settlement, but his work needs to be rethought to take account of the latest technologies, the new awareness of environmental wealth, the unpaid work of women and the intangible prosperity inherent in community. A new global economics is needed to challenge the very assumptions of international trade, competitive markets and unqualified growth.

Growth delusions 'Growth' is a theoretical representation of economic welfare. In some Western countries the gap between real welfare and 'growth' is widening to the extent that economic statistics are becoming as discredited as in the Soviet Union. The Index of Sustainable Welfare (see figure 4) is one measure of that gap. Purchasing power parties (see p. 107) are another indicator of the unreliability of cash as an economic measure. Just as growth in cars ultimately reduces mobility in congested cities, so crude economic growth can diminish prosperity.

The volume of goods available in the West is many times greater than at any time in history or throughout the entire Majority World. One per cent growth in Western economies is the equivalent of over $180 billion (1993 figures) more goods and services valued in hard cash, equivalent to 4 per cent growth in the entire Majority World. This is more than the total annual output of Austria, Denmark or Indonesia, and over three times that of Columbia, the Philippines, Pakistan, Egypt or Nigeria. One per cent growth in the West equals about $200 per person – 14 per cent growth per person in the Majority World.

Yet, when economic growth falters, Western societies experience severe crisis, because the model itself is inherently flawed. The Western Economic System is driven by the belief that there are no limits to growth. Profits, pay and GNP are all driven by the desire for the highest possible percentage increase. Percentages increase exponentially, so the amount added each year is several times greater than the year before. Exponential growth is deceptively rapid. Because we usually think in linear terms, it is hard to grasp the explosive potential of exponential growth. A growth rate of 1 per cent means an overall doubling in amount in seventy years. Seven per cent growth means a doubling in amount every ten years.

Sustained exponential growth is physically impossible, since the world is finite, so the drive for growth puts immense pressure on the global system. Energy use, greenhouse gases, deforestation, refuse and pollution are all growing exponentially. Many studies show that the world may be beyond its physical capacity to sustain the human population at current growth rates.[9] The aspiration of the Majority World to match Western levels of consumption is simply not viable on the present basis. It is certainly feasible for the Majority World to enjoy much higher material standards and greater economic welfare than the West, but only as a result of fundamental changes in economic organization.

Pressures of growth are absorbed to some extent through inflation, particularly in asset values (shares, property, land), luxuries (art, *haute couture*, cars), lotteries, arms production, and financial speculation. Some of this spurious growth is innocuous, but much has debilitating consequences. Illusions of growth are perpetuated by everything being sucked into the cash economy – replacing home cooking with eating out and ready-made meals, charging for formerly free services, privatizing public goods and making it necessary for everyone to work. Real growth in goods and services is much less than apparent growth, because it simply is not possible to continue to grow exponentially. But constant pressure for growth creates a treadmill which forces people to work for the use of money created by the West and its banks.

The ideological triumph of unregulated markets has a triple danger. First, many Western citizens believe it is their right to buy whatever they want at the lowest possible price regardless of the environmental and social costs. Second, Western leaders may believe their own rhetoric to such an extent that they reduce protection and abandon efforts to manage the market, causing social chaos. The third danger is that market liberalization produces political pressures to preserve one-sided Western privileges and that this causes a backlash against the Majority World. The challenge is to develop a framework for managing markets which provides equitable protection without weakening their creative potential.

Establishing equitable forms of collective sovereignty over market forces worldwide is a key task in challenging global apartheid. This means addressing the privileges of money, property, transnational companies and trade. The chief props of this ideology are numbers.

Ideology by numbers Numbers are often more powerful than words in decision-making, yet they can be less informative, more deceptive and less precise. Understanding numbers depends on context, assumptions and prior knowledge even more than with words. Yet as the world becomes increasingly integrated, decision-makers rely more and more on numbers abstracted from diverse circumstances. This was as true in the former Soviet Union as in the West, although the assumptions, theories and measures differ markedly. Today monetary measures are the most universal aid to decision-making in business and politics, with economics supplying the underlying lore. But in many respects they only work because people believe them. The entire edifice of credit and cash is built on credibility. It is a system of self-fulfilling prophecy, which works by redistributing resources by sleight rather than might.

For many practical purposes monetary units offer an acceptable approximation for use in everyday life, but aggregated into corporate balance-sheets, national income accounts or IMF data, they cease to be reliable. Economic data add up huge varieties of things which are scarcely comparable – apples, art, accountants' fees and accidents are aggregated into neat figures which are then invested with meaning. Comparisons between countries demand even greater leaps of imagination, and much technical adjustment. Although figures from different countries appear interchangeable, they can be as incomprehensible as Chinese characters in English text. Real comprehension consists of goods and services that change lands.

Aggregated numbers are enormously powerful in corporations, central banks, state treasuries and international agencies, so their consequences are colossal. This issue is beyond the scope of this book, but the sections on interest rates (p. 100), purchasing power parities (p. 107), and gross deceptive product and growth (p. 113) indicate why conventional economic numbers are insufficient to explain or manage the real economy.

Countries could be compared by many different numerical indicators – the number of religious buildings, the calorific value of food consumed per capita, free time per person, or the ratio of murders to mothers – but the most widely used is gross domestic product (GDP). This reflects a countries' purchasing power in international markets and is a benchmark for a wide range of decisions in global economic politics. The use of GDP is based on the dominant belief in trade as the engine of prosperity and money as a universal measure of value. Its power ultimately derives from the income, ownership and trade in property.

Privileges of property   Private property is the foundation of the market and Western ideology. As argued in chapter 7, property is a privilege, not a right. Modern property rights developed as a radical challenge to royal privileges and the established order in the seventeenth century, when men like Locke, Hume, Paine and Burke argued for a constitution based on contract, consent and the protection of life, liberty and private property. These concepts had a powerful influence on British politics, the United States Constitution, the French Revolution and the UN Charter. The underpinning assumption was that a 'free man' had independent means, so that only men of property could be citizens. Private property rights extend royal privilege to ordinary people, provided they have title to ownership. Although the power to vote has since extended citizenship to most adults in the West, independent means are still needed to exercise full citizenship.

In a global context, property rights are the ultimate basis of power. The West has been able to claim a disproportionate share of what is produced worldwide through ownership of companies, technology, intellectual property rights and above all, hard currency purchasing power. These privileges have been defined in such a way that most benefits flow back to the West. The West's shareholding in international finance and the World Bank/IMF as well as 'weight of trade' enables it to dominate international institutions, as argued earlier. Unlike in apartheid South Africa, property rights are not defined in racial terms, so that entrepreneurs and wealthy minorities in the Majority World can claim elements of global citizenship.

Reasserting social control over the privileges of property is a central challenge for a more equitable global settlement. Property relations are created and protected by society. They carry responsibilities towards society and the environment, which must be expressed in tangible ways. On a global scale this includes global taxation, currency management and international law governing global corporations, competition, investment, conditions of work and social responsibility. It also means enabling everyone to have a stake in property they can call their own, through redistribution and forms of tenure such as community land trusts, the Mexican *ejido* or other forms of common ownership appropriate to each society. Without this, global markets will condemn more and more people to economic serfdom. Social control is best asserted through democratic decision-making, an essential component of a market economy. Where democracy is diminished, markets become exclusive and oppressive.

Exclusive democracy and selective self-interest

The bottom line of these three core convictions is the self-interest of powerful people. The pursuit of personal profit and self-gratification through markets has become the core of Western ideology. This belief is repeatedly reaffirmed by the IMF, World Bank, G7 and Western elites, as well as through advertising and mass media. In a consumer culture identity is achieved by owning, not belonging. Loyalty is bought, not shared. Those too poor to own much are simply excluded. Without an underpinning sense of identity there is no basis for social cohesion or solidarity. National sovereignty provides a sense of solidarity and collective defence beyond the individual, but it creates an exclusive concept of humanity.

Democracy and freedom are watchwords of Western politics,

almost sanctified by histories of civil war and revolution in nearly every society, including white South Africa. When Dutch farmers left the Cape in 1836, one of their leaders, Piet Retief, declared 'We quit this colony ... to govern ourselves without interference ... We are resolved that we will uphold the just principles of liberty'.[10] The Boer War almost seventy years later was a desperate national liberation struggle, and apartheid itself was the ultimate defence of Afrikaner freedom. The vote was the crucial weapon with which poor white Afrikaners protected themselves against competition with the black majority on the one hand and exploitation by English employers on the other. Thus democracy for a few meant oppression for the many.

So it is for most people in the global economy. Western affluence, welfare states and military spending are paid for through the division of labour of global apartheid that encourages repression rather than democracy in the Majority World. Free trade and consumer choice for a few means low incomes, long hours and a struggle for subsistence among the many. While Western farmers, consumers and workers can lobby to protect themselves from the worst effects of global economic integration, the majority are swept along by tides of inevitability.

The struggle to create democratic institutions was essential for the evolution of the Western Economic System. They curbed powers of arbitrary authority and encouraged enterprise, enabling new ways of doing things to develop. They held rulers to account and mitigated the devastating consequences of economic competition. They created a framework of social security, economic management and regulation which enabled markets to thrive.

For all its rhetoric, the West has often been a poor role model in the practice of freedom. Democracy has little place in international politics except as a slogan. While G7 summit meetings praise democracy, their decisions frequently betray it. NATO, GATT, the European Council of Ministers and other treaty organizations make far-reaching decisions in secret, often with little deliberation by any elected assembly. Western resistance to national liberation struggles in former colonies and support for repressive authoritarian regimes, including white minority rule in South Africa, did more to undermine democracy than Soviet ambitions. Western intervention has repeatedly destroyed democratic development whenever people made the 'wrong' choice at the ballot box. Vietnam's democratic constitution of 1948 was thwarted by imperial France and its allies. In Guyana Britain replaced the elected government in 1953. In Iran the Mossadegh government was destabilized by the CIA and British agents. In Guatemala the Americans backed a coup against democracy in 1954. In 1973 Chile's elected Marxist president, Salvador Allende was overthrown with American encouragement. The US continued its illegal destabilization of Nicaragua after elections there in 1984. Western intervention eased with the end of the cold war, but trading interests still override concerns about human rights, democracy and the rule of law in international affairs.

Even in the West democracy rarely extends further than what is necessary for leaders to assume the mantle of legitimacy to control state power. 'Freedom' and 'self-determination' are often little more than an expression of collective self-interest, rather than an exercise in public participation to find the best possible solutions to social problems. Politics is a competition for voter support, in which party discipline and political realities are used to suppress the democratic processes of debate and considered decision-making. The combined pressures of security and economic management have eroded democratic participation in the West. Instead of using the potential of modern media to inform and engage people, the decision-making process is being withdrawn from local and national levels to non-elected bodies. The United States was in many respects the most democratic country in the world, with more than half a million elective offices in over 80,000 government units, from school boards and town meetings to the president. Yet America, more than any other Western country, put its faith in big business and allowed democracy to decay. A hundred years ago, voter turnout was consistently about 75 per cent, and stayed above 60 per cent until 1968. Today only half the electorate goes to the polls and the president is elected by less than a quarter of all adults. People with less education and income are also less likely to vote than more affluent, better-educated Americans. This shift in voting patterns means that most candidates pitch their policies towards the better-off 40 per cent of the population, eroding distinctions between political programmes. Thus Western political systems increasingly represent only the affluent, characterized by Kenneth Galbraith as the 'contented majority'.[11]

Decline in political participation has been matched by the dramatic rise of paid lobbyists, political advertising, television coverage and professional activists, turning the political process into a service industry in which influence is just another product to be bought and sold. At major political events journalists often outnumber participants, reflecting the transformation of politics into a spectacle. The takeover by the mass media creates a cash threshold which must be crossed to communicate with the public. Although the number of people voting in most Western countries has fallen, the cost of elections has risen. In US elections, most candidates for Congress now spend over $50 million on election campaigns. The 1992 presidential campaign cost more than $200 million, over $2 per voter.

Modern media make it impossible for anyone, even the most skilful politician, to communicate honestly with the public. David Gergen, media manager for Presidents Nixon, Ford, Reagan and Clinton, confessed that 'There have been so many lies told in the past, so many things oversold', and adds 'I plead guilty to doing a lot of it in the past.'[12] President Clinton felt obliged to hire Gergen, not to tell the truth, but to say what his administration needed to be heard. Politicians, too, have become prisoners of the system.

While the public is treated to a spectacle of caricatures, real politics continues in a hothouse of professional politicians, senior civil servants, pressure groups, lobbyists and corporate leaders. Battles within and between parties, companies and competing vested interests within the Western Alliance matter more than the hubbub of electoral democracy. As a result, the rules of trade dominate global politics while issues of the environment, poverty or justice remain secondary.

Democracy is not just a slogan, but a difficult and demanding process of collective decision-making. During the past two centuries, decision-making mechanisms in markets have developed dramatically. From a time when most people lived on the land, largely outside the market, the world has become a single interconnected market system in which almost everyone is linked through ceaseless flows of money, goods and information. Markets are governed by a vast range of rules, institutions and customs covering everything from weights and measures to futures and risk insurance. These rules are constantly evolving to cope with rapid changes in markets themselves. Compared with markets, democratic decision-making has scarcely developed beyond the invention of shares.

Democracy needs to work on many levels, from the neighbourhood, school, hospital and workplace to nations, regions, continents and humanity as a whole. The basis of democratic decision-making is inclusion and equal rights to participate in setting the frameworks which govern our lives. But for democracy to be effective people need access to decision-making, adequate information, and the power to participate. Information is the currency of democracy, just as money is the life-blood of markets. So long as control over information is dominated by corporate interests, democracy is diminished.

MASS MEDIA: FREE MARKET MINISTRY OF INFORMATION AND CULTURE

Mass media are less a source of information than of myth. They do not present reality, so much as self-contained worlds of prejudice and simple certainties. The Uruguayan writer Eduardo Galeano has bitterly commented that 'The majority must resign itself to the consumption of fantasy. Illusions of wealth are sold to the poor, illusions of freedom to the oppressed, dreams of victory to the defeated and of power to the weak.'[13]

Advertising is the world's biggest public education service and patron of the arts, entertainment and information. Advertisers' sole purpose is to persuade people to buy. Ernst Dichter, psychologist and 'father' of motivational research has described his work as the 'strategy of desire' in which the 'basic idea is that human desires are limitless'.[14]

Advertising is so pervasive it is taken for granted. It creates a colossal lie – that anything is possible, anything can be bought and happiness can only be found through consumption. Advertising fosters a permanent sense of dissatisfaction and yearning for more which can never be fulfilled. Advertising, entertainment, television, film and mass circulation press seep into the emotional vacuum within collapsing families and communities of the West, projecting imaginary worlds more real than the people next door.

Most media are an extension of commerce rather than a vehicle for citizenship. As television, newspapers and magazines depend more and more on advertising for income, they become agents for global companies and consumer religion. Advertising accounts for over four-fifths of media revenues, making the advertiser the client paying for readers' attention.[15] The main function of most media is not to inform, but to foster a climate of consumption. Even politics appears as an endless soap opera, a drama of clashing personalities and feuding factions, rather than a process in which people have a real stake and can take part.

Spending on advertising has risen dramatically since 1950, three times faster than world population and one-third faster than economic growth. Over $250 billion a year was spent worldwide on advertising in 1990. Americans are assaulted by more advertis-

Table 13 Ratio of advertising to education expenditure in five regions (US$ per head)

Country/region	Advertising (1)	Education (2)	Ratio (2/1)
USA	500	800	1.60
Japan	300	1,300	4.30
Western Europe	200	950	4.70
Mexico	25	100	0.25
India	1	10	0.10

Sources: Advertising: *International Advertising Association*, NY (1992); education: UN, *Human Development Report* (1993)

ing than anyone else, with companies spending almost as much per person as the state spends on education (see table 13). Deregulation of global television, diffusion of satellite broadcasting and the opening up of China, Eastern Europe and the former Soviet Union to advertising has made consumerism the fastest-spreading faith in history.

The world's media are controlled by relatively few giant firms. In 1981, forty-six companies controlled most US newspapers, magazines, book publishers, television and film. Ten years later just twenty-three companies dominated the industry. In 1945, 80 per cent of US daily papers were independently owned. By 1989 only 20 per cent were. American media control a high proportion of global information and entertainment, saturating public aware-ness with a relatively narrow spectrum of American values and concerns. News International's power is such that in 1995 Britain's prospective prime minister, Tony Blair, was flown to present his case to its global executives in Australia, much as activists in Britain's colonies used to go to London.

Most countries cannot afford to maintain extensive networks of foreign correspondents to supply their press and television, so they have little choice but to buy information from the West. This concentration of ownership over information dissemination ena-bles Western corporate interests to dominate the global agenda and creates a distorted picture of the world among Western citizens.

It's a small world for the West

People in the West are surrounded by images of the world. Television news begins with the revolving globe. Advertisers promise the earth. The tourist trade offers distant beautiful places. Environmentalists warn us 'not to spend it all at once'. Over and over, the message is: the world is at the West's disposal.

But people in the West are shown a highly selective view of the world. The Mercator map, on the walls of Western classrooms, newsrooms and war-rooms, puts Europe at the centre and shows the northern hemisphere occupying two-thirds of the globe's surface. Europe, with 9.7 million km², appears larger than South America, which is twice the area, at 17.8 million km². Scandinavia seems twice as large as India, which is in fact three times bigger. Africa looks smaller than the former Soviet Union, but in fact has an area over 25 per cent larger (30 million km² to 22.4 million km²). Most political boundaries on the map itself are Western inventions, etching imperial history into the very geography. Far-flung place names resonate with European identity – New York, not Land of the Iroquois, New Zealand instead of Aotearoa, or Lake Victoria in the heart of Africa. Naming was a process of appropriation, incorporating the world into Europe, so that distant places became extensions of home.

Television's apparently global reach is highly deceptive. Foreign news is a projection of domestic news – stories about American or European citizens abroad. The Majority World appears as a succession of calamities, interpreted by white presenters. Local people, mostly non-white, appear as nameless, voiceless evidence. Their deaths are numbers, hardly people. While the few Western aid workers and journalists killed in Somalia were big news, each individual life, work and tragedy featured prominently, the many Somali aid workers killed were silently added to the anonymous body-count. When four Western hostages were seized by Kashmiri secessionists in 1995, their plight was daily news, while an average of ten local people were being killed every day without comment. This difference in news coverage is understandable, but it inevitably projects distorted pictures of the world.

Black people are a small minority in the Western media, smaller even than their presence in the West itself. Their appearance is mainly linked with sport, entertainment or violence – riots in Los Angeles, Bradford or Marseilles. Successful black people reflect Western norms and successful assimilation. They contribute to illusions of equality and a non-racial society. The diversity of aspirations, lifestyles, poverty and wealth among peoples of every hue in the West, let alone the world, are omitted. Two-thirds of the world's people – the overwhelming majority – are almost invisible. They appear either as victims of disaster or exotic extras, their colour and context emphasizing 'otherness' to the white Western viewer. It has to be said that British broadcasting, private as well as public, is making real efforts to give greater insight into the Majority World, although there is still a long way to go.

Media images shape viewers' sense of reality almost as much as their daily experience. Their minds become trained to accept contradictions and conflicting perceptions. The effect of most images of people in the Majority World is to deny their humanity. People appear as an amorphous mass in distant settings with little in common with the West. This makes it possible for people in the West to accept suffering or the slaughter of war in ways that they would not tolerate among white people. Thus the war in Bosnia was almost permanently on Western screens, while the equally horrific bloodshed in Angola made only rare appearances. When Angola did feature, the news was mainly about Western aid getting through, not the causes of war and the West's complicity in it. The very same weekend as a mortar bomb slaughtered civilians in central Sarajevo in February 1993, a similar number of civilians were killed by UNITA forces in Angola. While Sarajevo dominated the headline news for days and provoked NATO airstrikes against Serbian targets, the Angolan atrocity received only brief reference inside the serious press. Yet the UN had equal responsibility for peace-keeping in both disputes. Even the secretary-general of the UN, Dr Boutros-Ghali, suggested that Western preoccupation with 'the war of the rich' in the Balkans at the expense of Africa was an expression of racism ('Maybe it's because I'm a wog that they don't listen to me').

After the Gulf War, the media curtain was quietly drawn as thousands of Iraqi men were bulldozed into mass graves and the 'turkey shoot' on the Basra road was shrugged off as a tragic necessity ('War is hell'). Oil and the returning heroes were all that mattered. In Afghanistan, Western concern lasted only as long as its geopolitical interest. Once the Soviets pulled out it ceased to be news, although fighting continued. The West turned away when the evidence of genocide was first reported in Rwanda, in contrast with swift intervention to protect Western lives in Algeria at about the same time. The few UN troops in Rwanda were withdrawn as the media watched the slaughter with helpless fascination.

Half-conscious differences in perception of white and non-white become even more evident when the images come closer to home and Haitians risk their lives to enter the United States or North Africans make their way into Southern Europe. The closer 'foreign faces' come, the more hostile the reaction. In Europe, racist parties are a significant political force in Austria, France and Italy, while gaining strength elsewhere. Neo-Fascists are in government in Italy and the European Union. In the US, racism is on the rise again and mainstream politicians campaign to defend the English language and American national culture from an alien invasion.

Racism is not respectable in the West. Nazi Germany left a genuine horror of racist ideology among Western leaders. Politicians across the political spectrum have taken a public stand against racism in America, France, Germany and the United Kingdom. Yet Western politicians tacitly, and sometimes openly, accede to populist racist pressures to increase immigration controls, curb imports or cut aid. The British home secretary used the threat from the far right to justify greater controls on immigration in 1992. In Germany all three major parties supported constitutional change to restrict refugees. The US racial filter means that over 100,000 Russians and East Europeans settled in the United States without question while Haitian refugees were turned away or interned. Distorted images of the Majority World foster an implicit belief in superiority which denies non-white people equal status with Europeans, not just politically, but as human beings. Racist movements do not even need to win seats to have power, because they tap deep currents within Western culture and politics.

SUMMARY

Western ideology is expressed primarily in the institutions of the postwar settlement, not words. It is manifest in the very different norms and principles which apply in domestic politics and international affairs, particularly between the West and the Majority World. While the West has espoused core values of democracy, free enterprise and the rule of law, these principles are often violated in the name of national security and national interests. Underlying Europe's global triumph is a sense of self-righteous certainty and the desire to maximize national economic benefits. Nation-states and the Western Alliance unite under a common identity to protect exclusive privileges which permit grossly unequal treatment of the world's majority.

These broad generalizations ignore great diversity and divisions within the West, but they seek to encapsulate the dominant themes of Western ideology in practice. As pressure of change forces people to redefine their core values in new contexts, and even to reform the institutions in which they are embedded, it is particularly important to think things through afresh. This is a moment of great opportunity and of danger which, over the coming decade, will shape a new global settlement.

Western politics are becoming both more polarized and fragmented, with bullish ferment on the radical right accompanied by tentative redefinitions of progressive politics on what used to be the left and centre, but may more usefully be called the new political holism. A new international community activism engages with the environment, human rights, global solidarity and local issues while the right targets power politics at a parochial and national level. As global competition intensifies there is a danger that national sovereignty, self-interest, employment protection and concern for the environment could continue to exclude the Majority World for the highest possible motives.

Many of the dilemmas facing the Western world can only be tackled on the basis of global cooperation. In this the remarkable transformation of South Africa from an exclusive state into a multiracial democracy may have lessons for the world.

Further Reading

Western certainty

Bacon, Francis, *The Advancement of Learning* (1605), Oxford University Press, 1868.
Bacon, Francis, *Novum Organuum*, (1620).
Descartes, René, *Discourse on Method* (1637), Penguin, 1968.
Shiva, Vandana, *Monocultures of the Mind: Perspectives on Biodiversity and Biotechnology*, Zed/Third World Network, 1993.

Nationalism

Davidson, Basil, *The Black Man's Burden: Africa and the Curse of the Nation-State*, James Currey, 1992.

Fanon, Frantz, *The Wretched of the Earth* (1961), Penguin, 1967.
Gellner, Ernest, *Nations and Nationalism*, Blackwell, Oxford, 1983.
Hobsbawm, E. J. *Nations and Nationalism since 1780: Programme, Myth, Reality*, Cambridge University Press, 1990.
Hutchinson, John, *Modern Nationalism*, Fontana, 1994.
Smith, Anthony D., *The Ethnic Origins of Nations*, Blackwell, Oxford, 1986.

Property

Brubaker, Elizabeth, *Property Right in the Defence of Nature*, Earthscan, 1995.
Dickinson, H. T., *Liberty and Property: Political Ideology in Eighteenth Century Britain*, Weidenfeld & Nicolson, 1977, Methuen, 1979.
Locke, John, *Two Treatises on Government* (1689), Cambridge University Press, 1963.

Critiques of economism

Daly, Herman E., and Cobb, John B. Jr, *For the Common Good*, Green Print, 1989.
Douthwaite, Richard, *The Growth Illusion*, Green Books, Bideford, UK, 1992.
Fromm, Erich, *To Have or To Be?* Jonathan Cape, 1978, Abacus 1979.
Hirsch, Fred, *Social Limits to Growth*, Routledge Kegan Paul, 1977.
Mishan, E. J., *The Costs of Economic Growth* (1967), Weidenfeld & Nicolson, revised edn, 1993.
Schumacher, E. F., *Small is Beautiful: A Study of Economics as if People Mattered*, Blond & Briggs, 1973, Abacus, 1974.
Waring, Marilyn, *If Women Counted*, Harper & Row, 1988, Macmillan, 1989.

New economic indicators

Anderson, Victor, *Alternative Indicators*, Routledge, 1981.
Jackson, T., and Marks, N., *Measuring Sustainable Development*, New Economics Foundation, 1994.
MacGillivray, Alex, *Environmental Measures: Indicators for the UK Environment*, New Economics Foundation, 1994.

Pearce, David, *Blueprint 3: Measuring Sustainable Development*, Earthscan, 1993.

Advertising, consumerism and media

Bagdikian, Ben H., *The Media Monopoly*, Beacon Press, Boston, Mass., 1983, 4th edn, 1992.
Clark, Eric, *The Want Makers: The World of Advertising and How They Make You Buy*, Viking, 1988.
Dichter, Ernst, *The Strategy of Desire*, TV Boardman, 1960.
Durning, Alan Thein, *How Much is Enough: The Consumer Society and the Future of the Earth*, Earthscan/Worldwatch Institute, 1992.
Herman, Edward S., and Chomsky, Noam, *Manufacturing Consent: The Political Economy of the Mass Media*, Pantheon Books, NY, 1988.
Leach, William, *Land of Desire: Merchants, Power and the Rise of a New American Culture*, Vintage Books, 1993.
Packard, Vance, *The Hidden Persuaders*, Longman Green, 1957.
Prendergrast, Mark, *The God, Country and Coca-Cola*, Weidenfeld & Nicolson, 1993.

10

Prospects for Improvement

> I have cherished the ideal of a democratic and free society in which all persons live together in harmony and with equal opportunities. It is an ideal which I hope to live for and achieve. But if needs be, it is an ideal for which I am prepared to die.
>
> Nelson Mandela, Rivonia Trial, 1964

> The time for fundamental change has inevitably arrived.
>
> President F. W. de Klerk, 22 December 1993

The profound parallels between apartheid and the global system mean that people in the West are as much part of institutional injustice towards the world's majority as white South Africans were towards their non-white neighbours. Culpability for inequality depends on how actively people support it and benefit from it, but everyone shares responsibility for ending it. The pattern is never static and in some areas it is changing dramatically. Rapidly industrializing countries like China and those of South-East Asia are challenge Western economic domination, while many people, particularly in Africa, experience severe hardship. Growing interdependence is forcing leaders of the West and the Majority World to seek common ground where once they were deadlocked. And internal difficulties within the West are causing many to rethink prevailing assumptions. These changes also had parallels in South Africa during the last decade of apartheid. Although South Africa's national liberation struggle was obviously very different from the new global politics, a surprising number of practical lessons can be learnt from the worldwide movement against apartheid.

THE UNRAVELLING OF APARTHEID

When F. W. de Klerk replaced P. W. Botha as president of South Africa in 1989, he frequently told journalists 'Don't expect me to negotiate myself out of power.'[1] His brother, a founder of the white liberal anti-apartheid Democratic Party, warned 'He is too strongly convinced that racial grouping is the only truth, way and life' to make any liberal leap of faith.[2] Yet within five years, the anti-apartheid opposition was unbanned, its leaders released from jail, exiles returned, the white minority had peacefully negotiated itself out of permanent political power and a government was elected by majority vote. White South Africa had the military and economic strength to rule for decades, although not indefinitely. What factors contributed to this momentous change?

The transition to democracy was no sudden conversion. No single moment marked the turning-point from white supremacy to majority rule. A myriad decisions in the lives of individuals and institutions marked the move away from inequality. When the white minority attempted to reform apartheid in 1984, it finally began to unravel, although it took another decade to die. Even if there were no parallels between South Africa and global inequality, there are important lessons in the process which brought apartheid to an end.[3]

The most important lesson is that no one strategy, action or group brought about change by itself. Apartheid did not end with the minority government fleeing from power in the face of irresistible opposition, although almost the entire strategy of the ANC was dedicated to this objective. The ANC-led liberation movement was central, but many groups, individuals and movements made a difference at particular moments. Against all the odds, people did not give up, and continued to find new forms of resistance. Sometimes resistance strengthened the regime's resolve, hardening the polarization, but it also shifted the balance of perception, particularly abroad. International solidarity, economic boycotts and symbolic actions such as the sports boycott made apartheid a major issue worldwide. It became harder for Western companies to support apartheid. The decision by international financial institutions to call in loans when township uprisings reduced South Africa's risk rating in 1985 was a major turning-point.

Splits within the ruling elite were also significant. The reactionary veto on reform was removed when the Conservative Party broke away in 1982. The Democratic Party breakaway in 1987 intensified the search for a way out. Theological opposition to racism was slow to grow within Afrikaner churches, but it caused soul-searching among the elite. Gradually, growing numbers of the white minority were prepared to jeopardize their privileges to side with justice. As the ruling minority lost conviction in its own mission it realized that apartheid had to 'adapt or die' and manœuvred to create a way out short of majority rule.

Broad-based alliances had a decisive role, starting with the African National Congress itself and the Communist Party within it, then the United Democratic Front and finally the awkward and extraordinary alliance between the ANC and its mortal enemy, the National Party. As the majority gained influence, white resistance grew in violence. The number of people killed during the transition to majority rule was greater than at any period during the entire liberation struggle, with over 15,000 killed in the final four years, compared with just over 5,000 in the previous four years,[4] almost all of them black people.

Perhaps the most remarkable lesson is the way in which an authoritarian, reactionary and repressive regime gradually discovered the intrinsic value of justice and integrity as a negotiating position, and how a disciplined, almost Leninist organization evolved into a broad, pluralistic movement as dialogue developed between these sworn enemies. Together they are creating a unique form of government in which all major interests take part, with none exercising a veto but the majority having ultimate authority. This pattern of government faces enormous difficulties and may not last, and the white minority still exercises disproportionate power, but it is very different from Western politics in which the winner takes all and losing parties are largely excluded from decision-making. In this respect the interim South Africa is more like the constant effort to achieve the maximum possible consensus in international treaty negotiations – except that the West has a veto which the majority dare not challenge.

Like the provincial run of an international epic, South African history played out a drama of European conquest, settlement, imperial consolidation, independence, cold war conflict and market liberalization. The West, too, fought liberation movements worldwide, in India, Indonesia, Ghana, Algeria, Vietnam, Angola and almost every part of the Majority World. But, unlike South Africa, the West seduced Majority World leaders into participating on unequal terms while keeping control of global governance. The West also faced internal opposition, but campaigns against the Vietnam War and nuclear weapons, and the movement for black civil liberties were more concerned with domestic issues than global justice.

GLOBAL NEGOTIATIONS

The West's refusal to address issues of global inequality has been as consistent as that of the minority regime in South Africa. Its ritual references to the needs of developing countries have been even more hypocritical than South African aid for black townships and homelands. In 1948 the US Congress refused to ratify an International Trade Organization (ITO), which could have established a fairer basis for trade. Proposals for a Special United Nations Fund for Economic Development (SUNFED) were rejected by the West in the 1950s. The UN Declaration and Programme of Action on the Establishment of a New International Economic Order in 1974, followed by more detailed agreements through UNCTAD in 1976 and 1979, were all sabotaged or dismissed by the West. In 1981 the moderate recommendations of the Brandt Report were summarily dismissed by British and US governments. Painstaking negotiations on the Law of the Sea, biodiversity and global climate change are still bedevilled by Western determination to protect one-sided privileges.

The 1992 Earth Summit, officially called the United Nations Conference on Environment and Development (UNCED), even had some similarities with the negotiations to end apartheid through the Conference for a Democratic South Africa (CODESA) taking place at the same time. Like CODESA, the Earth Summit brought together representatives of the rich minority and poor majority to draw up an agenda for a new future. Unlike South Africa, Western leaders did not even recognize there was a problem of legitimacy in global affairs. Like South Africa in the late 1970s, Western leaders know 'something must be done', but they cannot face the scale of the task. Western concessions at UNCED, GATT and climate negotiations were more parsimonious than even Botha's reforms, despite the generous rhetoric. The Rio Declaration and Agenda 21, signed at UNCED in June 1992, committed representatives of more than 150 countries to 'cooperate in a spirit of global partnership to conserve, protect and restore the health and integrity of the Earth's ecosystem'. They also undertook to 'cooperate in the essential task of eradicating poverty as an indispensable requirement for sustainable development' and to 'encourage public awareness and participation' in decision-making processes. Similar aspirations appear annually in G7 communiques, with no effect.

The UN Commission on Sustainable Development, set up to

follow up Agenda 21, may pass fine resolutions, draw up grand plans, exhort, wheedle and beg, but without political will by the West it can only offer ceremonial crumbs. The Majority World may be granted more administrative homelands, even diplomatic autonomy, with the trappings of international offices, conferences, perks and an occasional audience with the powerful. But until it can prevail over the combined might of the IMF/World Bank, Western central banks, financial markets and global corporations, they will be little more than political playgrounds. The global summits that really matter are the Uruguay Round of GATT, as outlined in chapter 3, and routine meetings of the G7.

Global environmental sanctions

At a global level, the natural limits of the planet are effectively imposing sanctions on the Western Economic System. Environmental threats to human habitation are a dramatic indication of the physical constraints on the current model of economic growth. These issues have been extensively documented[5] and need not be described here. But the accumulation of environmental problems of the atmosphere, biodiversity, chemicals, energy, forests, fish stocks, oceans, soil, waste and water affect everyone, inexorably forcing individuals, governments and companies to change their behaviour. As in South Africa, the costs of evading sanctions are increasing more rapidly than economic growth itself. Higher insurance premiums and risk ratings are already leading financial institutions to impose environmental conditions for good commercial reasons, much as they did in South Africa.[6] The risks of global environmental disaster could give the Majority World a new source of power in global politics. The West depends on the Majority World for intangible life-support services such as forests and wetlands which release oxygen from carbon dioxide, as well as for raw materials which are themselves environmental products. A Trilateral Commission report has pointed out that:

> increasing awareness of the threats to the environment has provided developing countries with leverage they didn't have before ... They can trade their participation in new international environmental arrangements against Western agreements to address the related issues that concern them most – better trade access to Western markets, debt reduction, technology transfer, and additional aid and investment.[7]

This leverage was evident during the Montreal negotiations on CFC emissions, when China and India insisted on resource and technology transfers as a condition of compliance. Malaysia forcefully resisted Western demands to preserve its rain forests, pointing to the deforestation still taking place in the West. The Trilateral Commission report comments that 'With this kind of negative power countries do not need to be rich and well armed to influence the behaviour of great states'. Ideally a new global settlement need not be achieved by force, but through mutual respect and determination to create a fair and sustainable world.

STRATEGIES FOR GLOBAL JUSTICE

[In Robben Island prison] We adopted a policy of talking to the warders and persuading them to treat us as human beings. And that is a lesson that one of our strongest weapons is dialogue. It has been a very powerful weapon.

President Nelson Mandela, July 1994[8]

We have also been liberated.

Former president F. W. de Klerk, May 1994[9]

People make things change. Everything we do has an effect on the global balance between the West and the Majority World, between humanity and our environment. Often the effect is unintended. Good deeds can have disastrous consequences, doing nothing can make a big difference, mistakes can bring blessings in disguise – or vice versa.

This section aims simply and directly to outline some of the things people can do to create a just, democratic and viable future. Whatever your starting-point, you can make a difference. The transition to majority rule in South Africa shows that change is possible. It may take a lot of effort over a long time, or it may happen suddenly. No single blue print will resolve the interrelated problems of our shared world, although plans will play a part. It is neither possible nor desirable to create a unitary world government to impose solutions, although some collective decisions may need to be imposed. Existing international institutions will be radically transformed whatever happens. The more this transformation actively involves people, the more likely it is to serve the whole of humanity, not just privileged minorities.

What is needed is a sense of strategy which enables individuals and organizations to decide for themselves how best to contribute to the momentous change which must take place for human life to thrive in the twenty-first century.

Restructuring for sustainable democracy

The goals of a campaign for global justice must be very clear and achievable. The task is immense, but the *scale* of institutional change is less than was demanded of the former Soviet bloc or than has been undertaken by global corporations over the past decade.

The greatest challenge is to enable a billion people living in absolute poverty to meet basic needs for water, food, shelter, security, good health and justice. They will never achieve this unless the West ends its unequal use of resources. It will take an immense transformation of production, consumption and decision-making. Real sacrifices have to be made for everyone to live better.

The cost of change is less than the cost of doing nothing. The new South Africa aims to spend between $12 and $24 billion dollars over five years to eradicate the worst iniquities of apartheid. This was equivalent to between 15 and 30 per cent of its GDP in 1990. At a global level this would be between $580 billion and $1,500 billion a year for five years. The West can afford similar sums and would find the money if it also had to answer to the global majority. The amount needed to restructure global institutions on a just and sustainable basis is within the order of magnitude of past commitments by the West. Britain and the United States spent half their national incomes to defeat German aggression at the height of the Second World War. The US committed $70 billion over five years (at 1991 prices) to rebuild Europe after the war. As a percentage of Western GNP, this is over $210 billion today. The US spent even greater sums on wars in Korea and Vietnam. The West continues to spend over $540 billion a year on the military, most of which is not needed for domestic defence. When West Germany absorbed East Germany it spent an average of $100 billion a year, levying a solidarity tax to pay for reconstruction, in addition to spending over $20 billion a year in aid for the former Soviet Union and substantial amounts for poorer regions of the EU. The West spends over $6 trillion a year on advertising, films and tourism. These are not more important than the basic needs of our fellow humans. The world can afford to eradicate gross inequality by the year 2010.

Demobilization after the war and the massive shift in Western industry from heavy engineering to services and new technologies prove that economic restructuring is possible. On a smaller scale, the utter transformation of Singapore from a disease-infested, overcrowded polluted city in the early 1960s to an affluent, efficient high-tech city in the 1980s shows what can be done, with determination, investment and political will. It may not be everyone's model of development, but it demonstrates that leaps are possible.

Nor should we forget that, by creating a large public sector, Western societies provided worthwhile services, an infrastructure and security for everyone, as well as jobs when fewer people were needed in agriculture and industry. Today's industrial revolution needs even fewer people and less energy to produce essential goods. Now we must ensure that the benefits of increased productivity are shared across the globe.

Many people feel helpless when faced with immense issues like global inequality and environmental destruction, but most of the changes required are worldwide rather than global. They can begin wherever you are. People learn by becoming involved, joining an organization and tackling issues that matter to them, then one thing leads to another. Starting at the local level is not just a question of tactics, but a recognition that all issues come together for each of us at a local level. That is where the global environment is, in all its messy, intricate reality. Neighbours threatened by road-building learn more about power, the state, vested interests, politics and planning by taking action than from books. Unique and complex relationships between soil, plants, people, politics and culture are rooted in specific circumstances understood by living and working in one place. Creating just and sustainable communities in one area gives inspiration to others.

The local is also linked with the global through air currents, trade, telecommunications and growing grassroots movements. This is not the same as the jet-setting officials and academics who dash from one international conference to another, but local initiatives linking together to learn from each other and join forces over specific issues. Some 5,000 groups have formed in the US to campaign against toxic waste dumps, linked through a state-wide network. Schools are using their own environment and global perspectives to reconstruct the curriculum. Local governments are using Agenda 21 to coordinate action on the environment and share experiences across the world. Human rights groups campaign for civil liberties and prisoners of conscience wherever they are. Women's groups are challenging their exclusion and lack of equal status in the global economy. Development charities are actively making connections between poverty and injustice. Trade-unionists are using electronic networks to build transnational solidarity on employment rights, education, the environment and economic change. Companies are taking positive steps to include environmental and ethical considerations in business decision-making. Some television and press in the West is improving coverage of the Majority World and global issues. Many of these movements have been celebrated by the Right Livelihood Award, the 'alternative' Nobel prize.[10] Since 1984, The Other Economic Summit (TOES), has pursued the annual G7 summit and media circus, giving activists in the Majority World a platform to challenge the West's most powerful leaders. These diverse movements are making a difference and there is a real sense that the tide is turning.

Global decision-making is a lot more accessible than many people imagine. Many international conventions allow non-governmental organizations to participate, and decision-makers in global agencies can often be reached more easily than their national counterparts. It is much harder organizing on global issues than defending local or national interests, which makes it essential to link global concerns with local issues.

The following sections set out elements of a successful strategy and specific goals around which people can organize. These twelve steps are not stages, but strands within a movement for a just global settlement that is already under way.

Recognition of the problem

At a strategic level, there needs to be widespread recognition that:

- the global crisis of poverty and the environment threatens human life and demands a fundamental transformation of worldwide political and economic systems;

- existing national and international mechanisms, including markets, companies, nation-states, regional power blocs and international institutions, have given rise to these problems and cannot solve them without far-reaching change;

- global inequality must end, not as a question of charity or reform, but of justice and survival;

- excess consumption and waste, particularly in the West, is linked with poverty and environmental degradation throughout the world;

- militarization increases instability and danger, not security;

- existing definitions of economic growth take no account of intrinsic natural, social and cultural wealth, the inestimable worth of each human being, nor the damage caused by industrial production;

- dominant Western values encourage greed, selfishness and envy, incompatible with security, community, public service, family life and harmony with nature.

There are many other problems within most countries, including those of the Majority World, but these strategic issues are a fundamental obstacle.

Recognition of these problems is growing, but so is narrow nationalism, xenophobia and the pursuit of short-term self-interest. Most political and business leaders are still driven by a desire for profit and growth regardless of the consequences for the environment or society.

Symbolic actions are particularly potent ways of highlighting problems.

Shared values

Values are the 'know why' of life. All faiths express historic values and the wisdom of our common humanity. Most contain beliefs unacceptable or oppressive to others. As we are brought closer together by communications and migration we need to respect different traditions and also create a shared ethic. The process of developing shared values is fundamental to coexistence on an increasingly crowded planet.

Visions of hope

In a world united by insecurity, competition and instant communications, we need a common statement of aspirations which can bring people together in a 'planetary patriotism' and global solidarity, much as the Freedom Charter did for many South Africans.

Most global declarations, including the Universal Declaration of Human Rights and Agenda 21, are a compromise between vested interests and aspirations towards truth. Any compromise with truth is an untruth and ultimately unworkable. All existing statements are inadequate for the unprecedented conditions we face. None take account of the ancestral wisdom of non-European peoples. The Charter of the United Nations, the Universal Declaration of Human Rights and the constitution of every state and international agency must be rewritten to take account of today's awesome realities. A worldwide Charter for Global Justice could become a focus for debate, education, coalition-building and action.

Practical programmes and projects

At a more day-to-day level there is a need for projects and programmes which put visions into practice. Many changes can begin on a local scale or within existing organizations without international agreement. Alternative models of development need to be tested and experienced before they will gain widespread support. In South Africa the most productive developments since majority rule were due to initiatives which began long before. The Programme for Reconstruction and Development for the new South Africa grew out of projects which struggled under the shadow of apartheid.

Clear goals

Clear and specific goals are essential. Vague aims can command a lot of support because they sound good and everyone can read their own meaning into them, but they are easily abused. Many liberation movements oversimplify their objectives into symbolic goals, such as national independence or seizing power, and then measure tactical activities rather than real progress. As a result, victory can be more symbolic than real. Successful struggles often produce the opposite of their original aims, like the revolutions in Mexico, Russia and many other countries. Goals are means to ends rooted in fundamental values and must therefore be consistent with them. The following five points summarize strategic goals for unravelling global apartheid:

First, Western governments, particularly Europe and the United States, must accept that they are part of an interdependent world. Responsibility for the global economy, environment, security and welfare must be shared. This means decision-making over resources and the rules of international relations must also be shared equitably.

Second, the institutions of world government – the G7, Security Council, NATO, central banks, IMF, World Bank, World Trade Organization, United Nations and its agencies – must be radically renewed to become more accountable, democratic, effective and efficient. UN agencies need to be strengthened in areas where global interdependence matters, such as the environment, global commons (air, sea, Antarctica, space), natural disasters, refugees, epidemic diseases (AIDS, bilharzia, malaria), and security. International Courts need greater powers to uphold international law and the Universal Declaration of Human Rights.

Third, global corporations and finance must be brought within a framework of international law, as set out in chapter 4.

Fourth, in order to pay for restructuring for sustainability we need global taxation, replacing discretionary aid with automatic transfers from rich to poor on the basis of need. Global taxes should aim to redirect economic activity along sustainable lines. This means taxes on CO_2 emissions, transport, pollution, extraction of non-renewable resources, carcinogenic products such as tobacco and pesticides, income from tariffs and on speculative currency transactions.

Finally, the most fundamental change needed is to rethink the principles of political economy upon which the Western world has developed. These are beyond the scope of this book, although many of the issues have been raised in earlier chapters. They include the principle that property ownership is a privilege which entails responsibilities; that the benefits of economic competition must be balanced by protection for those who lose as a result; and that markets created by society must be governed by society, so that every extension of markets must be accompanied by an extension of democracy. Greater debate and participation in decision-making is essential for the resources and intelligence of humanity to overcome the myriad problems of the twenty-first century.

Earlier chapters set out other changes needed in global institutions and the West itself. Local circumstances and opportunities will determine the most appropriate goals for each individual and organization.

Organizing for sustainability and survival

Organizing for change on a global scale is not the same as organizing a national liberation movement, such as the ANC. Most changes do not require global agreement so much as world-wide action that can be implemented without a central authority. Many organizations are working for a fairer and more sustainable future. They are more powerful when they act together, but diversity is also strength.

Different types of organization have different roles. Nation-states, political parties, faith communities, trade unions, voluntary associations (NGOs), interest groups, mass movements, think-tanks and pressure groups have different constraints and opportunities. The struggle for global justice is so big it needs all types of organization, from the one person gadfly to the maverick multinational corporation, determined local authority and pioneering nation-state.

The most important organizational principle is that joint work should be based on clearly stated objectives. It is not necessary for organizations to agree on long-term aims or even shared values in order to work together for specific goals, although the more values and aims are shared the more effective cooperation will be.

Networks are a more organic, creative model for organizing than the hierarchies which govern most organizations, including many liberation movements. Some features of effective networking are:

- a free flow of information;

- sharing experience, insights and skills;

- a core of shared values and principles;

- mutual respect and accountability;
- an evolving programme of key tasks and objectives.

The growth of non-governmental organizations and networks is a form of 'niche politics' that is both creative and powerful. This does not remove the need for integrating processes, including parties and parliaments, through which disparate interests are reconciled and reach collective decisions. Without forums in which all views and interests are represented and people are held account-able for their actions, important decisions are made by those with most power.

Alliance-building

Broad-based alliances have been central to almost every successful extension of democracy and overthrow of minority rule.[11] The role of alliances in political change is complex, but often follows three stages:

- forming and extending coalitions to oppose the existing order and promote a new one;
- weakening or disintegrating ruling coalitions, so that elements within them withdraw support or promote change from within, before switching allegiance and finally joining the movement for change;
- building pacts, either among all opposition forces or even between the regime and the opposition.

Heretical pacts played a powerful part in many revolutions. They can have a cathartic role in healing deep antagonism, as well as defeating intransigent resistance to any new settlement. South Africa was a classic example of this process of gradual but radical political change.

In the global transformation now taking place we need new alliances between communities and commerce, between local governments in the West with their counterparts in the Majority World, between officials employed by international institutions and the NGOs campaigning against them, between workers and management of transnational corporations and the people they affect. It is particularly important to forge closer links between the

West and the Majority World at every level, to create more opportunities for people of the Majority World to speak and work with people of the West on equal terms. Many Western problems are totally different when seen from the perspective of the Majority World.

Resources

It is more important to achieve something with few resources than to do nothing while trying to get more. Inner resources of courage, integrity, self-esteem and solidarity are a resilient basis for effective action. Do the best you can with the little you have. Match immediate goals to the resources available, but do not lose sight of the long term. Success attracts more resources, failure loses them. Building alliances pools resources. It can also drain them. Don't waste your resources on the opposition: build strength for your cause. Encourage or force the opposition to devote their resources to your goals.

Participation

People are the most valuable resource of any organization. This includes their understanding and experiences as well as their action and material support. Motivating people to participate is a vital source of strength. Broadening the base of the organization to include a diversity of people can also strengthen it. Different organizations need different kinds of membership and participation, but feedback and engagement with people beyond the inner core of active members is vital for any organization.

Indicators of success

You are more likely to achieve goals which can be measured and clearly identified. All indicators are proxies – money for wealth, rosary beads for prayers, qualifications for skills and knowledge, medals for bravery, infant mortality and longevity for the health of a nation. Appropriate indicators are a necessary tool for most human activities. Not only do indicators help to measure progress towards a goal, but they can be used to acknowledge and celebrate achievement, and encourage further development.

Appropriate measures for human liberation are needed at all levels, for public services, private enterprise and society as a whole. The United Nations' *Human Development Report* presents a valuable basis for international indicators. Regional, national and local indicators are also being developed.[12] At the same time, powerful and dangerous measures which inform most decisions by states, corporations and international agencies need to be abolished or radically transformed. These include the United Nations System of National Accounts (UNSNA), GNP/GDP, profit and loss accounting, and many forms of cost-benefit analysis.[13] Measures of success must go beyond the transformation of international institutions to redress the social, economic and environmental consequences of global separate development. The following ten targets provide specific measures for the end of global apartheid:

1   everyone has enough to eat;
2   access to clean water and sanitation is universal;
3   average life expectancy is equal, wherever you are born;
4   all have access to adequate housing, learning and health care;
5   adult literacy is universal for men and women;
6   everyone has an income sufficient to sustain life and income inequality is less than 1 : 15 worldwide;
7   average annual CO_2 emissions are below the sustainable level, estimated to be between 0.46 and 1.7 tonnes per person in every country;
8   all adults have a say in their government and equal representation in international institutions;
9   all have equal protection of the law;
10 all have equal freedom of movement worldwide.

Only when these goals have been achieved equally for men and women will it be possible to speak of one world.

Accountability

Be clear on whose behalf you are acting. At one level, we all act for ourselves and our own self-interest, which is bound up with the interests of particular groups. But we cannot assume that others agree with our view of shared interests or of how to achieve them. It is therefore essential to have appropriate forms of accountability to others, depending on the nature of the activity. In general, the greater the impact something has on people, the more formal and thorough accountability needs to be.

Sometimes it is necessary to act independently on one's own best judgement in defiance of received opinion, consensus or majority view. Nelson Mandela opened secret negotiations with the apartheid government from prison without a mandate. But he never broke faith with the mass movement to which he held himself accountable. Democratic accountability should not be allowed to impose injustice nor to give particular groups or individuals a veto over others acting in good faith.

Anticipate the opposition

Determined and powerful opposition forces are ranged against every movement for human liberation. Too many people have a vested interest in ignorance, inequality, injustice, exploitation and unsustainable industries to permit change without a struggle. Most people in the West benefit from low-paid work in the Majority World, one-sided protectionism and unrestrained use of natural resources. Many will resist change.

The Western political–economic system relies on illusions of growth for stability. When it loses momentum, it stumbles or even crashes. Although the West is materially richer than any society that has existed, every pause in the breathless rush for growth produces deep social spasms and despondency. Millions of people in the West are directly dependent on the deadly triumvirate of industries based on arms, money and oil. Have no illusions, but many powerful people are actively organizing to prevent greater justice and democracy.

The counter-action can be extreme – Chico Mendes and hundreds of people resisting the destruction of rainforests in Brazil, Thailand, the Philippines, Sarawak and elsewhere have been killed by landowners. The people of Vietnam, Chile, Cuba and Nicaragua paid a heavy price for overthrowing US-backed dictatorships and seeking their own development path. Tens of thousands of human rights activists, trade-unionists and democrats were executed by death squads in Latin America during decades of struggle against authoritarian rule. Workers demanding basic improvements in wages and conditions in the Majority World frequently face extreme force from employers and the state. The French government sent saboteurs to blow up Greenpeace's *Rainbow Warrior* in a New Zealand harbour. Non-violent opposition to road-building in Britain is met with violence and repressive laws. Opponents to environmental degradation by Shell Oil in Nigeria were executed by the military government.

Here are ten tried and tested ways of overcoming opposition:

- *Know your opposition*, preferably better than they know themselves. Understand their motives, decision-making processes and alliances. Talk with them, find out what their constraints are, what influences them, how far they might negotiate and how they respond to pressure (or flattery and seduction).

- *Anticipate their response.* Be prepared for a counter-attack with information, arguments or actions. Don't get too drawn onto their territory but ensnare them in their own rhetoric.

- *Be specific* about your immediate goals. Specific short-term goals will, if followed through, eventually transform the entire system. Attacking the whole system lays you open to total counter-attack. It is also demanding the impossible, since no system can be changed immediately or completely, even by those with most power in it. Choose a moment and a goal which will bring you closer to the ultimate aim and pursue the change you want clearly and precisely.

- *Act with integrity and honesty*, as openly as possible. Let people know what you stand for. Get public opinion on your side before the counter-attack begins.

- *Attack policies and actions*, not people. If you hurt people, they are even less likely to listen and more likely to hit back. Attack makes people defensive and potentially even more dangerous. Organizations can always change personnel to create the illusion of progress, without changing their underlying policies and actions.

- *Act through many leaders* and do not let particular campaigns become too identified with one person. A clearly identified personality is often necessary to communicate a message, but many voices travel further.

- *Give the opposition a way out.* Don't ask people to commit personal, political or industrial suicide. They will only redouble their resistance.

- *Make friends.* Creating enemies is a luxury no progressive movement can afford – there are enough without making more. The potential for creating alliances round specific goals is surprising, without collusion or capitulation. No one should be labelled 'enemy' unless absolutely necessary or they choose the label for themselves. Your aim is to turn everyone into allies. The test is whether they are capable of learning and what they do with what they know. There *are* enemies to the cause of equality and social justice. They can sometimes be very useful for tactical purposes, but do not let them waylay you or divert your energy.

- *Do not unite the forces of reaction.* Divide and undo is a strategy of the powerless. Some organizations with worthwhile goals are better at uniting people against them than achieving change.

- *Be persistent.* If you campaign about something you believe is important, and you put your case to the public and decision-makers clearly and persistently, you will be heard. Many campaigners eventually come in from the wilderness to advise or even implement their policies. Liberation movements throughout the Majority World entered government after decades of suppression. Opponents of totalitarian rule in the Soviet bloc are now ultimately responsible for their countries. Anti-racist activists become race equality officers, environmental campaigners become policy advisers and executives, community activists are employed as community organizers or stand for political office and get elected to carry out their ideals. You have to decide whether you are being coopted and neutralized, or whether you are capable of using a position in the system. Persistence may even persuade your opposition to adopt some of your ideas of its own accord.

If an organization is absolutely determined to block change, and all else has failed, it may be necessary to adopt more drastic measures. Violence and armed struggle are almost always counterproductive, because they give the opposition a licence to escalate violence against you, and this deforms political movements into quasi-military organizations, demanding discipline, loyalty and secrecy which erode democratic values. Violence also widens the gap between faithful adherents and potential supporters.

Rather than isolate yourself, isolate your opponent. Someone somewhere is responsible for blocking change. In a complex society it is always possible to pass the buck. Choose a powerful representative figure within the opposition whose decisions make a difference and focus the counter-attack on him. Pick a director or minister to *personalize and polarize the opposition*. The organization will eventually sacrifice that person to buy peace and signal a change in policy. It is unpleasant, but it works. They will do it to you. Do not do it unless absolutely necessary and your opponents have closed all opportunities for dialogue.

The most powerful forces of the existing order are far from unified. The end of the cold war removed one source of paranoia from US politics. Arbitrary authoritarian rule is being replaced by greater democratic accountability in many countries. There are many opportunities to shift the balance of power towards a more equitable, sustainable system.

The global regime will not change without engaging with the agencies and people who run it. Ultimately many of the changes needed will be the result of people in power deciding to do things differently, because they are pushed, deposed, removed, reorganized or undergo a change of heart. All revolutions have to work with existing institutions when they take power. What matters is that the goals are clear, just and widely supported. Global democracy begins from the bottom up as well as inside out.

CONCLUSION

Hereafter, perhaps, the natives of those countries may grow stronger, or those of Europe may grow weaker, and the inhabitants of all the different quarters of the world may arrive at that equality of courage and force which, by inspiring mutual fear, can alone overawe the injustice of independent nations into some sort of respect for the rights of one another. But nothing seems more likely to establish this equality of force than that mutual communication of knowledge and of all sorts of improvements which an extensive commerce from all countries to all countries naturally, or rather necessarily, carries with it.

Adam Smith, *Wealth of Nations*, 1776[14]

We have, at last, achieved our political emancipation. We pledge ourselves to liberate all our people from the continuing bondage of poverty, deprivation, suffering, gender and other discrimination ... My country is rich in the minerals and gems that lie beneath its soil, but I have always known that its greatest wealth is its people, finer and truer than the purest diamonds.

Nelson Mandela, 1994[15]

Adam Smith anticipated that global domination by Europeans would eventually wane, either through mutual force and fear, or through communication and commerce. China and Japan have the military and commercial capacity to challenge Western domination. Their success in industry and commerce is staggering, far greater even than it seems, since Chinese goods are undervalued in cash terms. But the 'injustice of independent nations' still persists through international institutions the West has created.

Smith was right when he identified markets and economic freedom as the most dynamic mechanisms for increasing prosperity, efficiency and liberty. He did not argue that markets or business should rule society, but that the sovereign (society) should lay down just laws to govern markets and prevent dealers from raising prices, suppressing wages or oppressing the public. To be effective, markets must be subject to a framework of law based on equality and justice. Democracy means that everyone must be able to participate in law-making to ensure that protection is equitable. When one section of society lays down the law to protect itself while excluding others, as in South Africa and in the postwar world, they create a system of separate development.

The anti-apartheid struggle in South Africa showed that victory is possible. When people focus on specific targets, they can influence even the most distant and powerful bodies in the world. Defiance campaigns, consumer boycotts and sporting bans raised specific issues in ways that general appeals to democracy and justice could not. Eventually the issue of apartheid in South Africa became a major preoccupation for the UN, international banks, Western governments and even transnational corporations until all agreed it had to end. The campaign against global apartheid deserves the same commitment.

Dialogue, diverse initiatives, persistence and a profound sense of humanity will eventually overcome systematic injustice and continue the long, slow process of freedom for all who share this beautiful planet.

Further Reading

The end of apartheid in South Africa

Mandela, Nelson, *Long Walk to Freedom: The Autobiography of Nelson Mandela*, Little Brown, 1994.
Sparks, Allister, *Tomorrow is Another Country*, Heinemann, 1995.
van Zyl Slabbert, Frederik, *The Last White Parliament*, Jonathan Ball/ Hans Strydom, Johannesburg, 1985.

Confronting environmental constraints

Bhaskar, V., and Glyn, Andrew, eds, *The North, the South and the Environment: Ecological Constraints and the Global Economy*, Earthscan/United Nations Press, 1995.
Brown, Lester R., et al., *State of the World*, Worldwatch Institute, Unwin Hyman, annual.
Friends of the Earth Europe, *Towards Sustainable Europe*, Brussels, 1995.
Holmberg, Johan, *Policies for a Small Planet*, Earthscan, 1992.
Houghton, J. T. et al., *Climate Change: The IPCC Scientific Assessment*, Cambridge University Press, NY, 1990.
MacNeil, J., Winsemius, P., and Yakuskiji, T., *Beyond Interdependence: The Meshing of the World's Economy and the Earth's Ecology*, Oxford University Press, 1991.
Meadows, Donella H., *Global Citizen*, Island Press, Washington, DC, 1991.
Meadows, Donella H., Meadows, Dennis L. and Randers Jørgen, *Beyond the Limits: Global Collapse or a Sustainable Future*, Earthscan, 1992.
Myers, Norman, *Deforestation Rates in Tropical Rainforests and their Climate Implications*, Friends of the Earth, 1989.
Schmidheiny, Stephan, *Changing Course: A Global Business Perspective on Development and the Environment*, MIT Press, Cambridge, Mass., 1992.
Smil, Vaclav, *Global Ecology: Environmental Change and Social Flexibility*, Routledge, 1993.

Challenging global inequality

Ekins, Paul, *A New World Order: Grassroots Movements for Global Change*, Routledge, 1992.
Karis, T., and Carter, G. M., eds, *From Protest to Challenge*, California, 1972.

O'Donnell, Guillermo, Schmitter, Philippe C. and Whitehead, Laurence, eds, *Transitions from Authoritarian Rule*, Woodrow Wilson Centre, Baltimore, 1986.

Rahman, Md Anisur, *People's Self-Development*, University Press, Dhaka/Zed Books, London, 1993.

Weisbord, Marvin R., and Janoff, Sandra, *Future Search: An Action Guide to Finding Common Ground in Organizations and Communities*, Berrett-Koehler, San Francisco, 1995.

Inspiring Change is an educational programme to improve personal and political effectiveness in your life and the world. Details from Inspiring Change, 32 Carisbrooke Road, London, E17 7EF, tel: 44+(0) 181–521–6977.

Sources

Where no place of publication is given the place is London or appears in the publisher's name.

Introduction: What is Global Apartheid and Why Does it Matter?

1 Policy Planning Study 23, partially reprinted in Thomas Etzold and John Lewis Gaddis, *Containment*, Columbia University Press, 1978, p. 226, quoted in Noam Chomsky, *Turning the Tide*, Pluto, 1986, p. 48.

2 Yehezkel Dror, *Ist die Erde noch regierbar?*, report to the Club of Rome, Bertelsmann, Munich, 1995; see also Yehezkel Dror, *The Capacity to Govern: A Report to the Club of Rome*, Circulo de Lectores, Barcelona, 1994.

3 The South Commission, *The Challenge to the South*, Oxford University Press, 1990.

4 Ernst Ulrich von Weizsäker, *Earth Politics*, Zed, 1994.

5 The Commission on Global Governance, *Our Global Neighbourhood*, Oxford University Press, 1995.

6 Gernot Kohler, *Global Apartheid*, Working Paper No. 7, World Order Models Project, New York, 1978.

7 Arjun Makhijiani, *From Global Capitalism to Economic Justice*, Apex Press, 1992.

8 Vandana Shiva, 'The New Environmental Order', *Third World Resurgence*, 20, Apr. 1992, Third World Network, Penang, Malaysia, pp. 2–3.

9 Clem Sunter, *The World and South Africa in the 1990s*, Human & Rousseau Tafelberg, Pretoria, 1987.

10   Group of Lisbon, *Limits to Competition*, Gulbenkian Foundation, 1993.

11   Anthony H. Richmond, *Global Apartheid: Refugees, Racism, and the New World Order*, Oxford University Press, Ontario, 1995.

Chapter 1: The World in One Country

1   Friends of the Earth Europe, *Towards Sustainable Europe*, Brussels, 1995, pp 51–2 and table 3.15.

2   Quoted in Walter E. Williams, *South Africa's War Against Capitalism*, Juta & Co, Kenwyn, South Africa, 1990, p. 23.

3   *The Wealth of Nations* (1776), 5th edn, ed. Edwin Cannan (1904), University of Chicago Press, 1976, bk IV, ch. vii, pt iii (vol. 1, p. 141).

4   Fernand Braudel, *The Wheels of Commerce*, Fontana, 1985, p. 568.

5   See Paul Kennedy, *The Rise and Fall of the Great Powers: Economic Change and Military Conflict from 1500 to 2000*, 1988, Fontana, 1989, ch. 1.

6   Quoted in Braudel, *The Wheels of Commerce*, p. 445.

7   Ibid. p. 432.

8   David E. Stannard, *American Holocaust: Columbus and the Conquest of the New World*, Oxford University Press, 1992, appendix.

9   Carlo M. Cipolla, *The Economic History of World Population* (1962), Pelican, 1974, p. 116.

10   Alfred W. Crosby, *Ecological Imperialism: The Biological Expansion of Europe, 900–1900*, Cambridge University Press, 1986, Canto edn, 1993.

11   Karl Polanyi, *The Great Transformation: The Political and Economic Origins of Our Time* (1944), Beacon paperback, 1957.

12   Donald Moodie, *The Record*, Cape Town, 1960, p. 206, quoted in Allister Sparks, *The Mind of South Africa*, Mandarin, 1990, p. 39.

13   Noël Mostert, *Frontiers: The Epic of South Africa's Creation and the Tragedy of the Xhosa People*, Pimlico, 1993.

14   L. E. Neame, *The History of Apartheid: The Story of the Colour War in South Africa*, London House & Maxwell, NY, 1963, p. 13.

15   F. A. van Jaarsveld, *The Awakening of Afrikaner Nationalism*, Cape Town, 1961, quoted in Sparks, *The Mind of South Africa*, p. 115.

16   David Welsh, *The Roots of Segregation: Native Policy in Colonial Natal, 1845–1910*, 1971.

17   Robert I. Rotberg, *The Founder: Cecil Rhodes and the Pursuit of Power*, Oxford, 1988.

18   J. A. Hobson, *Imperialism* (1902), 3rd edn, Allen & Unwin, 1938.

19   V. Lenin, *Imperialism* (1916) Progress Publishers, Moscow, 1978.

20   Alfred Milner, British high commissioner, 1904, quoted in Williams, *South Africa's War against Capitalism*, 1990 p. 16.

21 Premier Jan Smuts, quoted in David Yudelman, 'Lord Rothschild, Afrikaner Scabs, and the 1907 Strike', *African Affairs*, 81, 323, Apr. 1982, p. 257.

22 F. A. Johnstone, *Race, Class and Gold: A Study of Class Relations and Racial Discrimination in South Africa*, RKP, 1976, p. 72, quoted in Williams, *South Africa's War against Capitalism*, p. 50.

23 Quoted in Williams, *South Africa's War against Capitalism*, p. 54.

24 Anthony Sampson, *Black and Gold: Tycoons, Revolutionaries and Apartheid*, Coronet, 1987, p. 80.

25 Quoted in Williams, *South Africa's War against Capitalism*, p. 63.

26 B. J. Liebenberg, 'Herzog in Power', in *Five Hundred Years: A History of South Africa*, ed. C. F. J. Muller, Academia Press, Johannesburg, 1981, p. 417, quoted in Williams, *South Africa's War against Capitalism*, p. 42.

27 Sept. 1941; quoted in Williams, *South Africa's War against Capitalism*, p. 126.

28 Eugene P. Dvorin, *Racial Separation in South Africa: An Analysis of Apartheid Theory*, University of Chicago Press, 1952, p. 95.

29 Sparks, *The Mind of South Africa*, p. 227.

30 J. D. Fage, *A History of Africa*, Hutchinson, 1978, 2nd edn 1988, p. 442.

31 Sampson, *Black and Gold*, p. 131.

32 Ibid., p. 111.

33 *Financial Mail*, 11 Nov. 1983, quoted in Williams, *South Africa's War against Capitalism*, pp. 116–19.

Chapter 2: The Dynamics of Separate Development

1 Smith, *Wealth of Nations*, bk I, pt i (vol. 1, p. 15).

2 Karl Marx and Friedrich Engels, *Manifesto of the Communist Party* (1848), in *Selected Works*, Lawrence & Wishart, 1968, p. 40.

3 Smith, *Wealth of Nations*, bk I, ch. ii (vol. 1, p. 117).

4 Jeffrey A. Hart, *Rival Capitalists: International Competitiveness in the United States, Japan and Western Europe*, Cornell, Ithaca and London, 1992; M. E. Porter, *The Competitiveness of Nations*, Macmillan, 1990.

5 Smith, *Wealth of Nations*, bk I, ch. xi (vol. 1, p. 271).

6 Ibid., ch. xi (vol. 1, p. 102).

7 Ibid. (p. 103).

8 Ibid. (p. 108).

9 Ibid., ch. x (vol. 1, p. 111).

10 Ibid., ch. viii (vol. 1, p. 82).

11 Ibid. (p. 88).

12 Ibid., bk IV, ch. ix (vol. 2, p. 208).

13 Ibid., ch. vii (vol. 2, p. 125).

14 Adam Smith, *Theory of Moral Sentiments* (1790), ed. J. C. Bryce, Oxford University Press, 1976, II. ii. 3, 10.
15 Ibid., VII. iv. 37.
16 Smith, *Wealth of Nations*, bk V. ch. i, pt ii (vol. 2, p. 231).
17 Ibid., bk IV, ch. vii, pt iii (vol. 2, p. 102).
18 Ibid., bk V, ch. i, pt iii (art. i, p. 275); see also p. 157 n., and bk I, ch. viii (vol. 1, p. 82).
19 Ibid., bk I, ch. vii (vol. 2, p. 69).
20 Ibid., ch. x, pt ii (vol. 2, p. 151).
21 Ibid. (p. 143).
22 Ibid., ch. xi (vol. 1, p. 278).
23 Ibid., ch. viii (vol. 1, p. 75).
24 Ibid., ch. xi (vol. 1, p. 278).
25 Ibid., bk IV, ch. ix (vol. 2, p. 208).
26 Ibid., bk V, ch i (vol. 2, p. 305).
27 John Maynard Keynes, *The General Theory of Employment, Interest and Money* (1936), Macmillan, 1974.
28 Ibid., pp. 220–1.
29 Milton and Rose Friedman, *Free to Choose*, Pelican Books, 1980, p. 66.
30 Smith, *Wealth of Nations*, bk IV, ch. ii (vol. 1, pp. 481–3).
31 Ibid. (p. 475).
32 Ibid. (p. 477).
33 David Ricardo, *Principles of Political Economy and Taxation* (1817), Staffa, Cambridge, 1951, pp. 136–7, quoted by Herman E. Daly and John B. Cobb Jr, *For the Common Good*, Green Print, 1989, p. 214.
34 David Brion Davis, *Slavery and Human Progress*, Oxford University Press, 1984, p. 14.
35 Quoted in Peter N. Carroll and David W. Noble, *The Free and the Unfree: A New History of the United States*, Penguin, 1977 pp. 220–1.
36 Ibid., p. 223.

Chapter 3: The Economics of Global Apartheid

1 'A Century of Wrongs', *Review of Reviews*, London, 1990, quoted in Williams, *South Africa's War against Capitalism*, p. 126; Smuts was prime minister of South Africa, 1919–24 and 1939–48.
2 *Financial Times*, 13 Oct. 1993, Exporter Supplement, p. 31.
3 Edward Luttwak, Centre for Strategic and International Studies in Washington, quoted in Thomas A. Stewart, 'Sometimes Force is the Necessary Path to Peace', *Fortune*, 26 July 1993, pp. 122–30.
4 Walter Russell Mead, 'Bushism Found a Second Term Agenda Hidden in Trade Agreements', *Harper's Magazine*, Sept. 1992, pp. 37–45.

5 *Guardian*, 22 Sept. 1993, p. 18.

6 James Goldsmith, *The Trap*, Macmillan, 1994, p. 34.

7 Quoted in Alain Lipietz, *Towards A New Economic Order: Post-fordism, Ecology and Democracy*, Polity, Cambridge, 1992, pp. 123–4.

8 After meeting Jacques Delors, *Guardian*, 12 Jan. 1994.

9 G7 summit communique, trade, para. 4, p. 3.

10 Quoted in Kwame Nkrumah, *Neo-colonialism: The Last Stage of Imperialism*, Panaf, 1965, p. xvi.

11 Vanada Shiva, *Monocultures of the Mind: Perspectives on Biodiversity and Biotechnology*, Zed Third World Network, 1993, pp. 81–2.

12 Global Commons Institute, paper prepared for UN Climate Change Negotiations, INC7, New York, Mar. 1993.

13 Lydia Potts, *The World Labour Market: A History of Migration*, Zed, 1990, pp. 101–2.

14 Ibid., p. 210.

15 Susan George, *The Debt Boomerang*, TNI/Pluto Press, 1992, p. 123.

16 UNCTAD *Statistical Pocket Book*, 1994, p. 44, table 2.7.

17 Union Bank of Switzerland, cited in *Business Week*, 19 Dec. 1994, p. 42.

18 ILO data, cited in Colin Hines and Tim Lang, *The New Protectionism*, Earthscan, 1993, p. 77.

19 UNCTAD *Handbook of International Trade and Development Statistics*, 1976, p. 388 and 1983, pp. 485–90.

20 Adrian Wood, *North–South Trade, Employment and Inequality: Changing Fortunes in a Skill-Driven World*, Oxford University Press 1994.

21 Quoted in F. W. Taussig, ed., *State Papers and Speeches on the Tariff*, Harvard University Press, Cambridge, 1892, p. 213.

22 Ian Smillie, *Mastering the Machine: Poverty, Aid and Technology*, Intermediate Technology Publications, 1991, p. 14.

23 UNCTAD, *Uruguay Round: Papers on Selected Issues*, NY, 1989, pp. 349–50, table 4, quoted in Belinda Coote, *The Trade Trap*, Oxfam, Oxford, 1992, p. 94.

24 James Bovard, *The Fair Trade Fraud*, St Martin's Press, NY, 1991, p. 46–7.

25 Prbirjit Sarkar and H. W. Singer, 'Manufactured Exports of Developing Countries and their Terms of Trade since 1965', *World Development*, 19, 4, Pergamon Press, 1991, pp. 333–40.

26 Smith, *Wealth of Nations*, bk I, ch. xi (vol. 1, p. 278).

27 GATT, *Arrangements Regarding International Trade in Textiles*, Geneva, 1974, p. 9.

28 Chakravarthi Raghavan, *Recolonization: GATT, the Uruguay Round and the Third World*, Zed, 1990, p. 203.

29 Sheila Page, 'The Rise in Protection since 1974', *Oxford Review of Economic Policy*, 3, 2, 1987.

30 Estimates by the International Trade Commission, quoted in Robert B. Reich, *The Work of Nations: A Blueprint for the Future*, Simon & Schuster, 1991, p. 71.
31 Coote, *The Trade Trap*, p. 108.
32 Raghavan, *Recolonization*, pp. 83–9.
33 *Guardian*, 8 Oct. 1993, p. 17.
34 *Guardian*, 14 Apr. 1994, p. 17.
35 Vandana Shiva, 'TNCs Threaten Third World Farmers and Health through Free Trade', *Third World Resurgence*, 18 Jan. 1992, pp. 15–17.
36 Douglas Harbrecht, 'GATT: Tales from the Dark Side', *Business Week*, 19 Dec. 1994, p. 13.
37 World Bank, *World Development Report 1992*, Oxford University Press, p. 122.
38 EC Regional Policies, *inforegio news*, no. 1, Feb. 1994.
39 Coote, *The Trade Trap*, pp. 37–9.
40 Coote, *The Hunger Crop: Poverty and the Sugar Industry*, Oxfam, Oxford, 1987. See also World Bank, *World Development Report 1990*, Oxford University Press, p. 122.
41 UN Centre on Transnational Corporations, *The Impact of Trade Related Investment Measures on Trade and Development*, UN Publication No. E91.II.A.19, 1991, p. 74; E93 II, A.14, 1993; p. 227.
42 Harold M. Hubbard, 'The Real Cost of Energy', *Scientific American*, Apr. 1991, p. 10.

Chapter 4: Global Privileges of Private Enterprise

1 Smith, *Wealth of Nations*, bk III, ch. iv (vol. 1, p. 444–5).
2 N. Horn and J. Kocka, eds, *Law and the Formation of the Big Enterprises in the 19th and Early 20th Centuries*, Vandenhoeck & Ruprecht, Göttingen, 1979.
3 Robert A. G. Monks and Nell Minow, *Power and Accountability*, HarperCollins, 1991.
4 Laurence Kallen, *Corporate Welfare: The Mega Bankruptcies of the 80s and 90s*, Lyle Stuart, NY, 1991.
5 Monks and Minow, *Power and Accountability*, esp. ch. 4.
6 Daniel Yergin, *The Prize: The Epic Quest for Oil, Money and Power*, Simon & Schuster, 1991; Anthony Sampson, *The Seven Sisters*, Coronet, 1988.
7 Richard Thomas DeLamater, *Big Blue: IBM's Use and Abuse of Power*; Paul Carroll, *Big Blues, The University of IBM*, Orion/Weidenfeld, 1994.
8 Anthony Sampson, *The Sovereign State: The Secret History of ITT*, Hodder & Stoughton, 1973.

9   Duncan Innes, *Anglo American and the Rise of Modern South Africa*, Heinemann Educational, 1984.

10 Yergin, *The Prize*, pp. 263–6.

11 Tom Hilliard, 'Trade Advisory Committee: Privileged Access for Polluters', *Public Citizen*, Dec 1991, p. 12.

12 Natalie Avery, Martine Drake, and Tim Lang, *Cracking the Codex: An Analysis of Who Sets World Food Standards*, National Food Alliance, 1993. See also John Cavanagh et al., *Trading Freedom: How Free Trade Affects Our Lives, Work and Environment*, Institute for Food and Development Policy, San Francisco, 1992, p. 30.

13 *Fortune*, Aug. 1995.

14 UN, *World Investment Report 1994: Transnational Corporations, Employment and the Workplace*, NY, 1994.

15 Ibid., p. 5.

16 NUMAST, cited in *Financial Times*, 16 Aug. 1994, p. 15.

17 Russell Taylor, *Going for Broke: Confessions of a Merchant Banker*, Simon & Schuster, 1993 pp. 3, 236 ff.

18 UN, *World Investment Report 1994*, p. xxiii.

19 US Department of Commerce, *US Direct Investment Abroad: 1989 Benchmark Survey, Preliminary Results*, Washington, DC, 1991, table 31.

20 UN, *World Investment Report 1994*, pp. 313 ff.

21 George, *The Debt Boomerang*, p. 98.

22 UN, *World Investment Report 1993: Transnationals and Integrated International Production*, NY, 1993, annex table 2, p. 248; reinvestment data, p. 18; average profitability data, p. 19.

23 Ibid., p. 19.

24 UN, *World Investment Report 1992: Transnationals and Integrated International Production*, NY, 1992, p. 154, table VI.10.

25 B. D. Levine, *Inside Out*, Century, 1992.

26 Quoted in *Fortune*, July 1972, p. 49.

27 See James B. Stewart, *Den of Thieves*, Simon & Schuster, 1992; Levine, *Inside Out*; George Anders, *Merchants of Debt: KKR and the Mortgaging of American Business*, Jonathan Cape, 1992.

28 Keynes, *The General Theory of Employment, Interest and Money*, p. 351.

29 Smith, *Wealth of Nations*, bk II, ch. iv (vol. 12, p. 379).

30 See Benjamin Nelson, *The Idea of Usury: From Tribal Brotherhood to Universal Otherhood*, Princeton University Press, 1949.

31 Smith, *Wealth of Nations*, bk II. ch. iv (vol. 1, p. 378).

32 Keynes, *The General Theory of Employment, Interest and Money*, p. 235.

33 J. M. Keynes, *The Economic Consequences of Mr. Churchill* (1925), in *Collected Writings*, vol. 9, Cambridge University Press, 1972, pp. 207–30.

34 Peter F. Drucker, 'Trade Lessons from the World Economy', *Foreign Affairs*, 73, 1, Jan./Feb. 1994, p. 100.

35 Keynes, *The General Theory of Employment, Interest and Money*, p. 353; see also Silvio Gesell, *Die Reformation in Münzwessen als Brücke zum socialen Staat*, Buenos Aires, 1891; id., *Nervus rerum*, Buenos Aires, 1891; id., *Die Natürliche Wirtschaftsordnung*, Rudolf Zitzmann, Nuremberg, 1904 (9th edn 1949); id., *Verwirklichung des Rechtes auf dem vollen Arbeiterstrag*, Les Hauts, Switzerland, 1906; id., *Die Neue Lehre vom Zins*, Berlin, 1911; id., *The Natural Economic Order*, trans. Philip Pye, Free Economy Publishing Company, San Antonio, Texas, 1934.

36 Paul Ekins, *A New World Order: Grassroots Movements for Global Change*, Routledge, 1992, ch. 6.

37 UN, *World Investment Report 1993*, p. 19.

38 World Bank, *World Development* p. 296.

39 Ibid., p. 300.

40 Nancy Wagner, *A Review of PPP-Adjusted GDP Estimation and its Use for the Fund's Operational Purposes*, IMF Working Paper, Feb. 1995, Washington, DC.

41 IMF, *World Economic Output 1993*, Washington, DC 1993, pp. 116, 119.

42 See e.g. John Williamson, ed., *Estimating Equilibrium Exchange Rates*, Institute for International Economics, Washington, DC, 1994.

43 Orio Giarini, *Dialogue on Wealth and Welfare*, Pergamon Press, 1980.

44 See Victor Anderson, *Alternative Economic Indicators*, Routledge, 1991; UNSTAT, *Key Indicators and Indices of Sustainable Development* Geneva, 1993.

45 Michael Barratt Brown, *Fair Trade: Reform and Realities in the International Trading System*, Zed, 1993, p. 136.

46 Lars Anell and Birgitta Nygren, *The Developing Countries and the World Economic Order*, St Martin's Press, NY, 1980, p. 76.

47 See Stuart Corbridge, *Debt and Development*, Blackwell, 1993; Patricia Adams, *Odious Debts: Loose Lending, Corruption and the Third World's Environmental Legacy*, Earthscan Canada, Toronto, 1991, p. 165.

48 Congressional testimony of 29 Mar. 1984, reported in *Washington Post*, 30 Mar. 1984, and quoted in Arjun Makhijani, *From Global Capitalism to Economic Justice*, Zed, 1992, p. 37.

49 OECD, *Financing and External Debt of Developing Countries: 1989 and 1990 surveys*.

50 George, *The Debt Boomerang*, p. xvi.

51 Quoted in Sampson, *Black and Gold*, p. 29.

Chapter 5: Managed Markets of Global Apartheid

1 US Department of State, *Proceedings and Documents of the United Nations Monetary and Financial Conference, Bretton Woods, New Hampshire, July 1–22 1944*, Vol. 1, pp. 79–83, quoted in Bruce Rich, *Mortgaging the Earth: The World Bank, Environmental Impoverishment and the Crisis of Development*, Beacon Press/Earthscan, 1994, p. 54.

2 Fred Hirsch, *Money International*, Allen Lane, 1967, Pelican, 1969, p. 305.

3 See *Institutional Investor*, Mar. 1994, pp. 69–77; *Euromoney*, Mar. 1994, 178–9.

4 Graham Bird, *IMF Lending to Developing Countries: Issues and Evidence*, Routledge, 1995, pp. 14–18 (1985–92); Tony Killick, ed., *The Quest for Economic Stabilisation: The IMF and the Third World*, Heinemann, 1984, p. 2 (1974–82).

5 IMF, *Annual Report*, Washington, DC, 1991, p. 24.

6 IMF, *World Economic Outlook*, Washington, DC, May 1993 p. x.

7 Bird, *IMF Lending to Developing Countries*, ch. 1, esp. pp. 37–47.

8 Davison Budhoo, *Enough is Enough*, New Horizons Press, NY, 1990, p. 7.

9 Ibid., p. 49.

10 Ibid., pp. 54–5.

11 Ibid., p. 58.

12 Arthur Schlesinger, *One Thousand Days*, Houghton Mifflin, NY, p. 158.

13 Peter Koerner, Gero Maass, Thomas Siebold, Reiner Tetzlaff, *The IMF and the Debt Crisis*, Zed, 1992, p. 137.

14 Latin America Bureau, *The Poverty Brokers: The IMF and Latin America*, 1983, pp. 47–8.

15 Quoted in Anthony Sampson, *The Money Lenders: Bankers in a Dangerous World*, Hodder & Stoughton, 1981, Coronet, 1982, p. 169.

16 James Morrell and David Gisselquist, *How the IMF Slipped $464 Millions to South Africa*, Washington, DC: Centre for International Policy, Jan. 1978, quoted in Sampson, *The Money Lenders*, p. 170.

17 *1988 Annual Report*, quoted in Patricia Adams, *Odious Debts*, p. 81.

18 Quoted in Sampson, *The Money Lenders*, p. 302; Coronet edn., p. 344.

19 Quoted in Graham Hancock, *Lords of Poverty*, Macmillan, 1989, Mandarin 1991, p. 57.

20 World Bank, *World Development Report 1990: Poverty*, Oxford University Press, 1990, p. 3.

21 South African Bureau for Information, *South Africa 1988–89, Official Year Book*, 14th edn, Pretoria, pp. 178–9.

22 Ibid., pp. 411–13.

23 Quoted in Bernard Nossiter, *The Global Struggle for More*, Harper & Row, NY, p. 117.

24 Robert S. McNamara, speech given on 24 Sept. 1973, in *The McNamara Years at the World Bank: Major Policy Addresses of Robert S McNamara, 1968–1981*, Johns Hopkins University Press, Baltimore, 1971, p. 240.

25 Quoted in Rich, *Mortgaging the Earth*, p. 64.

26 World Bank *Annual Report*, Washington DC, 1991.

27 Michael H. K. Irwin, 'Banking on Poverty: An Insider's Look at the World Bank', in Kevin Danaher, ed., *Fifty Years is Enough: The Case Against the World Bank and the International Monetary Fund*, South End Press, Boston, Mass., 1994, p. 152.

28 Maggie Snider, 'Fighting Poverty at the World Bank', ibid., pp. 161 ff.

29 Quoted in Rosemary Righter, *Utopia Lost: The United Nations and World Order*, Twentieth Century Fund Press, NY, 1995, p. 195.

30 John Vidal, 'The bank that likes to say sorry', *Guardian 2*, 22 July 1994, p. 16.

31 Jan Rocha, ibid.

32 World Bank, *Brazil: Integrated Development of the Northwest Frontier*, Washington, DC, 1981, pp. xix–xx.

33 David Price, *Before the Bulldozer: The Nambiquara Indians and the World Bank*, Seven Locks Press, Washington DC, 1989, p. 158.

34 Derek Brown, *Guardian*, 5 Nov. 1993, p. 14.

35 Hugh Thomas, *The Suez Affair*, Weidenfeld & Nicolson, 1967, p. 25.

36 Sampson, *The Money Lenders* p. 271–2; Coronet edn, p. 299.

37 Quoted in Rich, *Mortgaging the Earth*, p. 100.

38 World Bank, *Sub-Saharan Africa: From Crisis to Sustainable Growth*, Washington, DC, Nov. 1989.

39 World Bank, *The World Bank and the Environment*, Washington, DC, 1993.

40 Ibid., p. 19.

41 John Clark, *Democratizing Development*, Earthscan, 1991; Bhuvan Bhatnagar and Aubrey Williams, *Participatory Development and the World Bank*, World Bank Discussion Paper 183, Washington, DC, 1992, World Bank, *How the World Bank Works with Nongovernmental Organizations*, World Bank, Washington, DC, 1990.

42 World Bank Group, *Learning from the Past, Embracing the Future*, World Bank, Washington, DC, 1994.

Chapter 6: Institutions of Global Apartheid: The United Nations System

1 Quoted in Noam Chomsky, *Deterring Democracy*, (Verso, 1991), Vintage, 1992 frontispiece.

2 UN Public Information, Jan. 1991, DP1/1098–41135.
3 UN Charter, Article 1.3.
4 *Official Year Book of South Africa*, 1986.
5 Ibid.
6 Robert D. Schulzinger, *The Wise Men of Foreign Affairs: The History of the Council on Foreign Relations*, Columbia University Press, 1984, p. 61.
7 Memorandum E-B18, 19 Oct. 1940, CFR, *War and Peace Studies*, Yale University Library, New Haven, Conn. quoted in Holly Sklar, ed., *Trilaterism*, South End Press, Boston, 1980, p. 139.
8 Memorandum E-B34 24 July 1941.
9 Memorandum E-B32, 17 Apr. 1941, CFR, *War and Peace Studies*, YUL, quoted in *Trilateralism*, p. 146.
10 Schulzinger, *The Wise Men of Foreign Affairs*, p. 109.
11 Minute of 6 May 1942, quoted in *Trilateralism*, p. 147.
12 See Ruth B. Russell, *A History of the United Nations Charter*, Washington, DC, Brookings Institute, 1958; Harley Notter, *Postwar Foreign Policy Preparation 1939–1945*, Washington, DC, 1949.
13 World Bank, *Annual Report 1992*, p. 254.
14 Shirley Hazzard, *Defeat of an Ideal*, Macmillan, 1973.
15 Patrick Moynihan, *A Dangerous Place*, Little, Brown, 1976, quoted in Chomsky, *Deterring Democracy*, p. 200.
16 Quoted in Righter, *Utopia Lost*, p. 223.
17 *Guardian*, 16 Oct. 1993, p. 14.
18 Brian Urquhart and Erskine Childers, *A World In Need of Leadership: Tomorrow's United Nations*, Development Dialogue 1990:1–2, Uppsala.
19 Erik Jense, ed., *The United Kingdom – The United Nations*, Macmillan, 1993.
20 Brian Urquhart and Erskine Childers, *Renewing the United Nations System*, Development Dialogue 1994: 1, Uppsala.
21 Erskine Childers, ed., *Challenges to the United Nations: Building a Safer World*, CIIR/St Martin's Press, 1994.
22 Amedeo Postiglione, *The Global Village Without Regulations*, Giunti, Florence, 1992.

Chapter 7: The Laws of Exclusion

1 Edward Roux, *Time Is Longer Than The Rope*, p. 16, quoted in S. E. M. Pheko, *SA: Betrayal of a Colonised People: Issues of International Human Rights Law*, ISAL Publications, 1990, Skotaville, Johannesburg, 1992, p. 9.
2 Sol T. Plaatje, *Native Life in South Africa*, (1916), Raven Press, Johannesburg, 1982, p. 61.
3 Johnson *v.* McIntosh, 21 US (8 Wheat) at 588 (1823), quoted in

Robert A Williams, Jr, *The American Indian in Western Legal Thought: The Discourses of Conquest*, Oxford and NY, 1990, p. 315.

4   Khattiso Ea, *Profile*, Lesotho, 1976, p. 26, quoted in Pheko, *SA: Betrayal of a Colonised People*, p. 9.

5   J. G. Riddall, *Introduction to Land Law*, Butterworth, 1974, 3rd edn 1983, pp. 389–90; Limitation Act, 1980.

6   H. S. Commager, *Documents of American History*, 8th edn, 1968, pp. 48–9, quoted in Williams, *The American Indian in Western Legal Thought* pp. 237–8.

7   Edward MacWhinney, *UN Law Making*, NY, 1984.

8   UN, *Basic Facts about the United Nations*, NY, 1992, p. 209.

9   Arnold McNair, *The Law of Treaties*, London, 1961.

10   Resolution 3068 (XXVIII), 30 Nov. 1973.

11   G. H. Sabine and Thorson, *A History of Political Theory*, Dryden Press, Ill., 1937; 4th edn, Tokyo, 1973, p. 154.

12   *Yearbook of the United Nations*, 1948, p. 528.

13   Carroll and Noble, *The Free and the Unfree* p. 133.

14   IMF, *World Economic Outlook*, May 1993, pp. 120–5.

15   Elizabeth Brubaker, *Property Right in the Defence of Nature*, Earthscan, 1995.

16   Francis Bowen (1838), Justice Joseph Story, Henry Clay, quoted in Daniel T. Rodgers, *Contested Truths: Keywords in American Politics since Independence*, Basic Books, NY, 1987, p. 124.

17   Amartya Sen, *Poverty and Famines*, Clarendon Press, Oxford, 1981, p. 166.

18   Albie Sachs, *Advancing Human Rights in South Africa*, Oxford University Press, Cape Town, 1992, p. 68.

19   John Locke, *Two Treatises on Government* (1689), ed. Peter Laslett, Cambridge University Press, 1967, p. 343.

20   Grotius, *Mare Liberum* (1609).

21   Quoted in Righter, *Utopia Lost*, p. 225.

22   Tommy T. B. Koh, of Singapore, president of the Third UN Conference on the Law of the Sea, official text, 1983, p. xxxvii.

23   General Assembly Resolution 2749 (xxv).

24   Mr Malone, speaking at the eleventh session, 182nd meeting, 30 Apr. 1982, pp. 155–6.

25   Righter, *Utopia Lost*, p. 226–7.

26   Official text, 1983, p. xxxiv.

27   J. T. Houghton, G. J. Jenkins and J. J. Ephraums, eds, *Climate Change, The IPCC Scientific Assessment*, Cambridge University Press, NY, 1990.

28   See Bjorn Larsen and Anwar Shah, *Global Tradable Carbon Permits, Participation Incentives, and Transfers*, Policy Research Working Paper 1315, World Bank, Washington, DC, 1994.

29   Samuel Fankhauser, *Global Warming Damage Costs: Some Monet-*

ary Estimates, CESERG GEC Working Paper 92–29, revised version 1993, p. 15.

30 Y. Fujii, 'An Assessment of the Responsibility for the Increase in CO_2 Concentration and Inter-generational Carbon Accounts', WP–90–55, International Institute for Applied Systems Analysis, Laxenburg, Austria 1990; K. Smith, 'Allocating Responsibility for Global Warming: the Natural Debt Index', *Ambio*, vol. 20, 1991, pp. 95–6.

31 Aubrey Meyer, *Energy Subsidy from South to North*, Global Commons Institute, 1993.

32 Kamal Nath, *Statement to the Conference of the Parties to the Climate Change Convention*, Berlin, 6 Apr. 1995.

33 UN, *Facts About the United Nations*, NY, 1992, p. 86.

34 Vandana Shiva, 'The Biodiversity Convention: An Evaluation from the Third World Perspective', in *Monocultures of the Mind*, pp. 80–1.

35 Ibid.

36 Friends of the Earth Europe, *Towards Sustainable Europe*.

37 Former deputy director, testimony before Senate Select Committee on Intelligence Activities, 1976, quoted in *New York Times*, 29 Apr. 1976.

38 Quoted in Jenny Pearce, *Under the Eagle: US Intervention in Central America and the Caribbean*, Latin America Bureau, 1981, p. 61.

39 John Stockwell, 'Wartime Interview: US Policy: The Need for War', *Open Magazine Pamphlet Series*, Westfield, NJ, 1991, p. 16.

40 Quoted in Pearce, *Under the Eagle*, p. 108.

41 Noam Chomsky, *Year 501: The Conquest Continues*, Verso, 1993, p. 254.

42 CODEHUCA, *This is the Just Cause*, Apex Trust, NY, 1991.

43 Stockwell, 'Wartime Interview: US Policy'.

44 Ramsey Clark, 'How Iraq was Decimated', *Third World Resurgence*, Penang, Malaysia, 1991, No. 7.

Chapter 8: The Western Alliance Government

1 *Guardian*, 28 Oct. 1992, p. 120.

2 Ivor Wilkins and Hans Strydom, *The Super-Afrikaners: Inside the Afrikaner Broederbond*, Jonathan Ball, Johannesburg, 1978. J. H. P. Serfontein, *Brotherhood of Power: An Expose of the Secret Afrikaner Broederbond*, Collins, 1979.

3 Sklar, ed. *Trilateralism*, pp. 10–17.

4 Schulzinger, *The Wise Men of Foreign Affairs*, pp. 145 ff., 166 ff.

5 Sklar, ed. *Trilateralism*, p. 170.

6 Zbigniew Brzezinski, *Between Two Ages: America's Role in the Technetronic Era*, Viking Press, 1970, p. 297.

7   Ibid. p. 298.
8   Executive Committee, 23 Oct. 1973, quoted in Robert Eringer, *The Global Manipulators*, Pentacle Books, Bristol, 1980, p. 8.
9   Jimmy Carter, *Why Not the Best?*, Nashville, Tenn., 1975, p. 127.
10 Richard Cooper, Karl Kaiser, and Masataka Kosaka, *Towards a Renovated International System*, Trilateral Commission Triangle Paper 14, 1977, pp. 7, 9.
11 *New York Review of Books*, 30 Apr. 1972.
12 Sklar, ed. *Trilateralism*, pp. 198 ff.
13 Adapted from Bertram Gross, *Friendly Fascism: The New Face of Power in America*, Black Rose Books, 1980.
14 World Bank *World Development Report*, Oxford University Press, 1992, pp. 238–9.
15 *OECD Observer*, Dec. 1990.
16 OECD, *Annual Report*, Paris, 1991, pp. 88–9.
17 *Our Global Neighbourhood*, Report of the Commission on Global Governance, Oxford University Press, 1995, pp. 153–62.
18 *1975 Defence White Paper*, pp. 3–4, quoted in Gavin Cawthra, *Brutal Force: The Apartheid War Machine*, IDAF, 1986, p. 27.
19 Allister Sparks, *The Mind of South Africa*, Heinemann, 1990, Mandarin 1991, p. 311.
20 *Jane's Defence Weekly*, quoted in *Race Relations Survey*, Johannesburg, 1987/8, p. 521.
21 Sparks, *The Mind of South Africa*, p. 356.
22 Quoted in Woodruff, *America's Impact on the World*, p. 65.
23 Kennedy, *The Rise and Fall of the Great Powers*.
24 Alan Wolfe, *The Rise and Fall of the 'Soviet Threat'*, Policy Studies Institute, Washington, DC, 1979.
25 Department of Defense, *Proceedings of the Low-Intensity Warfare Conference*, 14–15, Jan. 1986, p. 10, quoted in Jack Nelson-Pallmeyer, *War Against the Poor: Low-Intensity Conflict and Christian Faith*, Orbis Books, Maryknoll, NY, 1989, p. 8.
26 Michael P. W. Stone and General Carl E. Vuono, US Army, *Trained and Ready in An Era of Change*, speaking in 1990, quoted in Stephen Rosskamm Shalom, *Imperial Alibis*, South End Press, Boston, 1992.
27 Marine Corps Commandant General Gray, AM, *Marine Corps Gazette*, May 1990, quoted in Chomsky, *Deterring Democracy*, p. 31.
28 *Guardian*, 19 Aug. 1993, p. 7.
29 Quoted in the *Guardian*, 19 Oct. 1993, p. 20.
30 Ruth Sivard, 'World Military and Social Expenditures 1989', *World Priorities*, Washington, DC, 1989, p. 23.
31 William Hartung, *And Weapons for All*, HarperCollins, NY, 1994.
32 Stephen E. Ambrose, *The Rise to Globalism*, Penguin, 7th edn, 1993, p. 376.

33 Quoted in *Financial Times* survey, 18 July 1994, p. xi.
34 Quoted by David Beresford, in the *Guardian*, 25 Nov. 1994.
35 Sivard, 'World Military and Social Expenditures 1989, and NATO Information Service, *NATO Facts and Figures*, 11th Edition, Brussels, 1989.
36 NATO Handbook 1985.
37 NATO, *Facts and Figures*, 11th edn, 1989, p. 324.
38 Ibid. p. 185.
39 Ibid., p. 384.
40 Ibid., p. 109.
41 Ibid., pp. 444–50, paras 8, 9 and 32.
42 NATO, 'The Alliance's Strategic Concept', *The Transformation of an Alliance*, agreed Nov. 1991.
43 Presented to Congress, Mar. 1990, quoted in Chomsky, *Deterring Democracy*, p. 29.

Chapter 9: The West Knows Best: Values and Ideology of Global Apartheid

1 Address to Parliament, Jan. 1963, from Brian Bunting, 'The Origins of Apartheid', in *Apartheid*, ed. Alex LaGuama, International Publishers, NY, 1971, p. 36.
2 Frederik van Zyl Slabbert, *The Last White Parliament*, Jonathan Ball/Hans Strydom, Johannesburg, 1985, p. 104.
3 Ibid., p. 105.
4 Francis Bacon, *Novum Organuum*, (1620), aphorism 129, in *Selected Writings of Francis Bacon*, ed. Hugh G. Dick, Modern Library, NY, 1955,
5 René Descartes, *Discourse on Method* (1637), Penguin, 1968, p. 78.
6 Shiva, *Monocultures of the Mind*, 1993.
7 Ross Perot, *Save Your Job, Save Our Country: Why NAFTA Must be Stopped – Now!*, Hyperion, NY, 1993; see also id. *United We Stand: How we can Take Back our Country, A Plan for the 21st Century*, Hyperion, NY, 1992.
8 Ernest Gellner, *Nations and Nationalism*, Blackwell, Oxford, 1983. E. J. Hobsbawn, *Nations and Nationalism since 1780; Programme, Myth, Reality*, Cambridge University Press, 1990; Basil Davidson, *The Black Man's Burden: Africa and the Curse of the Nation-State*, James Currey, 1992.
9 Donella H. Meadows, *Global Citizen*, Island Press, Washington, DC, 1991, p. 55.
10 S. M. Pheko, *South Africa: Betrayal of a Colonised People, Issues of International Human Rights* (ISAL, London, 1990), Skotaville, Braamfontein, 1992, p. 7.

11   John Kenneth Galbraith, *The Culture of Contentment*, Houghton Mifflin, 1992, Penguin edn 1993.
12   Quoted by Michael Kelly, *NYT*, in the *Guardian*, 20 Nov. 1993, Weekend section p. 16.
13   Eduardo Galeano, *Days and Nights of Love and War* (1978), Pluto Press, 1983, p. 186.
14   Eric Clark, *The Want Makers: The World of Advertising and How They Make You Buy*, Viking, 1988, p. 70; Ernst Dichter, *The Strategy of Desire*, TV Boardman, 1960. See also Vance Packard, *The Hidden Persuaders*, Longman Green, 1957.
15   Ben H. Bagdikian, *The Media Monopoly*, Beacon Press, Boston, Mass., 1983, 4th edn 1992. See also Edward S. Herman and Noam Chomsky, *Manufacturing Consent: The Political Economy of the Mass Media*, Pantheon Books, NY, 1988.

Chapter 10: Prospects for Improvement

1   Quoted in Sampson, *Black and Gold*, p. 15.
2   Sparks, *The Mind of South Africa*, p. 370.
3   Allister Sparks, *Tomorrow is Another Country*, Heinemann, 1995; id. *The Mind of South Africa*: Francis Meli, *South Africa Belongs to Us: A History of the ANC*, Zimbabwe Publishing House, Harvare, 1988; T. Karis and G. M. Carter, eds, *From Protest to Challenge*, California, 1972; The Commonwealth Secretariat, *South Africa: The Sanctions Report*, Penguin, 1989.
4   *Financial Times*, 18 July 1994, p. viii.
5   V. Bhaskar and Andrew Glyn, eds, *The North, the South and the Environment: Ecological Constraints and the Global Economy*, Earthscan/United Nations Press, 1995; Houghton, Jenkins and Ephraums, eds, *Climate Change; Norman Myers, Deforestation Rates in Tropical Rainforests and their Climate Implications*, Friends of the Earth, 1989. UN Environmental Programme and the Economic Commission for Change *Forest Damage and Air Pollution*, 1988; Lester R. Brown et al., *State of the World*, Worldwatch Institute, Unwin Hyman, annual; Robert Bennet and Robert Estall, eds, *Global Change and Challenge*, RKP, 1990; GESAUP, *The State of the Marine Environment*, UNEP, Nairobi, 1990; Don Hindrichsen, *Our Common Seas: Coasts in Crisis*, Earthscan, 1990; Neil Middleton, Phil O'Keefe and Sam Moyo, *Tears of the Crocodile*, Pluto, 1993.
6   Jeremy Leggett, *Climate Change and the Insurance Industry: Solidarity among the Risk Community*, Greenpeace, 2nd edn, 1993.
7   J. MacNeil, P. Winsemius and T. Yakuskiji, *Beyond Interdependence: The Meshing of the World's Economy and the Earth's Ecology*, Oxford University Press, 1991, p. 111.

8 Quoted in the *Financial Times*, 18 July 1994, p. 11.
9 Talk at the Royal Albert Hall, London, 20 May 1994.
10 See Ekins, *A New World Order*.
11 Guillermo O'Donnell, Philippe C. Schmitter and Laurence White-head, eds, *Transitions from Authoritarian Rule*, Woodrow Wilson Centre, Baltimore, 1986.
12 UNDP, *Human Development Report*, Oxford University Press, annual.
13 See Marilyn Waring, *If Women Counted*, (Harper & Row, 1988), Macmillan, 1989; Victor Anderson, *Alternative Indicators*, Rout-ledge, 1981; David Pearce, *Blueprint 3: Measuring Sustainable Development*, Earthscan, 1993; T. Jackson and N. Marks, *Measuring Sustainable Development*, New Economics Foundation, 1994; Alex MacGillivray, *Environmental Measures: Indicators for the UK Environment*, New Economics Foundation, 1994; New Economics Foundation, *New Directions for Structural Funds: Indicators for Sustainable Development in Europe*, 1995.
14 Bk IV, ch. vii., pt. iii (vol. 2, p. 141).
15 Nelson Mandela, *Long Walk to Freedom: The Autobiography of Nelson Mandela*, Little, Brown, 1994, p. 613, 615; see also Schlack Pienaar and Anthony Sampson, *South Africa, Two Views of Separate Development*, Oxford University Press, 1960, p. 56; Merle Lipton, *Capitalism and Apartheid*, Temple Gower Smith, 1985; Brian Lapping, *Apartheid: A History*, Paladin, 1986; Williams, *South Africa's War against Capitalism*.

Index

independence, 173–4
isolationism, 149, 206
protectionism, 67, 73, 74–5
and South Africa, 176
and UN, 150, 153–4, 158, 161, 200,
 218

values, 231, 266, 269
 Western, 221, 229, 235
Verwoerd, Hendrik, 11, 208, 232
Vietnam war, 123, 199, 206, 237, 246,
 259

Wales, 181
Wapenhaus Report, 138
war, 17, 24–5, 214, 217–20, 224

Western Economic System, x, 35–41,
 242
Wilson, Woodrow, 149
women, 31, 49, 113, 141, 142, 158, 162,
 170
World Bank, 128, 133–41, 178–9, 197
 lending policies, 105, 133–5, 136,
 140
 and UN, 155, 157–8, 161, 166
World Court, 162–4, 166, 167
World Trade Organization, 2, 4, 47,
 75, 76, 231
 political body, 56–7, 59
 and UN, 155, 166
Wuppertal Institute, 3

Yemen, 159